FRANCIS THOMPSON
MAN AND POET

Francis Thompson
Drawn by the Hon. Neville Lytton 1907

FRANCIS THOMPSON

Man and Poet

by

J. C. REID

ROUTLEDGE & KEGAN PAUL
London

First published 1959
by Routledge & Kegan Paul Ltd.
Broadway House, Carter Lane, E.C.4

Printed in Great Britain
by Butler & Tanner Ltd.
Frome and London

TO
MY TEACHERS

Contents

Illustrations

Acknowledgements

IN 1953, while gathering material in the United States for my study *The Mind and Art of Coventry Patmore*, I spent some time at Boston College studying the Patmore papers there. On the same occasion, I was able, through the courtesy of Father Terence L. Connolly, S.J., to inspect briefly the unique collection of Thompson manuscripts, notebooks, letters and volumes which he has brought together in Boston College Library. It was then that the notion first came to me of writing a new study of the life and works of Francis Thompson. Although a good deal in the following pages is at variance with the published opinions of Father Connolly on the poet, I should like to acknowledge here his kindness and generosity in permitting me to make brief contact with the most complete collection of Thompsoniana in existence.

My thanks also go to the publishers named for permission to quote from the following books: *Life of Francis Thompson* by Everard Meynell (Burns and Oates, 1913); *Francis Thompson* by F. L. Mégroz (Faber and Gwyer, 1927); *Francis Thompson: In His Paths* (Bruce: Milwaukee, 1944), *Literary Criticisms by Francis Thompson* (E. P. Dutton; New York, 1948) and *The Man Has Wings* (Hanover House: New York, 1957) all by Father T. L. Connolly; *Francis Thompson and Wilfrid Meynell* by Viola Meynell (Hollis and Carter, 1952); *My Diaries* by W. S. Blunt (Martin Secker, 1919–20).

I should also like to thank my colleague, Dr. W. H. Pearson, for allowing me to read the typescript of his University of London Ph.D. thesis, 'A Comparative Study of Patmore, Hopkins and Francis Thompson', and for reading and making suggestions on my finished manuscript.

Last, but by no means least, my best thanks go to my wife for her forbearance, encouragement and practical help during the writing of the book.

I

The King of Infinite Space

IN 1857, Dr. Charles Thompson, a former house-surgeon in the Manchester Homeopathic Dispensary, married Mary Turner Morton. He was thirty-four, she a year older; both were converts to Catholicism, brought into the Church by those positive religious impulses and those reactions against lifeless creeds which, in mid-century, had found their focus in the work of the Tractarians. Seven years before their marriage the Catholic hierarchy had been restored in England, and the torrent of anti-Popish feeling unleashed by the Ultramontane Cardinal Wiseman's indiscreet Flaminian Gate pastoral had not yet subsided. But the number of seminaries and priests was growing, Pugin and Ambrose Philipps de Lisle were working to realize their dream of a revival of the architectural glories of medieval Catholicism, dead letter penal statutes had been removed from the law of the land, Irish immigrants, fleeing the potato famine at home, had come flooding in to swell the number of adherents in England, the Jesuits, the Cistercians, the Redemptorists and other religious Orders had established or re-established foundations, and between the old and the new Catholics that form of intellectual disputation which is one of the signs of health in a religious body had begun to flourish.

One memorable night in October, 1845, John Henry Newman, the genius of the Oxford Movement, had, after years of agonized doubt, made his submission to the Catholic Church, kneeling before the Italian Passionist, Father Barberi, drying his rain-soaked clothes at a fire at Littlemore. And, just two years before Charles Thompson married, Newman, now a

Catholic priest, had preached his famous 'Second Spring' sermon at Oscott, prophesying a glorious future for the Church after the three-centuries-long winter. It was a time of surging optimism for the half-million Catholics of England, who saw their ranks daily increased by conversions.

Not only Charles Thompson, but his sisters and most of his brothers were among those who, from conviction, so changed their religion. One brother, Edward Healy Thompson, who had been an Anglican clergyman, after his conversion taught English literature at the Catholic University of Dublin, became a sub-editor of the *Dublin Review*, and wrote some pedestrian poetry, devotional works and studies of such marginal mystics as Marie Lataste. Another, John Costall Thompson, published a volume of undistinguished verse. Charles himself, upright, kindly, and a conscientious doctor, had little interest in or feeling for literature, but practised his religion with the fervour of a convert, suffering somewhat in his profession from the anti-Catholic prejudice prevalent at the time in Manchester. Whenever there was a possibility that a new-born infant would not survive, he would himself baptize it at once, which hardly made for increased popularity with his non-Catholic neighbours.

His bride, Mary Morton, was no less assiduous in her acceptance of her adopted religion. Born in Manchester, she had at the age of thirty moved with her family to Chelsea, where she became friendly with a Catholic family and engaged to the son, who died, however, before the marriage. Soon after his death, Mary Morton had embraced his religion, to which she had long been attracted, a step strongly disapproved by her family. Relations became even more strained when, as a postulant, she entered the convent of the Holy Child Jesus, recently established at St. Leonards. This Order was a progressive teaching sisterhood founded by Cornelia Connelly, the wife of a convert American clergyman. Despite her piety, Mary Morton found she could not adjust herself to the requirements of Cornelia Connelly's rule, and, leaving the convent, worked as a governess at Sale, where she met her future husband.

After their marriage, the Thompsons went to Preston, in Lancashire, where Dr. Thompson set up in practice, first in St. Ignatius Square, later at 7 Winckley Street, a flat, three-storied, featureless house, giving directly on to the pavement.

Here on December 18, 1859, Francis Thompson, their second child, was born. Charles Joseph, who preceded him, lived but one day, and of the three girls born afterwards, one died in infancy. Francis was baptized in the Jesuit church of St. Ignatius, close by the Thompsons' first Preston home. After living also in Winckley Square and Latham Street, the Thompsons moved with their two little daughters and the five-year-old Francis to Ashton-under-Lyne. Here in the manufacturing town which so belies its charming name, at 226 Stamford Street, another plain, drab residence, Francis was to spend the next twenty-one years of his life.

Except for a couple of months at a school run by the Nuns of the Cross and the Passion, the young Francis was educated at home by private tutors and a governess. Their religion cut the Thompsons off from close contact with their neighbours; few visitors, except for occasional priests, came to the home. Charles Thompson's competence as a physician assured him of a steady practice, and, in his professional capacity, he had a fair circle of acquaintances. But the Thompson children were driven pretty much in on themselves; they saw few other youngsters, they existed in a rather hot-house atmosphere of provincial piety, for the religious fervour of their parents was, if anything, deepened by the near-hostility of the worthies of Ashton-under-Lyne. Considering the religious training he received from his parents, and the whole atmosphere of convert piety with which he was surrounded, young Francis could hardly not have been impelled towards the religious life, still more so because of ample precedents in his family. The elder of his sisters, Mary, became a nun, as did two of his father's sisters and a niece, while several other relatives, like his mother, failed in their attempts to enter convents. Since Francis himself was to be rejected for the priesthood, and as the urge towards the religious life was a powerful environmental influence on him, his failure here was surely one important element in the shaping of his mature personality.

Thompson's Victorian childhood had nothing in common with those grimly recorded by Samuel Butler and Edmund Gosse. His parents, especially his mother, were indulgent, perhaps over-indulgent. The general impression given, unwittingly, by Thompson's own later musings on childhood is of a spoiled,

3

sheltered child, wrapped as in soft cotton-wool by generous affection. Charles Thompson was no Moulton-Barrett, a tyrant of the hearth, but a generous man, always anxious to do his best for his children, and perhaps somewhat lacking in the firmness which may have served the adolescent Francis better. Certainly, Thompson looked back upon his infant days as the true 'paradisus vitae'. The childhood of poets is always important, but there have been few whose young experiences became so interwoven with the nature of the man as Thompson's did. In his first eleven years spent in the nursery with Mary and Margaret, lasting traits of his personality were shaped as in hot wax and many of his enduring emotional drives determined. His own unreal, sentimental, 'fairy' concept of children was derived from his sheltered nursery days; much of his later nostalgia for a 'Lost Eden' bears the stamp of their pleasures.

In the warm womb of his Ashton home, he lived as in a dream universe; here, cut off from all but the most glancing contacts with the everyday world of strenuous reality, he learned to accept an interior fantasy as the prime actuality; here he developed that instinct for make-believe which indelibly marks his poetry. In later life Thompson often wrote about childhood. Much of this shows clear signs of adult rationalizing, as when he muses on Shelley, 'the enchanted child':

'Know you what it is to be a child? It is to be something very different from the man of to-day. It is to have a spirit yet streaming from the waters of baptism; it is to believe in love, to believe in loveliness, to believe in belief; it is to be so little that the elves can reach to whisper in your ear; it is to turn pumpkins into coaches, and mice into horses, lowness into loftiness, and nothing into everything; for each child has its fairy godmother in its own soul; it is to live in a nutshell and to count yourself the king of infinite space; it is

> To see a world in a grain of sand,
> And a heaven in a wild flower,
> Hold infinity in the palm of your hand,
> And eternity in an hour;

it is to know not as yet that you are under sentence of life, nor petition that it be commuted into death.'

4

So speaks the adult who has never had children of his own, romanticizing his infancy. Alice Meynell, mother of a vigorous, gifted brood, knew better than this. In her essay on 'Childhood' she points out that youngsters do not spend their time listening to elves. Although rich in make-believe, they know very well what they are doing, and far from 'believing in belief', it is facts that they trust and cherish.

Yet, even if we make allowances for the adult feelings which Thompson projects back into his childhood, enough remains to show how deeply those nursery days involved him in the world of fantasy. In one of his notebooks, we find this revealing passage:

'There is a sense in which I have all my life been and even now remain a child. But in another sense I never was a child, never shared children's thoughts, ways, tastes, manner of life and outlook on life. I played—I never ceased to play,— but my sport was solitary sport. Even when I played with my sisters, from the time I began to read (about my sixth year) the game often, I think, meant one thing to me and quite another to them—my side of the game was part of a dream-scheme invisible to them.'

From the comfortable, loving home around him, Francis retreated into his private 'dream-scheme', building for himself a secret paradise chiefly through games and reading. He played with puppets and with a toy theatre which he treasured all his life—it was still his at his death; he made up the rules for the games with his sisters; and their dolls were among the main objects of his fantasies. 'I dramatized them; I fell in love with them.' One was selected as a goddess, named Princess of Puppetdom, and worshipped, the first example of that bloodless divinity Thompson was, in later life, to adore as a statue, Alice Meynell, the Mistress of Vision, and as the girls with floating hair in a set of illustrations to Shakespeare which enchanted him as a boy.

Although, in itself, this kind of infantile idealization is neither unusual nor abnormal, the young Francis Thompson clearly lived a dream-life of quite exceptional intensity. This visionary existence in which, dominating his sisters in the nursery, he reigned supreme in his kingdom of dreams, became for him as an adult a constant point of reference, a cool, dark cave of self where he could find refuge from obligations of manhood.

> Yet am I to the dead years' riches heir;
> Not wholly poor, nor bondslave to my fears.
> My spirit feeds, although my body fast,
> Amid the garnered memories of the Past.

he wrote in an early poem, 'Adversity'; and elsewhere, of his childhood: 'I did not want responsibility, did not want to be a man. Toys I could surrender, with chagrin, so I had my great toy of imagination whereby the world became to me my box of toys.' In much of his poetry, the adult Thompson was to exploit again and again what Alice Meynell called his 'terrible or tender trick of likening great things to small', but which others might regard as a degrading of nature, a child's scaling down of the universe to the dimensions of a play-box, the earth to be swung a trinket at the wrist, and the stars to serve as bijoux for cherubim to pelt each other with. The young Francis, absorbed in his nursery games, locking himself in his room against meal-time to complete a fantasy with his toy theatre, looks forward to the self-absorbed adult, forgetful of meals and appointments, manipulating his dreams while about him men confronted real life in all its earnestness.

The boy's excessive love of play was bound up with another form of dream-life, passionate immersion in reading. Books were ever to be precious to Thompson, often more real to him than people. He was a 'great reader' all his days, which was to stand him in good stead when, towards the end of his life, he became a book-reviewer and literary essayist, but which was also to be one of the curses of his poetry, when a tenacious memory packed it with echoes, paraphrases and disguised quotations from other poets. Seated for hours on the stairs, he devoured Shakespeare, Shelley, Coleridge, Macaulay—especially Shakespeare. His description of his response to 'A Midsummer Night's Dream' is especially interesting as showing the intensely escapist character of his reading pleasures.

'I experienced profoundly that sense of trance, of dream-like dimness, the moonlight glimmer and sleep-walking enchantment, embodied in that wonderful fairy epilogue

6

"Now the cat &c.," and suggested by Shakespeare in the
lines, "These things small and indistinguishable, like far off
mountains turned into clouds." I did indeed, as I read the
last words of Puck, feel as if I were waking from a dream and
rub my mental eyes.'

He knew that what was involved was a shaping of basic
personality, rather than merely of literary sensitivity. 'But
never, in any individual passage, did I sense the poetry of the
poetry, the poetry as poetry. . . . I was, in fact, as a child, where
most men remain all their lives. Nay, they are not so far, for
my elemental perception, my dawn before sunrise, had a passion and prophetic intensity which they (with rare exceptions)
lack. It was not stunted, it was only nascent.'

Thompson's delight in reading and nursery games seems in
great part to have blinded him to the beauties of nature. There
is hardly a trace, either in his poems or in his writings about his
childhood, of a child's response to the sights and sounds of the
valley of the Ribble or of the sea, which he saw often on holiday.
Just two or three years before Thompson learned to read, another little boy, named Arthur Rimbaud, in Northern France,
was building out of his reading of fairy-tales and adventure
stories a secret life of inner fantasies, fused, however, with events
and scenes drawn from the world around him. Where Thompson, familiar with the sea from infancy, virtually ignored it as a
reality, Rimbaud, who had never seen the ocean, dreamed constantly of it and wove from it an exquisite symbol of beauty and
freedom. The poetic visions of Thompson and Rimbaud are
more alike than the difference in the pattern of their lives and
in the respective quality of their achievement at first suggests.
But, in recognizing the superiority of Rimbaud's poetry, it is
important to emphasize that, whereas Thompson was content
with his fantasies, in the French boy interior imaginings and
tangible reality blended together in an obsessive vision.

There are occasional hints in Thompson's notes that he knew
something of the miseries of childhood, the 'world-wide desolation and terror' of being lost, and the 'long tragedy of early
experiences', but these are infrequent, and suggest more than
anything else the despair-laden adult's attempt to assimilate his
childhood to his mature mood. The only traces of the physical

7

interests of a normal, reasonably healthy boy are found in his
delight in war-games, when he would act out current sieges and
battles with the aid of chairs and planks, and his joy in cricket,
which he played with his sisters on the sands at Colwyn Bay.
Cricket was to become a lasting passion with him, always however as an observer, only once, after infancy, as a participant.
Perhaps here, too, through the elaborate ritual of English
cricket, the slow trance-like ballet of the game, he could project
himself into a somnolent activity with no relation to the demands of everyday life.

For his first eleven years, then, Francis Thompson enjoyed
the swaddling warmth of a fairly-well-to-do provincial Catholic
home, with his governess, his tutors, his indulgent parents, his
compliant sisters, his dolls, books, toy theatre, and, above all,
his dreams. His home-life was, as he termed it, his 'refugium
or sanctuary of fairy-tales'. His first contact with the brutal
realities outside this cosy enclave came when, in 1870, his
parents sent him to the Catholic College of St. Cuthbert, at
Ushaw, near Durham. A photograph dating from the same
year shows a shy little boy, dressed in the stiff adult-style suit of
the period, one sensitive hand resting on the back of a chair, the
other holding a straw hat by his side, and looking inwards,
while his two sisters, each clutching a doll, confront the camera
with direct childish confidence. This same timid youngster with
protruding shoulder-blades, delicate face and odd, sidling walk,
unused to the company of boys and so baited by the Ushaw lads
in the railway train that the tarts in his pocket were smashed
to pulp, found the rude world of college a horrid nightmare.
'Fresh from my tender home, and my circle of just-judging
friends, these malignant schoolmates who danced round me
with mocking evil distortion of laughter . . . were to me
devilish apparitions of a hate now first known; hate for hate's
sake, cruelty for cruelty's sake.'

So he recorded his first impressions of school in a notebook,
and he projected on Shelley the burden of his resentment at
these 'testimonies to the murky aboriginal demon in man', when
he wrote of the earlier poet's schooldays:

'That he escaped for the most part bodily violence is
nothing to the purpose. It is the petty malignant annoyance

8

recurring hour by hour, day by day, month by month, until its accumulation becomes an agony; it is this which is the most terrible weapon that boys have against their fellow boy, who is powerless to shun it because, unlike the man, he has virtually no privacy. His is the torture which the ancients used, when they anointed their victim with honey and exposed him naked to the restless fever of the flies. He is a little St. Sebastian, sinking under the incessant flight of shafts which skilfully avoid the vital parts.'

Although several of Thompson's schoolmates expressed surprise in later life that he had been so unhappy at school, the young boy found nearly all his companions vicious, unfeeling and uncouth. His reaction against them and back to nursery fantasy he transfers to Shelley: 'He threw out a reserve, encysted in which he grew to maturity unaffected by the intercourses that modify the maturity of others into the thing we call a man.' One of the earliest analysts of Thompson's personality, the psychologist, Dom Thomas Verner Moore, O.S.B., wrote, 'At Ushaw he manifested that shut-in reaction type which might readily have developed into a full-grown *dementia praecox*', and went on to show the young Thompson shrinking 'from the activity of the conscience principle which would direct the energies of the organism away from the self to the call of common, ordinary duty'.[1]

For many people during some part of their lives, and for most children, pleasure lies in inactivity, in a life of dreams, in excessive love of ideals above reality. The normal person shakes off these impulses when he enters into real life. But others in whom the shut-in tendency is abnormally developed, shrink back from contact with reality, closing up like a sea-urchin touched by an exploring finger. All the records that remain of Thompson's schooldays, including his own notebook jottings, proclaim that his was the super-sensitive, excluding reaction. This abnormal sensitivity, together with a capacity for finding calamity lurking beneath the business of every day and a catastrophe in an inconvenience, form part of the scaffolding for Thompson the man.

[1] 'The Hound of Heaven', *The Psychoanalytical Review*, Vol. 5, No. 4. October, 1918, p. 348.

Among 'Tommy's' schoolfellows at Ushaw was Henry Pat-more, the son of the poet to whom the adult Thompson was to owe so much, a shy, pious, delicate youth who died young, leaving behind him a handful of poems whose promise amply justified his father's printing of them with his own, and Lafcadio Hearn, at that time with no suspicion that his destiny was to transform him into Yakumo Koizumi, subject of the Emperor of Japan, authority on the art and culture of the Nipponese and professor of English literature at the University of Tokyo. There were, too, many high-spirited boys whom it would have needed sibyllic powers to see as future leading figures of the Catholic Hierarchy. But Thompson made few friends. He played hand-ball, not without some skill, but seldom handled a cricket-ball, or took part in other games.

Here, at Ushaw, one of three hundred boys, many of them gifted above the average, Francis could no longer dominate his fellows as he had his sisters and the cardboard figures of his toy theatre, nor could he fall back upon the sustaining comfort of his mother. So most of his leisure time at school was spent in trying to recapture his fantasy world through books. One of his masters, noting the boy's unusual interest in poetry, introduced him to the works of several poets, among them the French Romantics. In the reading-room, Francis used to erect a barri-cade of books as protection against pellets of paper, the sling-shot ammunition of his warring schoolmates, and, thus sealed off, bury himself in a volume of verse. This delicate-looking lad, with a somewhat pinched expression, very quiet and unob-trusive, and perhaps a little melancholy, as one of his teachers described him, was regarded by the other boys as queer and self-absorbed, fair game for occasional mild 'rags', yet liked for all that, especially for his gentleness of manner.

He did make some attempt to translate his dreams into reality, for, his head filled with ideas from Fenimore Cooper, Marryat and Ballantyne, he organized a pirate band, which lasted, how-ever, but a short while. He was fond, too, of tales of wars and sieges and one of his essays, 'The Storming of the Bridge of Lodi', written when he was fourteen, caused a stir among masters and pupils when recited by a schoolfellow in the Hall on a College Speaking Day. Here we can see, in its earliest form, the clash in Thompson's spirit between the two contrary impulses which were to tear him apart for most of his life—the urge to come to terms with the world of things, actions and obligations and that which drove him deeper and deeper into an illusory world where activity and obligations were irrelevant. His libido turned inwards on itself, making his own emotions the centre of his interest, at the same time outer-directed impulses moved him towards the extravert activities of pirate-games and war-mimicries.

It is hardly surprising that Thompson should, at this time, have found as much relief in the writing of poetry as in the reading of it. Poetry was much on his mind; a Ushaw story records that he was given to reciting Latin and Greek verses in his sleep. For many adolescents, the writing of poetry serves as a means of escape and of self-dramatization and is part of the process of emotional growth. Even as a schoolboy Thompson had begun to appreciate the value of poetry as a repository of dreams and as a confessional. He begins to look back, as he was to look back in his adult verses, to vanished pleasures. Already the adult Thompson's omnipresent symbols of sun and moon, as well as his nostalgia for a childhood refugium, in which the infant is priest of esoteric mysteries, are shadowed forth in such Ushaw verses as:

> Think, my Soul, how we were happy with it in the days of yore
>> When upon the golden mountains we saw throned the mighty Sun,
>> When the gracious Moon at night-time taught us deep and mystic lore,
> And the holy, wise old forests spoke to us, and us alone.

And the characteristic mixture of self-pity and the conviction that suffering is the price that must be paid for the poetic gift appears in an early form in:

> Lay aside thy useless grief and brood not o'er thy aching smart,
> Wherefore but for sick heart's healing came down poesy divine?

The other Ushaw poems are adolescently romantic or frigidly classical, more or less what we would expect from a talented schoolboy of the time; some, like the 'Lamente Forre Stephanon' a Chatterton-like fake-mediaeval ballad on a sick teacher, exhibit the facetious and forced humour of his later light verses. We cannot attach too much importance to these schoolboy effusions, but they certainly help to confirm the impression that, as an adolescent, Thompson displayed acute self-centredness, lack of spiritual toughness, and a refusal to adjust himself to the demands life was making on him. How different is the import-ance he gave to the mysteries of childhood from the attitude of a modern Catholic romantic poet, Patrice de la Tour du Pin. At the beginning of the vast *Somme de Poésie*, La Tour du Pin celebrates his own childhood visions:

> Voila mon terrain et ma nourriture
> J'ai cherché là-bas ce qui devait naître,
> Pour en composer un monde privé,
> Ce que voudrait bien posséder tout être,
> Ce qu'a tout enfant avec la joie pure
> De créer la vie qui peut le sauver.

But realizing that such a life is now in the past, that the mature man, no longer the uncomplicated, single being the child is, can-not now simply enjoy the memory of childhood ('Je ne suis pas mon seul habitant, et mon ciel changeant est clair d'amitiés'), he moves out of the child-world of innocence and joy into the complex world of adulthood, of male and female. What for La Tour du Pin is merely a starting-point is for Thompson a goal, a vanishing vision at which he grasps as at a life-line.

During his college days another very important influence was operating on him—that of religion. In his home he had ab-sorbed the basic principles and practices of Catholicism. At Ushaw, the training was continued, deepening and extending his faith, and finding a ready response in his sensitive nature. Whatever view we finally take of Thompson's character and of his poetry, we cannot doubt the sincerity of his religious feeling. What the quality of that feeling was and what the extent of his intellectual grasp of Catholicism, are less certain. At Ushaw, under the tutelage of priests, he was nourished by a Counter-Reformation type of Catholicism, in which ritual played a lead-ing part. In the College chapels, where priests and pupils prayed together, he assisted at Mass and Benediction, and, in the month of May, dedicated to the Blessed Virgin, he took an absorbed part in the elaborate twice-daily ceremonies in her honour. Devotion to the Blessed Virgin remained an important element in his emotional life; she is a recurrent theme in his poetry.

Above all, the liturgical splendours of the Church's ceremonial fascinated his eyes, already trained in ritual of play. He
was to remain haunted by the boy's memory of splendid vest-
ments, of incense, of lighted tapers, of Latin hymns, of the sacred
vessels. Those images drawn from church ceremonial which
weigh down some of his poems, as with the elaborate Benediction metaphor which opens the 'Orient Ode' are relics
mainly of his impressionable adolescent years. At times we get
the feeling from Thompson's poetry that the externals of the
Catholic religion mean more to him than the religious ideas they
incarnate. Certainly he was always as fascinated by ritual as
Rimbaud was by magic; through ritual, in his dreams, he
would dominate the universe, as Rimbaud would through
occultism push his way into the very presence of God. 'Ritual is
poetry addressed to the eye', he wrote, with its implication that
poetry, too, is ritual. The preponderance of images in his poetry,
which dance in a kind of intoxicated ritual, suggest that he
found in ceremonial an end in itself rather than a means, that
the rite was at least as important as, perhaps more important
than, the creed.

Thus to label Thompson a 'ceremonial-taster' is to be grossly
unfair to him. Although traces of the ritual-entranced youngster were to remain almost to the end, his religious experience
deepened greatly in his mature years and we may put down
much of his emotional response to his religion at Ushaw to normal adolescent piety. Yet the place ceremonial occupies in his
poetry does stubbornly recall the boy who played with dolls and
directed the play of his sisters, seeing himself as a purveyor of
arcane truths, a being apart, as the priest is apart by his celibacy
and his calling.

For the aim of Thompson at Ushaw was Holy Orders. After
spending four years as a junior in the seminary, he entered
College in the department known as 'Little Lads' for the three-
year course there. His school record was good; especially in
Latin, Greek and English; his teachers spoke of him as a 'good,
quiet, shy lad'. There seemed no obstacle to his advancing to
minor Orders. But, if there had been any idea in the young
Thompson's head that the priesthood would offer another
dream-world of escape, this avenue was to be closed to him. For
in his nineteenth year, his teachers decided, regretfully, that he

was unsuited for ordination. The chief reasons given to his parents by the President of St. Cuthbert's were 'his strong, nervous timidity' and 'a natural *indolence* which has always been an obstacle with him'. The wisdom of this decision of masters skilled in detecting the positive and negative qualities in the personalities of their charges was vindicated by Thompson's subsequent career, for it is impossible to imagine him conscientiously fulfilling even the simplest of pastoral duties.

What the priests called 'indolence' was more than Thompson's temperamental disinclination to apply himself to routines and duties which did not appeal to him, more even than his life-long inability to rise from bed, where he so often sought escape from the reality of time. Several writers on Thompson have explained this 'unnatural reserve'[1] as the self-absorption of genius, so possessed with the magnitude of an imaginative vision as to be indifferent to the petty routines of other less endowed beings.

Yet Thompson's poetry, unlike Rimbaud's, did not begin to flower until a decade later, and, although Thompson told Blunt in his last months that from youth his ambition was to be a poet, he did surprisingly little to realize that ambition. The indolence of Ushaw remained with him all his life, showing itself as a refusal to honour appointments, to meet deadlines, to remember which hour, even which day, it was, that perpetual negative inversion of will which was the exasperation and the despair of those who loved him. A psychologist might, with justice, diagnose Thompson's indolence as a psychoneurotic state—acabolia —or the unwillingness to make decisions, a self-absorbed view of the universe, resulting from a suppressed awareness of the incompatibility of fantasy with reality. Adler's definition of a neurotic as a person who knows what he should do, but who devotes his energies to finding reasons for not doing it, fits Thompson like a glove. The insistent note of melancholy which pervades his later verse may indeed be governed in part by his religious attitudes, but it is also unmistakably temperamental, compounded of an immature resentment at a cosmos which refused to allow itself to be shaped to the demands of fantasy and of a constant desire to evade the imperatives of ordinary

[1] Rev. T. H. Wright: *Francis Thompson and His Poetry* (Harrap & Co., 1927), p. 26.

adult life. At school, the praecox tendency did little more than single him out as 'different', and spoil his chances of becoming a priest; more drastic were the consequences when he was launched out into the world to make his own way without the support of boarding-school or home.

Yet, any such psychological explanation goes only part of the way to define Thompson's character. Many of his critics have tended to glide over his defects of personality, to sentimentalize them, or to rationalize them as religiously-conditioned asceticism. Others have found sexual infantilism as the source of his malaise. In a sense, all of these are right. Thompson demonstrably possessed an undeviating religious faith, and his intellect and his sensitivity were above the ordinary. It is perhaps unfashionable today to mention the will when so much blame is so easily laid on neurosis or environment; yet Thompson's deficiency was largely one of will; his was the weakness of a temperament which seeks to surrender itself without obligation, which looks for an object outside itself to become subservient to, which will go to immense pains of its own to avoid taking the lesser pains of others; which takes an almost masochistic pleasure in willing not to will.

His failure to become a priest most certainly influenced his later behaviour. J. M. Cohen says: 'His was a religious vocation, which led him, half-unconsciously, to make a total sacrifice of his volition.'[1] But such impulses, as we have seen, preceded as well as followed the disappointment of the seminary. Between the two sides of Thompson, the intelligent one aware of the world around him and sensitive to its compulsions and the dreaming one in flight from the concrete, there was from the beginning of the Ushaw period a tension which spills over into the pain of his poems. Not for many years was Thompson to attain a religious awareness acute enough to enable him to recognize and confront reality on its different levels and to reconcile the claims of poetry, life and religion. In the meantime, we find him returning home to Ashton-under-Lyne, in July, 1877, after seven years at Ushaw, a failure in his own eyes and a disappointment to his parents.

[1] 'Francis Thompson', *The Month*, Vol. 2, No. 6, N.S., December 1949, p. 392.

II

My Little-Worlded Self

THE Thompsons received their eighteen-year-old son back without reproaches or recriminations. Francis was not the first among their friends and relations to be rejected for the priesthood, and the knowledge that at Ushaw he had received a sound Catholic education went some way to moderate their disappointment. Amidst the scenes of his happiest days, Francis, although approaching manhood, took up again his games with his sisters, devising new plays for his toy theatre and fresh conjurer's tricks; he was back in the nest. It was now that the conflict between his egocentricity and everyday life began to assume a serious form. For Charles Thompson decided that Francis should follow in his footsteps and become a doctor. The boy bowed to the letter of his father's wish, and, after passing the entrance examination with distinction in Greek, was admitted in 1878 as a student of Owen's College, Manchester. But he had no intention of surrendering his soul to medicine. For six years he was to keep up an elaborate pretence of studying at the College, commuting each day from Ashton-under-Lyne, but seldom visiting the lecture-halls and at home acting the part of the earnest student. He told Blunt later that the details of doctoring were abhorrent to him and that an insurmountable repugnance always stood in the way of his immersion in the subject. The dissection of dead bodies he came to endure, but he could never accustom himself to the sight of blood flowing.

Such an admission may represent a rationalization of his sense of guilt for the deceptions he practised for so long on his

tolerant father. He had become, as he confessed, 'expert in con-
cealment, not expression, of myself. Expression I reserved for
my pen. My tongue was tenaciously disciplined in silence.' The
fact remains that, during these six years, it never seems to have
occurred to him to broach the idea of a literary career to his
father, who was indifferent to literature, but not hostile. The
record suggests that the idea of making his living by writing
never crossed his mind until Wilfrid Meynell proposed it to
him. Everard Meynell tells us that Francis 'was far less ready
than my father to believe that he was fitted for the writing
career'.[1] Yet he made no protest against his father's choice of
vocation and advanced no alternative proposal, but spent the
thousands of hours when he should have been conning his text-
books and attending lectures, tramping round the Manchester
streets with his shoe-laces untied, drowsing in the sun on a
bench, reading his favourite poems in the Manchester Public
Library, and sitting long afternoons at the Old Trafford
cricket ground, indulging his passion for the game. He made a
hobby of remembering cricket scores and celebrated teams, and
his sister, Polly, later Mother Austin, whom he had persuaded
to play the game with him in their back garden, was led by
his example to memorize such details, too, and retain them for
thirty years and more.

This delight in cricket is one of the most endearing traits of
the poet. It was, however, largely an academic thing, perhaps
as I have already suggested, a stimulus to day-dreaming; certainly his several verses on the game are drenched in his
characteristic moods. The ritual of cricket is almost invariably
the occasion for nostalgia, melancholy and *tedium vitae,* as in his
poem on the historic encounter between Lancashire and
Gloucestershire in 1878.

> It is little I repair to the matches of the Southron folk,
>   Though my own red roses there may blow;
> It is little I repair to the matches of the Southron folk,
>   Though the red roses crest the caps, I know.
> For the field is full of shades as I near the shadowy coast,
> And a ghostly batsman plays to the bowling of a ghost,
> And I look through my tears on a soundless-clapping host

---

[1] *The Life of Francis Thompson,* Burns & Oates, 1913, p. 91.

As the run-stealers flicker to and fro,
    To and fro:—
O my Hornby and my Barlow long ago!

Thompson must have done some reading in medicine, if only
to carry off the deception he was practising on his father. That
he did also pay some attention to the fossils and geological
specimens in the University is plain from the traces of acquaint-
ance with contemporary science seen in his poems, as, for
instance, the picture of prehistory given in 'An Anthem of
Earth'.

Thou hast devoured mammoth and mastodon,
And many a floating bank of fangs,
The scaly scourges of thy primal brine,
And the tower-crested plesiosaure.

Robert Graves says 'As an instance of a poet who has been up to
date in science since Shelley, what about Francis Thompson?
At one time it was his chief interest.'[1] This over-states the case,
however, since the references to science, described by him as
'old noser in its prideful straw', which can be found in his poetry
form meagre enough harvest for six years at a University.

Day by day he would wander around the factory city, a
familiar sight with his careless dress and odd, ruminating gait.
With his brisk sharp steps, punctuated with sudden hesitations
or full stops, all the time muttering abstractedly to himself, the
erratic student became an object of gentle smiles to the neighbours, smiles, which we may be sure, he never noticed. Museums
as well as libraries attracted his attention, and he would fill in
many a lecture-hour ambling purposelessly through the art
galleries of Manchester. It was while on a stroll through a
gallery that he fell in love with a cast of the Vatican Melpomene,
of which he wrote later in the most extravagant terms, reminiscent of Pater's famous description of the Mona Lisa. This
statue, he says, thralled his youth

'in a passion such as feminine mortality was skill-less to in-
stigate. . . . With her leaf-twined locks, she seems some
strayed Bacchante, indissolubly filmed in secular reverie. . . .

[1] *The Common Asphodel*, Hamish Hamilton, 1949, p. 55.

Thither each evening, as twilight fell, I stole to meditate and worship the baffling mysteries of her meaning: as twilight fell, and the blank noon surceased arrest upon her life, and in the vaguening countenance the eyes broke out from their day-long ambuscade. Eyes of violet blue, drowsed-amorous, which surveyed me not, but looked ever beyond, where a spell enfixed them,

> Waiting for something, not for me.

And I was content. Content; for by such tenure of unnoticedness I knew that I held my privilege to worship: had she beheld me, she would have denied, have contemned my gaze.'

For most of his life, Thompson was to project his love on to people and things incapable of returning it, selecting his love-objects, in fact, for the very reason that they could not reciprocate, since shared love involves responsibility, but a love for dolls, pictures in a book of Shakespeare, a plaster cast, Alice Meynell, wife and mother, and the little Meynell girls, does not. All this is of a piece with his unwillingness to abandon his world of dreams for adulthood. One weakness of his poetry is the lack of conviction in his treatment of sexual love. He desires, even yearns for, love, yet despite his poetic record of two tentative approaches to the love of woman, it is the love of love, and not the love of woman, he is mainly concerned with. 'It was my practice,' he wrote, 'from the time I left college, to pray for the lady whom I was destined to love—the unknown She. It is curious that even then I did not dream of praying for her whom I was destined to marry, and yet not curious. For already I previsioned that with me it would be to love, not to be loved.'

In his love for inanimate objects and unattainable women we may see another form of egotism. This kind of love is no sublimation, nor is it the robust uxorious love of Patmore, but a projection of the self, so that what is loved is not anything with a will and feelings of its own, but the ego reflected back. In it Narcissism blends with Masochism. And it is not surprising perhaps that the young man who adored the Melpomene cast should be the same young man who felt no sense of obligation to his parents.

In this indolent way, with the streets and the museums his

university, two profitless years slipped by, before Francis went to
London to sit his examinations. Whether he actually presented
himself is doubtful. In any case, he announced to his father,
in due course, that he had failed. Two more similar years passed
by, with Thompson mastering, in his quick-witted way, just
enough medical jargon to engage in conversation with his father;
and with the English and French poets claiming the rest of his
attention. At the end of the period came another trip to London,
and the same judiciously-timed announcement of failure. Dr.
Thompson, not unnaturally perplexed at his intelligent son's
lack of success, and with no suspicion at all of Francis' complete
inner repudiation of a medical career, was moved to enquire at
Owen's College about his son's progress, and learnt to his con-
sternation of the long record of non-attendance at lectures and
unsatisfactory work.

Charles Thompson was nothing if not a patient man. In later
years, when Francis had made his name as a poet, he said 'If the
lad had but told me!' Nothing is known of him that stamps him
as over-bearing or insensitive in personal relationships; nothing,
in fact, to suggest that Thompson refused to tell his father that
he hated medicine because he feared his anger or his contempt.
Only a determination not to exercise will, with perhaps a jealous
guarding of his inner privacy, can account for Thompson's
continued ignoring of his moral obligations. He seems at the
time to have felt no remorse for the anxiety he caused his father.
Blunt reports that Thompson told him that it was a mistake to
suppose that his father had treated him harshly.

'I was incredibly vain,' he said, 'it makes me blush now to
remember what I thought of myself. Neither my father nor
my mother had the least appreciation of literary things or the
least suspicion that I had any talent of any kind, but I was
devoured with literary ambition, all my medical studies were
wasted because I ran off from my classes to the libraries to
read. If my father had known it, he would not have forced me
to go on. . . . I was in every way an unsatisfactory son.'

But this was said after years of pain and suffering and when
the fact of his poetic achievement has perhaps cast a romantic
veil of hind-sight over his actual motives at the time.

Charles Thompson's immediate reaction to the discovery of

Francis' indolence was to set him to study for two more years, after reproving him for his wasted opportunities. But the patrimony of this borrowed time was frittered away, too. Sent at length for examination to Glasgow, where it was believed that the examiners were less exacting, Francis returned with the inevitable report of failure. However much indulgence we may be ready to grant Thompson as a potential poet being forced to spend his time half-studying a subject in which he had no interest, it is hard not to sympathize with the elder Thompson, who was not a wealthy man, over the expenditure of hundreds of pounds on six years of dreaming indolence. Exasperated, puzzled and dismayed by the latest failure, he determined that his twenty-five-year-old son should at last be flung in to sink or swim in the ocean of work.

Francis's first essay into the world of labour consisted of one abortive fortnight in a surgical instrument-maker's business, followed by two months as a hawker of encyclopaedias, which he spent, not in selling, but in reading, the volumes. Then, as if to anticipate one of the odder happenings in a story by Franz Kafka, Thompson, of his own volition, took a curious step. Perhaps because his father told him that no other avenue was open to him, perhaps in a fit of desperation, perhaps to cast himself romantically in the kind of role about which he had woven military fantasies at school, Francis Thompson went for a soldier. He was medically examined, put through a process of basic training and then rejected as physically unable to bear the life. He returned home to Ashton-under-Lyne, as uncommunicative as ever. 'What does one want with a tongue when one has silence?' he set down in a notebook.

Then, for this young man who had surrendered his sense of moral purpose to a scale of values that prized unconsciousness above activity, there approached one of the supreme crises of his life, a cloud which was to blot out the sun of innocence and joy from him. For when Thompson offered himself as a soldier he had already for five or six years been secretly addicted to laudanum. It is not known when he began taking the drug. Perhaps it was administered to him as part of the treatment when, in 1879, he fell ill from a lung fever, the first signs of the weakness which was later to develop into full-scale tuberculosis, and this medication gave him a taste for the opiate. But more likely causes of his addiction were the gift to him by his mother of Thomas de Quincey's *Confessions of an English Opium-Eater*, and her death soon afterwards in December, 1880.

Little purely biographical data remains by which we can gauge the strength of the ties binding Francis to his mother. He wrote and spoke of her hardly at all, yet his happy nursery days must have been made so in great part by her love. We cannot overlook the fact, either, that his poetry abounds in maternal imagery, of the breast, the womb, the suckling child, the solacing mother, and that a search for a mother-substitute underlies his timid relations with women, with Alice Meynell, for instance:

> For this was even that Lady and none other,
> The man in me calls 'Love', the child calls 'Mother'.

His mother's embracing and protective love formed the only real pattern of love he was to know; for him the universal symbol of love is that of a parent for a child;

> 'All which thy child's mistake
> Fancies as lost, I have stored for thee at home:
> Rise, clasp My hand, and come!'

the Hound of Heaven says to the naked soul, and a little poem, 'Love and the Child' ends

> To the tender God I turn:—
> 'Pardon, Love most High!
> For I think those arms were even Thine,
> And that child was even I.'

Poignant evidence of Thompson's love for his mother is found in the only poem he wrote about her death—'This is My Beloved'. Here, with unusual self-denigration which may be taken as a measure of the poem's sincerity, he imagines the terrible sight presented to the spiritualized eyes of his mother in heaven as she gazes upon the blackness of her son's soul.

> Son of the womb of her,
> Loved till doom of her,
> Thought of the brain of her,
> Heart of her side,

She joyed and grieved in him,
Hoped, believed in him:
God grew fain of her,
        And she died.

Died, and horribly
Saw the mystery,
Saw the grime of it—
        That hid soul;
Saw the slime of it,
        Saw it whole.
O mother, mother, for all the sweet John saith,
O mother, was not this the Second Death?

A sense of guilt at his wasted years, and contrition at having let
his mother down here outweigh ordinary human sorrow at her
passing. This does not mean that Thompson's life was to be
decisively altered by such a reflection; it is a recurrent feature of
his life that sincere remorse at things left undone was not
followed by a firmer course of action.

It seems likely, then, that the death of Mrs. Thompson was
one of the several factors which impelled Francis along the path
to opium. We will be considering these matters more closely in
the next chapter. In the meantime, it is enough to say that,
during the years of time-wasting at Owen's College, from about
1881, Thompson was taking laudanum regularly, using some of
his father's allowance and selling books and instruments to purchase the drug. The indolence of these years has its source in his
natural habit of withdrawal intensified by the narcotic. It gradually dawned upon the forbearing Charles Thompson that the
manner and conduct of his son had deteriorated. Seeking for a
reason, he hit upon alcohol, and one Sunday in November,
1885, he confronted Francis directly with the accusation. He
was met with a torrent of vehement denials, but with no explanation. Here was a chance for Thompson to speak out, and throw
himself on the mercy of a tolerant parent; but, jealous of his
inner privacy, and perhaps abysmally ashamed, he kept his dark
secret to himself. What his father said on this occasion can only
be conjectured. He would have been hardly human if, even in
the midst of his bafflement at Francis' unexplained behaviour,
he did not present the young man with an ultimatum.

On the following day, Thompson left a note for his sister

saying that he had gone to London. Here, it seems, was, at last, a decision made on his own initiative. Yet the resolve was as tentative as anything he had so far undertaken. He did not go at once to the capital, but to Manchester, where he hovered indecisively for a week among familiar haunts, disposing of more books to sustain him and purchase his liquid opium. Then he wrote home for his fare. When it was sent, he took the train to London. Did he set out, like the young Chatterton, for a metropolis of promise where the art of poetry could be pursued among people who appreciated the gifted? Or was his journey merely another escape from obligations, which now, his father's patience exhausted, confronted him with a challenge he dared not meet, but, were he to remain at home, could not evade? Certainly he had never given thought to any practical means of becoming known as a poet, nor had he any other occupation in view. He came to London not in expectation, as an adventure, or with the eager confidence of a man certain of his own gifts, but as a fugitive, in despair. 'I made the journey to the Capital', he wrote, 'without hope, and with the gloomiest forebodings, in the desperate spirit of an *enfant perdu.*' Into the city of dreadful night he plunged like a night-hunted refugee into a black river, abandoning home and family, and all obligations save his devotion to his religion, and calling not upon old artificer Time to forge anything in his soul but only on the daemon who dwelt in the swirling mists of opium.

III

The Amaranthine Weed

TO Thompson, de Quincey's *Confessions* came as a revelation, and grew into an obsession. That he consciously modelled his behaviour on that of the opium-eater, that he often identified himself with him, cannot be questioned. And, in a very real sense, Thompson's poetry was to become a species of 'confession' as de Quincey's prose is. While recognizing this, we must remain doubtful how much of what Thompson later told Wilfred Meynell, and his biographer, Everard Meynell, was the unadorned truth, and how much, not a conscious lie, but a confusion between wishful thinking, fact and dreams clung to for so long that they had ceased to be distinguishable from reality.

There are certainly many curious parallels between the lives and characters of the two men, too close to be all accidental. De Quincey was born in Manchester, where Thompson spent the significant years of his youth; Thompson's own description of de Quincey as a child might be a portrait of himself: 'shy, small, sensitive, dwelling in corners, with a passion for shunning notice, for books and the reveries stimulated by books; without the boy's love of games and external activities'. Both writers, in childhood, before taking opium, lived in a dream world, half-neurotic and half-literary. Both read copiously in the Manchester libraries, were unhappy and solitary at school, became opium addicts, set off for London, lived there in desolation and were befriended by a golden-hearted prostitute. Like Thompson, de Quincey refused to apply to relatives for assistance and invented elaborate, unconvincing excuses to explain why. Both shook off the drug-habit, only to resume it, 'never again entirely to be mastered', as Thompson wrote of his master.

Thompson, like de Quincey, was an unstable personality who translated his inner tensions and indecisions into the form of dreams. Both were careless in answering letters and keeping appointments, yet would write laborious, periphrastic apologies for slight social errors and omissions. Almost everything the two wrote was an anagram of themselves. Much of Thompson's prose and not a little of his poetry shows the mark of de Quincey's mellifluous lushness. De Quincey has his Lady of Sorrow; Thompson has his 'pale Ashtaroth', Lady of Pain, and his Mistress of Vision. Both, too, shared more than they ever admitted in the literary malaise of the century—de Quincey showing that exhaustion of spirit which followed the initial Romantic exuberance, Thompson the decadence which was the literary inheritance of the last decade of the century.

Thompson's devotion to de Quincey was well-known to his relatives. His uncle, Edward Healy Thompson, commented: 'We had often said his experiences would surpass those of de Quincey.' The opium-eater's name appears often as an authority in Thompson's prose: he reviewed the *Confessions*, he wrote a short study of the man. And many of the phrases he selected to describe de Quincey so exactly apply to himself as to indicate a conscious or unconscious identification with his master: 'shy little creature', 'diffuse, ostentatious in many words of distinctions which might more summarily be put', 'shy as a hermit-crab, and as given to shifting his lodgings; much-enduring, inconceivable of way, sweet-hearted, fine-natured, small-spited, uncanny as a sprite begotten of libraries'.

The example of de Quincey and the seductive dreams of escape bred by his hypnotic prose, the death of Mrs. Thompson, the taste of laudanum during an illness—here are three converging reasons for Thompson's addiction. Are they sufficient? Did Thompson resort to opium with some half-realized notion of liberating his poetic self, of tapping the subconscious wells of truth, as Rimbaud did? In his poetry, Thompson has much in common with those nineteenth-century writers who treasured the Image as the key to special truths reserved for the artist alone, and who put a very high value on the image-making powers of the mind at the expense of its rational powers. He cultivated the 'art of revery', and tended to substitute sense for thought. By temperament he was at one with those of his contemporaries who cherished the notion of the inevitable isolation of the poet by virtue of his possession of the secret of the Image, and who, by opium like Coleridge, or by alcohol like Verlaine, sought to cut themselves off from the world of pragmatic action, and to come closer to the terrible and joyous revelation of the image. Was laudanum Thompson's way of obtaining access to that translucent universe of the imagination, an artistic world beyond the concerns of common life and the operation of the reason?

Certainly he never claimed this to be so, but then he hardly ever spoke of his enslavement to the drug, save obliquely when condemning it in others. There is, however, insufficient indication of a conscious artistic purpose in his earlier years, or at any time, of a desire to plunge into the dark forests of the subconscious in search of poetry, to justify our accepting a poetic aim as a factor in his addiction. Thompson's actions give less the impression of the pursuit of a vision, however deviously, than of an escape. Dreams become not a means to romantic revelation, but ends in themselves; inertness rather than creative activity is his apparent goal. Perhaps he dimly sensed a relationship between the purpose of his adolescent verses and his fantasy-life; but this was never explicit to him; his aloneness was not a tribute paid to the calling of *poète maudit* but a quality of personality which both preceded and followed the flowering of his poetic gift.

Here we may look a little more closely at some aspects of opium-addiction to see if they throw any light on Thompson's personality. His continued taking of laudanum is something which most of his commentators, when they have faced it at all, have been inclined to explain away. The frankest consideration, that of Everard Meynell, suggests as causes the seductions of de Quincey, the relief opium gave from the assaults of tuberculosis, to which Thompson had, it appears, a hereditary weakness, and which had killed a sister, the strength it gave him to cushion the distresses his sensitive nature received from the workaday world, and the fact that opium was 'in the air' in Manchester, where cotton-spinners used it, and where it was easy to obtain. Others have been less searching and precise. One writes: 'His first consent to opium, and his final flight to it, a short while before his death, were dictated by a lamentably weak body. Opium, though it took devil's toll of him, certainly prolonged his life',[1] which not only accepts the legend of a 'cure', but gives physical weakness as the sole cause. On the other hand, Father Terence Connolly finds the 'ultimate explanation' in 'Thompson's natural indolence, his consciousness of failure at Ushaw and Owens, his bodily weakness as a result of illness and his weakness of will as a consequence of having the drug administered to him'. 'These facts', he says, 'reduce Thompson's moral culpability to a minimum in acquiring the habit of drug-taking, and they prove that his subsequent mastery of it was the achievement of a man such as Mr. Wilfrid Meynell described him—possessed of the strongest will he had ever encountered.' [2] This is palliation with a vengeance.

Thompson began taking opium about 1880, underwent treatment in 1888, which effected a temporary cure, reverted after a couple of years, went to Pantasaph, where he was deprived of the drug, either wholly or partially, for perhaps four years, then in 1896 began using the drug again, and continued until his death in 1907. So, from the age of twenty-one to the age of forty-eight (with the exception of six or seven years) Thompson was a regular user of laudanum. Wilfrid Meynell, always charitable in his estimate of his beloved protégé, told T. H. Wright, 'He was indeed a doctor of himself, and the discipline to which he subjected himself in his doses after intervals of complete abstention strengthened rather than weakened his moral character',[3] a judgment which must be examined in the light of Thompson's whole career. Alice Meynell went still further: 'Of his alienation from ordinary life laudanum was the sole cause, and of laudanum early and long disease.'[4] This is, as we shall see, putting the cart before the horse.

One problem in coming to grips with Thompson's personality is the fact that again and again in his essays and notebooks he shows that he is aware of the moral implications of various

[1] Philip John: 'A Poet of the Church', *Catholic World*, June, 1940, p. 323.
[2] *Francis Thompson: In His Paths*, Bruce, 1944, p. 150.
[3] Quoted in Wright: *Francis Thompson and His Poetry*. Harrap. 1927, pp. 30–1.
[4] 'Some Memories of Francis Thompson', *Dublin Review*, January, 1908, p. 161.

actions from the responsibility for which some of his admirers would excuse him. Nowhere is this clearer than in his comment in a review of de Quincey's *Confessions*, when he discusses 'vulgar prejudices' about the drug: 'That opium has the effect of stupefying; that it has the very contrary effect of making drunk; that it harries its victims rapidly to the grave; that it is to some unknown extent and in some vaguely-conceived way more deadly than alcohol—all these things are as much matters of faith as ever they were. If only to establish the true effects of the singular drug, to clear it from its fanciful, and confine it to its quite sufficiently real evils, this book would be worth reading.' He knew that laudanum had 'quite sufficiently real evils' and that it offered a refuge from normal life, and he clearly suffered pangs of conscience about his enslavement to it. When he was dying, he erroneously thought his decline was the result of laudanum poisoning, and in declaring so to Wilfrid Meynell, 'spoke a word', writes Everard Meynell, 'from which both had refrained for ten years'. Meynell knew that Thompson had reverted to the drug once more, and Thompson knew that he knew, but neither spoke of it to the other, the one from charity, the other from secretiveness and guilt.

Opium, then, cannot be brushed off lightly as a temporary aberration or something of little relevance to Thompson's life and poetry. Alice Meynell thought she had determined for good the extent to which laudanum coloured his poetry when she wrote, probably accurately: 'Not one of Francis Thompson's poems, except perhaps "Dream Tryst" . . . was written with the aid of opium.'[1] But the matter is not as simple as that. Most of the nineteenth-century beliefs, even among medical men, about opium came from the records of imaginative writers like Baudelaire, Poe, de Quincey and Coleridge. Elisabeth Schneider in *Coleridge, Opium and 'Kubla Khan'*, in support of her thesis that *Kubla Khan* is not a poem 'given' in a drugged dream, but a deliberate, conscious composition, has gone deeply into the modern scientific literature on the subject of drugs and opium addiction, and her findings conflict on many points with the literary myths woven about the subject. The ideas that opium invariably produces dreams and visions, that it leads to moral degeneration, and deterioration of the intellect, and that it

[1] Ibid.

begins by giving pleasure and ends by creating pain—these derive in great part from the records of literary drug-takers. Gothic fashions in literature, highly imaginative temperaments, the Romantic interest in dreams, visions and hallucinations are as relevant to any consideration of supposed responses to opium as the physiological effects of the drug itself. In fact, Dr. Horatio C. Wood suggests that de Quincey's dreams may have been 'pure fiction'.[1] 'Some of the writing about opium has been almost as imaginative as the effects attributed to it', says Miss Schneider.[2]

Many of the popular conceptions of the effect of drug-taking on the character come from confusing the physical effects of the drug with its social and legal aspects. In countries like the United States, where the taking of certain drugs is a crime, drug-addiction becomes closely associated with depravity; the cost of the narcotic causes the addict to substitute drugs for food, and the health almost invariably suffers. But that no serious effect follows inevitably from regular drug-taking within the limits of tolerance, that is by those who keep their dosage stable, is seen from the careers of the poet Crabbe, Wilberforce, Lord Erskine, Sir James Mackintosh and others who were opium-eaters throughout their lives. Although addicts quite often deteriorate, the cause of this is now believed to lie in factors other than the drug itself. Some confirmation of this is given by the researches of Dr. Lawrence Kolb, who, after investigating the histories of a great number of persons who had become addicts for one reason or another, found that three-quarters had good employment records, and none who were originally normal persons had had their efficiency impaired by opium.[3]

It is now widely held that those most likely to become addicts are people of unstable psychological make-up. A modern authoritative medical text says, 'The vast majority of addicts are persons classified as neurotic or constitutional psychopathic inferiors, and addiction is only one manifestation of their fundamental personality defect. . . . Since motivations relating to hunger, sexual urges and pain are reduced by morphine, use of

---

[1] 'The Story of the Use and Abuse of Opium', *American Journal of Pharmacy*, CIII, 1931, p. 19. Quoted Schneider, pp. 46–7.

[2] *Coleridge, Opium and Kubla Khan*, University of Chicago Press, 1953, p. 28.

[3] 'Drug Addiction—a Study of Some Medical Cases', *Archives of Neurology and Psychiatry*, XX, 1928.

the drug provides an escape mechanism from reality, a way of release from the failures and disappointments of everyday life, a means of bridging the gap between ambition and accomplishment.'[1] A more recent statement substantiates this opinion. The report of the Study Group of the World Health Organization on the treatment and care of drug addicts, published in 1957, describes the largest group of addicts and the most difficult to treat as those

'who suffer from a basically pathological character structure. In these people, the more the drugs are used to solve their deep-rooted personality problems, the more malignant the addiction. . . . Among the causative factors are frequently found immaturity of character development, a desire to live only in the present, a narcissistic attitude, or a destructive— even a self-destructive—tendency. The lack of a sense of meaning in life and the desire to escape from reality characterize many of this group, who often show a low capacity for dealing with frustration, anxiety and stress.'[2]

All of these symptoms may be discovered to a greater or a lesser degree in Thompson's poetry. Those who deteriorate under addiction, Kolb and others have found, are those who were abnormal before taking the drug. Users like Crabbe were able to establish a maintenance need considerably below the limit of tolerance, and below the amount that could be taken without deterioration. Less stable users have a continued temptation to increase their dosage beyond the maintenance level, in search of a still further flight from reality. Yet this compulsion does not appear to lie in the drug itself: it has been doubted by more than one writer on the subject whether an unusually strong will is required to control one's addiction.

For all the ecstatic apostrophe of de Quincey to 'just, subtle and all-conquering opium', modern research indicates that the craving for opium is nearly always an emotional impulse. 'The habitué adjusts himself psychologically to the support of his

---

[1] Louis S. Goodman and Alfred Gilman: *The Pharmalogical Basis of Therapeutics*, 2nd edition, Macmillan Co., 1955, p. 242.
[2] *Bulletin on Narcotics*, Vol. IX, No. 3, July–September, 1957, United Nations European Office, Geneva.

drug; he finds in it an agent that artificially fortifies him for meeting pain or difficulties. . . . The greater number of habitués have drifted into narcotism because of inherent mental instability; the majority of all addicts have become victims during adolescence, before character, even in normal youth, could become stabilized.'[1] We may draw from such evidence two conclusions relevant to our discussion of Thompson. First, what is commonly regarded as the necessary product of opium, namely, kaleidoscopic visions, represent rather false generalizations from the cases of sensitive literary addicts such as Coleridge and de Quincey whose 'dream' writing, in Miss Schneider's words, 'derives far more from the coalescing of individual temperament with literary tradition than from consumption of opiates.'[2] Second, many other apparent consequences of opium-addiction prove in actual fact to be the factors which led to the taking of the drug, heightened by the opiate. Baudelaire, a particularly acute and self-analytical witness, believed that drugs merely accentuated an already existing character: 'L'oisif s'est ingénié pour introduire artificiellement le surnaturel dans sa vie et dans sa pensée; mais il n'est, après tout, et malgré l'energie accidentelle de ces sensations, que le même homme augmenté, le même nombre élevé à une très-haute puissance.'[3]

All this, which may have seemed a lengthy digression, is particularly relevant to Thompson's case. Nearly all the causative factors described by Gordon and Gilman operated, as we have seen, in Thompson's childhood. Dr. Kolb, too, found that many addicts used opium to facilitate a regression towards infancy. If it be granted that the person who most readily allows the euphoria of opium to be a substitute for real life is already predisposed to regressive fantasies and narcissistic attitudes, Thompson's taking to opium was no aberration, nor was it a cause of his abstraction. Opium-addiction is a logical consequence of Thompson's personality, another escape-hatch from the tangible, another door slammed against responsibility.

Opium, of course, does not generate literary talent. But the euphoria produced by the drug, which is at its most intense in

[1] G. C. Wholey: 'The Mental and Nervous Side of Addiction to Narcotic Drugs', *Journal of the American Medical Association*, Vol. 83, No. 5, August 2, 1924, p. 324.

[2] Schneider: p. 78.

[3] *Œuvres Complètes*, p. 445.

the most unstable, affords some relaxation of tension, releasing for a time the addict's capacity for imaginative vision. Roger Dupouy in a book published in 1912, *Les Opiomanes*, which in many respects anticipates later medical findings, declares that opium reveries are voluntary and not hallucinative. He insists that only dreamers dream under opium, but that the relaxation brought by the drug helps to give the reveries fuller and easier release. Traits already present in the addict become highly developed, especially in the direction of egocentricity. Rather than stimulating the ordinary senses, opium has been shown to dull them,[1] just as it tends to inhibit sexual desire. As Wholey says in the article already quoted, 'Both sexes, in extreme addiction, are practically rendered emotionally asexual.' The vagueness of Thompson's poetic world, his practice of dealing in large abstractions, the absence from his poetry of all but a very few images drawn from precise observation of the everyday world suggest that his sensibilities were habitually dulled by the drug, a hypothesis supported by the many eye-witness accounts of his abstracted manner and odd conversational habits.

An addict who indulges beyond maintenance level, as Thompson did, for part of his life at least, has his passivity increased, is detached from other people and maintains less and less control over his will. At the same time, de Quincey and others assert, he develops an illusion of power over things and mastery over circumstance. 'Space, also, it amplifies by degrees that are sometimes terrific. But time it is upon which the exalting and multiplying power of opium chiefly spends its operation. Time becomes infinitely elastic, stretching out to such immeasurable and vanishing termini that it seems ridiculous to compute the sense of it, on waking, by expressions commensurate to human life', as de Quincey writes in *Suspira de Profundis*.

In this seeming acquisition of domination over time and place lies the Artificial Paradise of Baudelaire, where the opium-taker is lord of his supra-mundane kingdom, where 'L'universalité des êtres se dresse devant nous avec une gloire non soupçonnée jusqu'alors.' Here, too, is the sense of domination which Aldous Huxley claimed to have found in mescalin, and the conviction of superhuman powers which Rimbaud expressed in 'Matineé

[1] Krueger, *Pharmacology of the Opium Alkaloids*, Suppl. No. 165, I, 29–32.

d'Ivresse', that state in which he wrote the silences, and the darkness, and recorded inexpressible and fixed frenzies in their flight.

In such circumstances, the writer often sees himself as God, the great spirit dominating the cosmos, swinging planets like bracelet-ornaments, using stars as playthings, precisely as Thompson treats the universe in his poetry. Yet it must be remembered that de Quincey begins his *Confessions* with the comment that 'if a man "whose talk is of oxen" should become an opium-eater, the probability is that (if he is not too dull to dream at all) he will dream about oxen'. While the body of the addict dreams, while his will is suspended, while what goes on in the outside world ceases to be of importance, since he counts himself the king of infinite space, his intellectual activity is in fact suspended, and his creative powers inhibited. De Quincey, a man of stronger will than Thompson, managed his copious journalism by rigidly controlling and timing his drug-taking. Thompson, temperamentally more susceptible to the seductions of opium, was unable to do this in his earlier phase, and seems to have pushed his dosages up to the limits of tolerance in pursuit of the imagined cosmic and spiritual harmony which narcotic trance offered. For most addicts agree that the appeal of escape through drugs is so strong that on return to a reality that is for them unreal, their main desire is to retreat back from it into the self-sufficient universe they have ordered in fantasy.

We don't know how much laudanum Thompson took before he met Wilfrid Meynell. Laudanum, or opium tincture, is a hydro-alcoholic solution containing ten per cent of opium. Blunt tells us that the poet took six ounces daily in the extremity of his final weeks. Compared with de Quincey's fifty-three ounces on peak days, this seems little enough. Against this must be balanced Thompson's weaker constitution and his advanced tubercular condition. The most we can say is that, in the early years of his addiction, he shows every sign of having been slavishly devoted to opium, pushing his maintenance need higher and higher, whereas after his 'cure', he seems, like de Quincey, to have kept the drug reasonably under control.

Yet, in all, we can hardly doubt that laudanum confirmed Thompson in his emotional pattern and his mental habits, and that in it he found a substitute for the lost world of childhood. At home, conditioned, no doubt, by fear of his family's discovering his vice, he controlled the dosage so that the effects did not become too noticeable, although it was evidently a deterioration in 1885 which led his father to suspect alcoholism. In London, he abandoned restraint, and plunged not only into the lower depths of the city but into the lower depths of addiction as well.

IV

Under those Dread Wheels

WITH little more luggage than a few extra pieces of clothing and with Blake and Aeschylus stuffed in his pockets, Thompson arrived in London in December, 1885. He was nearly twenty-six years old, and carried the marks of the provinces on him in his Lancashire accent which Viola Meynell calls 'slight' but W. S. Blunt 'broad'. He was thin, with ill-covered shoulder-blades, although he carried himself bravely upright, a large, self-indulgent mouth, not yet veiled with the straggly moustache and beard of later years, and large, melancholy eyes. Although he did not know it, he was to become spiritually one of a band of young literary men, the 'beat generation' of the late eighties and nineties, including Lionel Johnson, Ernest Dowson, Aubrey Beardsley, who were pursuing the decadent muse through the sinuous corridors of disordered lives.

His arrival in London was the beginning of three years of desolation which have done most to create the Thompson legend and have provided the occasion for much purely sentimental writing. The general tendency is to excuse, or at least to mini-mize, the lack of moral stamina these years reveal by associating them either with religious asceticism or with the self-oblivious dedication of the artist. Some, too, are much concerned to separate him from the decadents. 'No one looks upon him as a *fin de siècle* poet', writes one Catholic critic.[1] The argument seems to be, in part, that while Wilde, Beardsley, Dowson, Lionel Johnson and others were drunkards or drew obscene

[1] Calvert Alexander, S.J.: *The Catholic Literary Revival*, Bruce, 1935, p. 150.

pictures or practised sexual vice, Thompson remained faithful to his religion and retained, despite his opium-addiction, his purity of spirit. The latter point may well be true, although there seems little to choose between Dowson's drunkenness and 'curious disregard of personal tidiness', and Thompson's abandonment to opium and personal unkemptness. At the same time, we know very little of Thompson's inner religious life at this time. If we may trust 'The Hound of Heaven', his religion in his London slum days, although not abandoned, was clung to largely out of habit and was less of a haven and a dynamic force than it was to Dowson. In point of fact, as Osbert Burdett recognized, 'he was, critically considered, the most decadent of writers'.[1]

Was it his muse he was seeking in the London gutters? As we have seen, he set out in desolation, not in hope, and during the years in which he moved evasively through the arches of the Metropolis, he made little attempt to be a writer. His initial offerings to Meynell were very meagre, and Meynell himself described Thompson's discovery of his own poetic gifts as a surprise to him. 'I gave him Mrs. Meynell's little volume of *Poems*', he told Mégroz. 'He took it away to his lodgings, and when he came back he told us how he had sat up reading it that night, and finally had thrown it down in his excitement, and said aloud "Then I, too, am a poet!" He found she had said things he wanted to say, and *it came to him as a revelation that they were sayable.*'[2] We must assume that Thompson, however much he later attributed his misfortunes to his hidden pursuit of the poetic vocation, had, during his Manchester and London period, only the dimmest of ideas about his talents; positive development of his gift was inhibited by the conflict between the intelligent man who acknowledged the world and the fact of communication and the secretive dreamer who wanted only to feed silently upon the manna of his illusions.

In any case, he made no attempt to get in touch with relatives in London who might have helped him. His father sent him seven shillings a week to a reading-room in the Strand, which he collected for a short while. Then he began to erect the familiar

[1] *The Beardsley Period*, The Bodley Head, 1925, p. 174.
[2] R. L. Mégroz: *Francis Thompson. The Poet of Earth in Heaven*, Faber and Gwyer, 1927, p. 28. [Italics mine.]

wall of excuses and rationalizations between himself and the allowance, persuading himself either that it had not arrived, or that he was too suitably dressed to collect it, or that it was the wrong day, and so on. Thompson's compulsion to cast himself outside society, a desire to declass himself more complete than that of the hero of John Wain's *Hurry On Down*, prevented him from collecting the money even when he most needed it, until at length his father discontinued the payments.

Since he still had to have funds for food and laudanum, his love of books drew him to the job of 'collector' for a bookseller in Panton Street. His task was to gather in a sack the volumes required daily by his employer from the wholesalers. He soon lost this job, partly through indolence, partly through being more interested in reading some of the books than in speedily delivering them. It was not long before he ceased to find any regular work at all, and, since laudanum took precedence over food and lodgings, he was reduced to ragged, unclean penury; the respectable doctor's son had transformed himself into a piece of human flotsam. So careless of his personal appearance did he become that Bernard Kettle, then librarian of the Guildhall Library, recalled: 'He was so poorly clad that it fell to my lot to have to perform the painful duty of asking him to forgo his visits here. He always came in with two books in his pocket. One, I think, was Sophocles; and had I known I was entertaining an "angel unawares", I should perhaps have been more reluctant to eject him.' [1]

The chances of the late Victorian streets provided Thompson with a mockery of a livelihood. He tried a boot-black stand, unsuccessfully, which is not surprising in view of his diffident nature and lively Cockney competition; he ran behind luggage-laden cabs in the hope that at their destination he might earn a few coppers helping to unload the cargo; he held horses for sixpence; he sold matches and newspapers. Time and again he had not enough for a bed even in the meaner doss-houses, so he spent the night sometimes in a shelter provided on the Embankment for the homeless, sleeping on a mattress in a box like a lidless coffin, with a leather blanket, sometimes in the crypt of St.

[1] *An Encyclopaedia of London*, edited by William Kent, J. M. Dent & Sons Ltd., 1951, p. 358.

Martin's-in-the-Fields on a wooden bench, sometimes under the arches of the Adelphi, enduring

> through watches of the dark
> The abashless inquisition of each star.

When he had the price of a bed, he would mingle with the down-and-outs in a doss-house, finding them kind and friendly in their rough way to this obvious 'gentleman' down on his luck, although their language offended his Ushaw-trained ears. ('For naked bestiality you must go to the modern *bête humaine*', he wrote.) It is said that one of those he chatted with around a lodging-house fire was a murderer, and there were other criminals, too, with whom he innocently rubbed shoulders. He learned the economies of the poor, where to buy the cheapest food, and how to make a drink from a pennyworth of tea added to boiling water from the doss-house kettle. He shared the rude companionship of the gutters, sheltering from the elements in doorways and porches and wandering the streets by day and by night, in a limited area, mainly the City and the West End. Years later, in 1897, he was commissioned to write a book on London, but, despite elaborate plans ('My design is to give impressions of London, such as present themselves to a wanderer through its streets') it was never written, partly, at least, because his knowledge of the city was restricted to a few localities —the Strand, Covent Garden, Trafalgar Square, the Embankment, Blackfriars Bridge. It is doubtful, anyhow, whether, despite his years in the open, his inward-looking eyes observed enough of the details of his environment to give life and body to such a book.

Something of the mood of these black outcast days comes across to us, however, from a review Thompson later wrote of General Booth's *In Darkest England*, where the grinding misery he saw in the slums, the deforming pressures of environment and the sense of agonized humanity prompt him in retrospect to rhetorical flights:

> 'Misery cries out to me from the kerb-stone, despair passes
> me by in the ways; I discern limbs laden with fetters impalp-
> able, but not imponderable; I hear the shaking of invisible
> lashes, I see men dabbled with their own oozing life. . . . Our

39

destitute children . . . are brought up in sin from their cradles, they know evil before they know good, the boys are ruffians and profligates, the girls harlots in the mother's womb . . . If Christ stood amidst your London slums, He could not say: "Except ye become as one of *these* little children." Far better your children were cast from the bridges of London than they should become as one of these little ones.'

It is hard to imagine Thompson forming anything like a friendship with the outcasts with whom he shared lodgings and beds; but they tolerated him, perhaps, even, for his talk, respected him, and they passed on to him their own painfully learnt ways of earning a few coppers to ward off absolute destitution. Sometimes he had a stroke of fortune which he was sure was Providential; once a policeman gave him money, one of the Rothschilds tendered him a florin for a newspaper and on an unforgettable occasion he found two golden sovereigns in his path.

From such a miserable condition, he was first rescued through the charity of a bootmaker, Mr. McMaster, a devout Anglican solicitous for the souls of the unfortunate. The ragged, dirty Thompson, dazedly withdrawn into his secret world, was wandering one day in Wardour Street after about nine months in London, when he was confronted by a man who said to him abruptly, 'Is your soul saved?' 'What right have you to ask me that?' Thompson replied. And McMaster, recognizing something unusual in the way of vagrants, said, 'If you won't let me save your soul, at least let me save your body.' This good man had already rescued more than one crushed soul from the miseries of the gutter, and Thompson became the latest to whom he gave employment in his shop at Panton Street. Learning on enquiry from the Thompsons at Ashton-under-Lyne that Francis' story of his origins was true, Mr. McMaster found him lodgings, clothed him, gave him food and five shillings a week for his services as messenger and odd-job man and putter-up of shutters. The question of proselytizing never arose. Thompson made it plain from the beginning that he was a Catholic; he had his medal round his neck and a crucifix in his room, and he said his prayers, 'his Mass', as McMaster described it, every night.

The kindly bootmaker found that his new protégé was much
better at talking and at asking questions than at his simple tasks.
But he grew fond of the poet, lent him books to read, including
the Iliad and Bulwer-Lytton, and entrusted his children to him
to take on walks, admiring his tender ways with them. One result of McMaster's communication with Charles Thompson was
that, at Christmas, 1886, Francis, neatly dressed for the occasion,
paid a fortnight's visit to his family. But the barriers already
thrown up by Thompson at home, which had been reinforced
by his year in London, prevented any real contact between
father and son. Apparently Dr. Thompson had despaired completely of his son's ever making anything of himself; 'a dawdling,
sauntering sort of life', as he put it, was what the lad had chosen
for himself. No confidences being offered, it was taken for
granted that Francis had now obtained some simple job which
gave him sustenance. The family was breaking up; Mary was
early in 1887 to enter a convent in Manchester, where she spent
over sixty happy years; Charles Thompson married his second
wife, Anne Richardson, in the same year. The only other time
Thompson was to return home was on his father's death ten
years later. There was nothing now left for him at Ashton-under-
Lyne save memories and regrets. The 'Paradisus Vitae' had
vanished for ever.

When he returned to London, he became an even less satisfactory employee than before. It is easy to understand why. His
brief contact with his family, on the point of dissolution, had
re-awakened that consciousness of reality he had been striving
to stamp out, and made him realize that he had lost what might
be—and in fact was—the last chance of making reparation to
his father for his wasted years. Back in the city, the industrious
McMaster and his thronging family reminded him, too, of the
obligations of manhood. So by increased doses of laudanum he
strove to cut the ropes that bound him to hateful reality.
His inefficiency, his clumsiness, his jerky movements and his
abstractions increased, and Mr. McMaster, as Dr. Thompson had before him, put them down to alcohol. Francis had
been back at Panton Street merely a few days when his shift-
lessness wore down even the bootmaker's forbearance, and
they parted company in the middle of January, 1887.
McMaster spoke of Thompson as 'my only failure'; he did

not learn of the poet's later fame until after Thompson's death.

Thompson mentioned McMaster to Wilfrid Meynell and said that he was kind, but dwelt more upon the rebuff he gave the evangelical question put to him in Wardour Street. That he felt grateful to McMaster is plain, but he never went back to Panton Street to visit his first London friend, to tell him of his later success, or to express his gratitude. This is consistent with his character. He was unable or unwilling to give concrete expression to his feelings; even to perform the normal action of translating a sentiment into an act of gratitude; to the Meynells, who did so much for him, he could not manifest by ordinary domestic courtesy any awareness of his debt to them. This seems to be more than high sensitivity, of the kind which makes some people avoid a dear friend on occasions so as to be spared the strain of responding to him; it was part of his emotional indolence and odd scale of values in which ordinary personal relations occupied a very low place.

If Thompson's condition before McMaster threw a life-line to him had been bad, his state when he loosed his hold on it was even worse. He now lived for nothing but laudanum; most of his wages from the bootshop had gone for it (to be sure the wages were meagre, but laudanum was dirt cheap); now food, shelter and clothing were sacrificed on the same altar. Back in the lower depths, haunting Covent Garden and the archways, he resumed his life as a vagrant in 'a region whose hedgerows have set to brick, whose soil is chilled to stone', as he wrote, 'where flowers are sold and women, where the men wither and the stars; whose streets to me on the most glittering day are black'.

Not even the unfortunate Simeon Solomon, stumbling dirty and tattered through London slums at this time, sank deeper into destitution than Thompson did now. In the squalor of the gutter he sought his private paradise. His sufferings were as acute as a sensitive nature could bear, not only the physical and psychological torments when absolute poverty deprived him for periods of the drug for which his spirit craved, but also agonies of white-hot irons of guilt pressing upon his Catholic conscience. He was twenty-eight years old; he had achieved nothing; he had left a legacy of sorrow behind at home; a handful of indifferent verses were all he had to show for it. We have the word of McMaster that Thompson scribbled poetry in the shop's old account-books, and that he had sent his work to several magazines. However, nothing was published, and nobody knows how seriously Thompson took this scribbling or what was the worth of the pieces thus written. What seems more than likely, given his early history, is that the notion of a poetic vocation burned very dimly at this stage, and that the verse of this period was produced less with the aim of a literary career than with the intention of purgation, of unpacking his dream-laden heart with words. Now he gave himself almost wholly to the embraces of the Dark Mistress, from shabbiness sinking to rags, from poverty to beggary, from unkemptness to dirt. The Embankment saw him more often than the meaner doss-houses; time and space were dissolved for him in a narcoticized state in which he was commander of the cosmos, superior to all other men. The future was of no account beside the drugged present. It is surprising how very little of the external world seems to have penetrated to his consciousness. Out of the thousands of lines of poetry he was later to write, fewer than fifty have direct reference to his physical sensations or his concrete surroundings at this time; but the poems are crammed with recollections of his dreams.

Picking up a few pence again from matches, newspapers, horse-holding and from the charity of passers-by, shivering under newspapers on the Victoria Embankment, huddled in an alley or doorway in Covent Garden, nourished on scraps from the vegetable-wagons, kicked and frequently moved on by the police, Francis Thompson had reached his nadir, when charity came to him, on his own account, from an unexpected quarter. A prostitute took pity on him, and when her transient lovers no longer claimed her attention, would take him home, feed him and give her bed to him. She lived in Chelsea but her beat was in streets near the Strand and she would take her forlorn charge from there in a cab. In her lodgings, Thompson found a companionship and warmth which filled the gap left by the death of his mother. In his relations with the prostitute he exhibited the pattern of love which was consistently his, that of a child for its parent, although sometimes it is he who is the parent and the other who is the child. There was no sexual contact between the two; not only does opium inhibit sexual desire, but Thompson, apart from his religious regard for sexual purity, hardly ever evinces in his poetry any but immature and undeveloped erotic feeling. As he told it, the prostitute became his friend and saviour, she listened to him talk, heard him read his fumbling lines, and cherished him. Everard Meynell, translating Thompson's account, describes their relationship thus: 'Weakness and confidence, humility and reverence, were gifts unknown to her except at his hands, and she repaid them with graces as lovely as a child's, and as unhesitating as a saint's.' [1]

It all makes a touching story, the most romantic episode in Thompson's life, which has provided the basis for two highly imaginative plays about the poet. Yet the golden-hearted prostitute, from la Dame aux Camélias onwards, is a prettified stereotype much more frequently found in literature than in life; it is one of the persistent literary myths of the century. Suspicion deepens when it is recalled that de Quincey claimed exactly the same kind of relationship with his 'noble-minded Ann', a sixteen-year-old prostitute who was his companion night after night in Oxford Street, who gave him money for food from her slender purse, and who, like Thompson's unnamed daughter of joy and charity, vanished when he would seek her out to repay her. This remarkable coincidence does not mean that Thompson's story was a mere fabrication, an attempt to push still further the parallel between himself and the opium-eater, but a stubborn doubt remains whether, in his frequent confounding of dream with reality, he may not have unconsciously heightened, on the deep-sunk model of de Quincey's experience, a chance association of less consequence than he made it appear. His own account reads too like his ecstatic description of the Vatican Melpomene or his high-falutin poems to Alice Meynell to be taken wholly at its surface value.

Years later, in lines from *Sister Songs* addressed to little Monica Meynell, he told the story thus:

> bled of strength,
> I waited the inevitable last.
> Then there came past
> A child; like thee, a spring-flower; but a flower
> Fallen from the budded coronal of Spring,
> And through the city-streets blown withering.

[1] *The Life of Francis Thompson*, Burns & Oates, 1913, p. 82.

She passed,—O brave, sad, lovingest, tender thing!
And of her own scant pittance did she give,
     That I might eat and live:
Then fled, a swift and trackless fugitive.
     Therefore I kissed in thee
The heart of Childhood, so divine for me;
     And her, through what sore ways,
     And what unchildish days,
Borne from me now, as then, a trackless fugitive.
     Therefore I kissed in thee
     Her, child! and innocency,
And spring, and all things that have gone from me,
     And that shall never be;

The comparative directness of this passage as compared with the flamboyance of the rest of *Sister Songs* gives it the ring of truth—since Thompson is nearly always at his most sincere when he is writing simply. We may, too, respect his sentiment concerning the fundamental innocence of his prostitute. Yet 'a flower fallen from the budded coronal of Spring', so resembling Oscar Wilde's frigidities, is surely a strange and inadequate description of any street-walker, suggesting rather a remoulding of some actual happening by the hands of fantasy.

It was while Thompson was receiving help from this girl, in whatever circumstances, that he tried again to sell some of his poems. They were rejected, not surprisingly, for such fragments and pieces as survive are almost completely without distinction, and in any case were written on any grimy, tattered scraps of paper that came to hand. In his extremity, perhaps in despair, he remembered *Merry England*, a Catholic paper he is likely to have seen in his uncle E. H. Thompson's house, when he stayed there on his fruitless examination-visits. This illustrated monthly, priced at one shilling, had been founded in 1883 as an organ to propagate Catholic principles, expecially as they concerned working-class conditions, but taking in literature and art as well. Among the contributors was a solid core of Catholics, most of them in sympathy with the social ideas of Cardinal Manning, including Lionel Johnson, Hilaire Belloc (whose first-printed poem appeared in its pages), Coventry Patmore, E. H. Thompson, Aubrey de Vere, Sir William Butler and Cardinal Manning himself. W. S. Blunt, George Saintsbury, St. John Adcock, and

45

W. H. Hudson also wrote for the paper. For the editor and proprietor was an able young journalist in his thirties with a talent for making friends, Wilfrid Meynell, a convert from Quakerism, who in 1877 had married a poet, Alice Thompson. Ten years later both were busy journalists, toiling indefatigably to support their fast increasing family.

In February, 1887, Francis Thompson had some kind of windfall, and, as he himself said: 'With a few shillings to give me breathing space, I began to decipher and put together the half-obliterated manuscript of "Paganism" '—that is, an essay called 'Paganism Old and New', which contains in its opening paragraphs the words 'those who, like the present writer, tread as on thorns amidst the sordidness and ugliness, the ugly sordidness and sordid ugliness, the dull materiality and weariness of this unhonoured old age of the world'. Putting the article and some poems in an envelope, he dropped them one night into the letter-box of 43, Essex Street, the offices of *Merry England*, apologizing in his accompanying letter for 'the soiled state of the manuscript' which was, he said, 'due, not to slovenliness, but to the strange places and circumstances under which it has been written', and enclosing an envelope for reply, bearing a stamp bought with his last penny. But Wilfrid Meynell was too busy an editor to read every unsolicited manuscript, especially when it looked as unpromising as this one. So for six months the package remained unopened. When it was finally examined, Meynell was struck by the quality of the essay, although the poetry did not impress him. He wrote at once to the only address Thompson had supplied, the Charing Cross Post Office, asking him to call and discuss using some of the work. But no reply came and the letter was eventually returned as unclaimed. Accordingly, after more delay, the poem 'The Passion of Mary' was printed in *Merry England* in April, 1888, fourteen months after its submission, in the hope that the elusive poet would see it and get in touch with Meynell.

In the meantime, Thompson, who, as the tone of his covering letter showed, had no real expectation of publication, had gone further down the ladder of despair. Even the friendship of the prostitute, whatever part she played in his life, proved insufficient for his consolation. Alternating with the euphoria of opium were the dreadful waking lucid moments of self-pity and abysmal despair. He came at last to the state where the tensions within him so rent his spirit that only one solution seemed possible—self-destruction. Meynell passed on to W. S. Blunt the poet's own account of his action.

'It was in an empty space of ground behind the market where the gardeners throw their rubbish that, just before, he had resolved on suicide. He then spent all his remaining pence on laudanum, one large dose, and he went there one night to take it. He had swallowed half when he felt an arm laid on his wrist, and looking up he saw Chatterton standing over him and forbidding him to drink the other half. I asked him when he told of it how he had known it was Chatterton. He said, "I recognized him from the pictures of him—besides, I knew that it was he before I saw him—and I remembered at once the story of the money which arrived for Chatterton the day after his suicide." Just the same thing happened to Thompson, for a friend, having seen the copy of *Merrie England* [*sic*], told him about it the very next morning.'

As with the story of the prostitute, there is something a little too pat about the details of this business. The date is impossible to ascertain, and the story of the just-too-late arrival of money for Chatterton is, in any case, a fiction. More than one attempt has been made, by Catholics shocked at the idea of a suicide-attempt by the author of 'The Hound of Heaven', to challenge the whole account.[1] Certainly the episode is not mentioned by Everard Meynell, and rests upon Blunt's account of a conversation with Wilfrid Meynell, which, however, he recorded in almost identical terms in both an obituary article in the *Academy* and his published *Diaries*. Yet Wilfrid Meynell, asked about the incident in his extreme old age, when his memory was failing, was unable to deny that Thompson had told it to him.

The suicide-attempt story bears all the marks of typical Thompsonian self-dramatization, as well as of that half-unconscious activity prompted by the drug and of his characteristic indecision. That his will had not completely atrophied is seen from his posting his manuscripts to *Merry England*; it is possible,

[1] See, for instance, Doyle Hennessy, 'Did Francis Thompson Attempt Suicide?' *Catholic World*, February, 1950, pp. 346–50.

indeed, that he could will himself to the verge of suicide. But it is not surprising that, even in his extremity, his Catholic training which had taught him that suicide is the final sin of blasphemous despair should have caused him to draw back. The apparition of Chatterton we can safely dismiss as an opium fantasy or a piece of rationalizing; nor need we accept the melodramatic touch of the discovery, next morning, of the poem in Meynell's paper. For one thing, there is good evidence that Thompson knew beforehand that *Merry England* was to print his poem. Canon John Carroll (later to become the Bishop of Shrewsbury) had been a close friend of the family in Preston and Ashton-under-Lyne. He kept in touch with Thompson during part of his London days, supplied him with money then as later, and tried to serve as a link between the poet and his family. Just before 'The Passion of Mary' appeared in *Merry England*, the Canon got in touch with Thompson and asked him if he knew that Meynell intended to print the piece. When Thompson told him 'No', the priest asked him to call at the office of *Merry England*. This the poet would not do, but instead took the step of surprising decisiveness for him, a step which was to change the entire course of his life. On the 14th of April, Wilfrid Meynell received a letter written in a disorderly scribble on grubby paper, which ran in part,

DEAR SIR—

   In the last days of February or the first days of March, 1887 (my memory fails me as to the exact date), I forwarded to you for your magazine a prose article, 'Paganism Old and New' (or 'Ancient and Modern' for I forget which wording I adopted), and accompanied it by some pieces of verse, on the chance that if the prose failed, some of the verse might meet acceptance. . . . To be brief, from that day to this, no answer has ever come into my hands. And yet, more than a twelve-month since the forwarding of the manuscript, I am now informed that one of the copies of verse which I submitted to you (i.e. 'The Passion of Mary') is appearing in this month's issue of *Merry England*. Such an occurence I can only explain to myself in one way, viz., that some untoward accident cut off your means of communicating with me. To suppose otherwise—to suppose it intentional—would be to wrong your known honour and courtesy.... I therefore enclose a stamped and addressed envelope for an answer, hoping that you will recompense me for my long delay by the favour of an early reply. . . .

I remain,

Yours faithfully,

FRANCIS JOSEPH THOMPSON

P.S.—Doubtless, when I received no answer, I ought to have written again. My excuse must be that a flood-tide of misfortune rolled over me, leaving me no leisure to occupy myself with what I regarded as an attempt that had hopelessly failed. Hence my entire subsequent silence.

Hidden beneath the formal English Thompson could write so fluently even in the tightest grip of opium is the pain and misery of a sunk soul, as well as a diffidence and an agonized self-mistrust which must have struck a sensitive chord in Meynell. What prompted Thompson to write this letter? To find an explanation other than the natural response of somebody about to see a poem of his own in print for the first time, we must look beyond the tangled psychology of this neurotic dreamer to the fact of his religion. In practice, though well-intentioned, he was, both in his London days and later, inclined to be lax; at Ushaw he had given no evidence of particular piety. Yet, from McMaster's evidence, we know that, even in the darkest days, he remained faithful to the prayers learnt at home and Ushaw. Throughout his entire life, his faith is the only constant thing that stood between him and complete surrender to self, the only tie that bound him to the world of obligations. Intellectually, he seems to have had, in the time we are now considering, merely a limited apprehension of his religion. Later he was to add a richer spiritual intuition to his youthful love for the externals of Catholicism. But, emotionally, he was deeply involved, from childhood days, in religion. 'The Passion of Mary' is a genuine *cri de cœur*, written from the depths of 'this cold tomb of life', and the envoy is a strenuous prayer for help in his agony, as well as a statement of hope:

O Thou who dwellest in the day!

Behold, I pace amidst the gloom:

Under those Dread Wheels

Darkness is ever round my way
With little space for sunbeam-room.

Yet Christian sadness is divine
Even as *thy* patient sadness was:
The salt tears in our life's dark wine
Fell in it from the saving cross.

Bitter the bread of our repast;
Yet doth a sweet the bitter leaven:
Our sorrow is the shadow cast
Around it by the light of Heaven.

O light in Light, shine down from Heaven!

This undistinguished poem contains hardly a trace of what were to be recognized as characteristic Thompsonian affectations; but it affords striking proof of that religious trust which, even in his most befogged state, kept him from total surrender. In any case, whether we choose to regard his action in writing to Meynell as an answer to prayer, or as a manifestation of the other man hidden within him, Thompson, after a long flight from his fellows, took the step which was to bring him from darkness into light.

On reading Thompson's letter, Wilfrid Meynell sent a reply at once to the chemist's shop in Drury Lane whose name appeared on the enclosed envelope. When he received no reply, he went in person to enquire. He learnt that the poet did not lodge there, the chemist's chief connection with him being as a supplier of laudanum. There was, in fact, a debt of three and ninepence, which Meynell, as a supposed relative, was expected to pay. For this and something extra, the chemist promised to pass a message on should Thompson call again.

Some days afterwards, Meynell was working in his office at 43 Essex Street, from which he edited the *Weekly Register* and *Merry England*, when Thompson was announced. Outside the door, the poet hesitated, as at 'Fate's dread portal', like Kafka's K. approaching the Advocate, or, in his own words:

Like one who sweats before a despot's gate,
Summoned by some presaging scroll of fate,
And knows not whether kiss or dagger wait.

Then, as Meynell told Blunt:

'When he came into the room, he half opened the door and then retreated and did so twice before he got courage to come inside. He was in rags, his feet, without stockings, showing through his boots, his coat torn, and no shirt. He seemed in the last stages of physical collapse. I asked him how, being in such a condition, he had been able to consult the books out of which he had gathered the quotations for his essay. He answered: "Books I have none, but Blake and the Bible." All the quotations had been made from memory.'

The ragged poet, terrible in his destitution, was more than Meynell had bargained for. His pity was stirred by the forlorn spectacle, but the thirty-six-year-old editor and the twenty-nine-year-old derelict did not become intimate at once. There was diffidence on both sides, aggravated by Thompson's natural evasiveness. Meynell, who did not at this time suspect the effort it had cost Thompson to visit him, gave him a cheque for his poem, but was unable to persuade him to accept a small weekly sum. However, he succeeded in obtaining Thompson's promise to come again, and a few days later the poet reappeared to talk about possible future work for *Merry England*.

A little later, thanks to Meynell's tact, a breach was made in Thompson's secretiveness and the poet came to dine at the Meynells' home in Upper Phillimore Place, where, for the first time, he met Alice Meynell, the goddess of his later verse. On this initial visit, the forerunner of countless others, the two men sat talking until about ten, when Thompson said that he had to leave. When Meynell asked why, Thompson replied that he was obliged every day to earn at least tenpence on which to live. This he did by calling cabs for theatre-goers and selling matches near Charing Cross. Even to the gentle Meynell, Thompson was reluctant to surrender his pain-racked independence; the way of the streets had become as much a part of him as a limp to a lame man. Perhaps, too, he feared that too close contact with the Meynells would mean that the spring-doors of reality's trap would close behind him. He was cagey, elusive; he talked freely enough of books but sparingly of himself; he responded tepidly to Meynell's assurance that he could make a livelihood by writing. The editor even offered to take Thompson into his own home, and, when the poet refused, pressed him for a reason. At last it came out. He had told his prostitute-friend of his first interview with Meynell, and she had said that his new friends would not understand their relationship. The next day she disappeared from her customary beat and changed her lodgings without a word to Thompson. He was haunting the streets, hoping to catch a glimpse of her; he never did. So at least is what he told Wilfrid Meynell. Perhaps one can be too sceptical about stories of this kind, but, to me, the noble renunciation of the woman of the streets, so like fiction, so unlike life, while not impossible, carries, as does so much of Thompson's poetry, strong overtones of romanticization, wish-fulfilment and de Quinceyism.

Certainly, Meynell was finding it hard to persuade the ragged poet either to accept help or to write more for him. Two more pieces from the original manuscripts—'Dream Tryst', a poem, and 'Paganism Old and New'—were printed in *Merry England* for May and June; but six months elapsed before Meynell could wring from Thompson another contribution, this time an essay on Bunyan. Some have expressed surprise that Thompson, with the pages of a journal now open to him, wrote no poetry during this period. The explanation is that he was still taking copious draughts of laudanum which, far from producing imaginative work, actually, in the abstracted state, inhibits it. What does one want with poems when one has dreams?

Still, Meynell's generosity and the atmosphere of Upper Phillimore Place succeeded where the inquisitions of Charles Thompson had failed. Opium was at last mentioned. Meynell's immediate response was to fit Thompson with a new suit of clothes and persuade him, not without great labour, to visit a physician, who pronounced his case a hopeless one of narcotic poisoning. All that could be done, he advised, was to permit Thompson to continue taking the drug to smooth his speedy descent into the grave. This did not satisfy Meynell, now assuming complete responsibility for his discovery, and late in 1888, he managed to manœuvre Thompson, still unwilling to do anything to help himself, into a private hospital. Here, for several weeks, the derelict underwent the excruciating pangs of deprivation. 'Not Even in Dreams' and 'Non Pax-Expectatio' probably date from this period; the latter poem, in particular, reflects his torment during this treatment.

> Hush! 'tis the gap between two lightnings. Room
> Is none for peace in this thou callest peace,
> This breathing-while wherein the breathings cease.
> The pulses sicken, hearkening through the gloom.
> Afar the thunders of a coming doom
> Ramp on the cowering winds. Lo! at the dread,
> Thy heart's tomb yawns and renders up its dead—
> The hopes 'gainst hope embalmèd in its womb.

Finally discharged and believed 'cured', Thompson was so physically weak and mentally depressed, a mere shell of a man, that Meynell, after taking him under his roof for a while, arranged for him to convalesce in the Premonstratensian Monastery at Storrington in Sussex. There Thompson went early in 1889 and remained until about February, 1890, tended by the devoted monks. Meynell had two motives in sending the poet to Sussex. One was to make him free of the invigorating air and therapeutic atmosphere of the countryside, to wash his lungs clean of London's tainted air, and to withdraw him as far as possible from the memories associated with the withering streets of the slums; the other was to make sure that he was cut off completely from access to opium.

This enforced abstinence had an astonishing effect. From this man of thirty who had had only two rather mediocre poems printed, poetry now poured in a turbid torrent. The flood-gates were opened, and images cascaded from his brain; the quiet Downs at Storrington echoed with the surges of his tumultuous song. Now that he no longer had laudanum to seal him within the placid garden of his dreams, the whole universe of his stored fantasies spilled out on to paper.

V

Withered Dreams

THE part played by the withholding of the drug in liberating Thompson's muse has been recognized. 'The renunciation of opium, not its indulgence, opened the doors of the intellect', writes Everard Meynell. The method of 'cure' adopted in Thompson's case was apparently abrupt withdrawal of the narcotic without substitution therapy. The physical and emotional consequences of such a cure have been made familiar to the general public in our own day by books like Nelson Algren's *The Man with a Golden Arm* and plays like Michael Vincente Gazzo's *A Hatful of Rain*. The release of the nervous and muscular systems from the inhibition of the drug results in exaggerated physiological activity, expressed in such effects as retching, sneezing, tears, twitches, convulsions, fever, diarrhœa and alternation of chills with excessive sweating, as the tortured body cells strive to readjust their metabolism.[1] As Sir William Henry Willcox says, describing withdrawal symptoms in his article on 'Drug Addiction' in the *Encyclopaedia Britannica*, 'Pains in the body and limbs may occur and mental symptoms of restlessness and apparent mental suffering are exhibited in a marked degree.' Physical exhaustion allied to nervous exhaustion often produces in the patient fits of acute mental depression, even suicidal tendencies. (Was it after a spell of abstinence or involuntary deprivation that Thompson made his abortive attempt at suicide?)

One effect of abrupt withdrawal is hyperaesthesia; the former addict's sensibility becomes abnormally acute, noises, especially

[1] See Goodman and Gilman, op. cit., p. 245.

the curious whispering sounds described by de Quincey and others as part of opium dreams, become intensified, the skin itself becomes very sensitive to the touch. For a long time, as Elisabeth Schneider points out,[1] the effects of withdrawal symptoms were confused with the effects of opium itself. When Alice Meynell, defending Francis Thompson, said once that none of his important poems was written under the influence of opium, she was missing the point. While doses above maintenance level prolong the passive state in which the mind of the compulsive neurotic dreamer surrenders to his fantasies, there is no evidence that opium is itself responsible for the tortured visions commonly attributed to it. Joris-Karl Huysmans, having assiduously cultivated his delicate sensibilities on decadent literature and art, found, in the person of his hero Des Esseintes, that, when he was very ill from dyspepsia and nervous stomach troubles, many of the characteristic hyperaesthetic effects of drug withdrawal showed themselves. Without the aid of drugs, Des Esseintes, in *A Rebours*, experiences nightmares, hallucinations of smell, disturbances of vision; he hears the sounds of running water and buzzing wasps melting into a single noise like the whirring of a lathe, and finally changing into the silvery tinkle of a bell. Then he would be rolled along on billows of harmony, while he would appear to smell incense and see vast sanctuaries with lofty vaults. These and other sensations so closely resemble the twisted, exquisite experiences recorded by Coleridge, Poe and de Quincey that one is strongly inclined to regard them as the psychological consequences of the drug's withdrawal in the mind of highly imaginative people. Such withdrawal symptoms can, of course, occur during the course of addiction, if the addict reduces the amount of his usual dose or if he abstains beyond the time when he is accustomed to take his regular amount. Since during his vagrant days Thompson was often in a situation where he could not afford opium or when he could buy merely a limited quantity, he must have experienced many of the excruciating effects of withdrawal before he met Wilfrid Meynell.

The point I am making is this: Thompson, a natural dreamer, was enabled by opium to place himself more readily in the passive state for dreaming; his fantasies were elaborated by opium rather than produced by it; in the period of enforced

[1] *Coleridge, Opium and Kubla Khan*, p. 61.

abstinence in hospital, the hyperaesthesia and other consequences came to dominate his sensibilities, and, mingling with his memory of earlier withdrawal hallucinations, went to form a large part of the content of his newly-liberated verse.

According to some modern studies of the effects of drugs, the acuteness of withdrawal symptoms varies according to the instability of the temperament of the patient. Jean Cocteau, describing his own feelings while undergoing a cure, writes: 'Opium leads the organism towards death in euphoric mood. The tortures arise from the process of returning to life against one's wish. A whole springtime excites the veins to madness, bringing with it ice and fiery lava.' [1]

Several medical authorities regard most of the phenomena associated with disintoxication as mainly psychological in character. [2] In some lines on 'The Pains of Sleep', Coleridge gave a classic description of the phantoms that haunted his mind when he was attempting to do without opium:

> But yester-night I pray'd aloud
> In anguish and in agony,
> Awaking from the fiendish crowd
> Of shapes and thoughts that tortur'd me!
> Desire with loathing strangely mixt
> On wild and hateful objects fixt.
> Sense of revenge, the powerless will,
> Still baffled and consuming still;
> Sense of intolerable wrong,
> And men whom I despis'd made strong!
> Deeds to be hid that were not hid,
> Which all confus'd I might not know,
> Whether I suffer'd or I did:
> For all was Horror, Guilt, and Woe,
> My own or others still the same,
> Life-stifling Fear, soul-stifling Shame!

Thompson escaped none of these psychological and physical effects in hospital and at Storrington; while, under the deprivation, 'trains of forgotten thought rose up from their living

---

[1] *Opium*, translated by Margaret Crosland and Sinclair Road, Peter Owen, 1957, p. 22.
[2] For instance, Arthur B. Light and Edward G. Torrance, *Opium Addiction*, Philadelphia, 1930, p. 211.

catacombs', in Coleridge's phrase, and streamed into his poetry.

The period Thompson spent in hospital is often described as a 'cure'. But to be fully cured, he needed psychiatric treatment as well as physical care. As the United Nations Bulletin on the treatment of drug addiction says: 'The main characteristic of treatment will therefore be its psychotherapeutic nature, and it will not be fundamentally different from that used in the psycho-therapeutic management of other personality problems. Such treatment should aim at giving the patient more insight into his neurotic fears and wishes, and a better judgment of situations, thus enabling him better to respond to the unavoidable stress of life.'

Without such adjustment, the chances of relapse are very great, since the prime cause of addiction has not been removed; and hence it is not surprising that Thompson's so-called cure was temporary only. The kind of therapy he needed was to come later, through the growing influence of Alice Meynell, and, more particularly, of Coventry Patmore, from whom he was to learn enough about himself and his religion to complete the adjustment begun on only one level in Storrington.

Through Thompson's letters to Wilfrid Meynell from the Sussex Priory run, like the dull booming of a drum, the agonies of a man deprived of drugs, whose body and spirit are crying out in what Cocteau calls 'the worst moment, the worst danger'.

'I am, as I expected to be, very ill just now. . . . It is severer and more obstinate than I hoped would be the case. I am often fairly sick of the being that inhabits this villainous mud-hut of a body. I received the medicine all right. I was, for four or five days, much better, but I am sorry to say it did not last. Having noticed that the attacks came on principally during the half-sleep of early night or early morning, I sat up the greater part of the night in order to tire myself into heavy sleep. The device was successful during the four nights that I kept it up; but the first night that weariness caused me to drop it, the attack returned.'

And, in a letter written to Canon Carroll just after he returned to London from Storrington, he explicitly recognized the intimate connection between the pangs of withdrawal and the poetry:

> 'The fact is that I have been for months in a condition of acute mental misery, frequently almost akin to mania, stifling the production of everything except poetry, and rendering me quite incapable of sane letter-writing. It has ended in my return to London, and I am immensely relieved; for the removal of the opium had quite destroyed my power of bearing the almost unbroken solitude in which I found myself.'

The celebrated essay on Shelley, to which we shall return later, was one of the products of the Storrington period, written 'with quite agonizing pain and elaboration'. Bishop (later Cardinal) Vaughan, who had known Thompson at Ushaw, on meeting him again at the Meynells, had suggested that he write something for the *Dublin Review*, which the Bishop owned. This lush, rhetorical piece mingling miasmic self-projection with sensitive literary comment was rejected by the editor of the *Review*, and remained unprinted until after Thompson's death. But the main harvest of Storrington was poetry, bushels of it. The first piece, which so excited the Meynells that they hastened by train to Storrington to congratulate the author, was the elaborate 'Ode to the Setting Sun' which was followed by other pieces of the same characteristic style, from which the *Poems* of 1893 was later compiled. In the meantime, they were published by Wilfrid Meynell in successive issues of *Merry England*.

Despite the kindness of the monks, Thompson was overwhelmed with loneliness at Storrington. His whole being cried out for the grimy comfort of the slums, for the bleak companionship of the vagrants, for the life-in-death of the Embankment by night, and above all for the dulling clasp of the drug. He hugged the trees in passionate attempts to dispel his loneliness, and his long-winded letters to Meynell show his desperate need to cling to his memories of London, just as the verbal elaborations of the 'Shelley' essay indicate his attempt to recapture the fantasies of his tranquillized days. Spells of pride in his writing alternated with even more frequent fits of depression. The 'Shelley' essay, for instance, 'seemed to me dreadful trash when I read it over before sending it', although he was later to call it 'the picked fruit of three painful months'.

Dispossessed hermit-crab as he was, Thompson actually saw and absorbed very little of the Sussex countryside. Only a handful of precisely seen aspects of nature figure in his works; Blunt recorded that, in 1898, when the poet visited him at Newbuildings, he was quite ignorant of the names of the commonest trees, 'even the elm, which he must have seen every day in London. I pointed out one to him, and he said, "I think, a maple." ' A tireless walker, he spent a great deal of his time tramping over the Downs. One of his favourite walks was up a steep chalk path known as Jacob's Ladder, leading to the top of the Downs, from which a magnificent view of the valley can be seen. On one ascent of this path, he completed the 'Ode to the Setting Sun' which he had begun in a part of the priory grounds called the 'Field of the Cross' from a life-sized crucifix erected on a mound. On another of his walks he met the child 'Daisy', one of a family of nine, which encounter he described in the poem of that name.

By February, 1890, he was judged well enough to return to London and resume his friendship with the Meynells, who were now living in Palace Court, Bayswater. Here, with their seven gifted children, Wilfrid and Alice Meynell had established a power-house of journalism. Alice, queenly, sensitive, intellectual, with a somewhat remote and chilly beauty, was writing her lucid, cool, poised essays, and at the same time helping her husband with his multifarious journalism. For Francis Thompson, she became a new idol to be worshipped; she replaced the nursery dolls, and Shakespeare heroines, the prostitute of the Strand, the museum Melpomene; she became his remote fair one, the 'Unknown She' of his prayers. At her feet, the poet, self-starved of human affection, poured his vials of worship, making her the focus of his elaborate sequence, 'Love in Dian's Lap', which he wrote for her in spring, 1891, in one of those cheap little exercise books where his poetry and meditations were confusedly pencilled.

The Meynells, bearing vigorously the burden of rearing their family on the proceeds of journalism alone, were producing the *Weekly Register* and *Merry England* as well as scores of articles, by Herculean efforts. To this busy circle, Thompson, now living at

Paddington, a mile or so away, a short distance for such a tireless walker, was admitted as co-worker. He took his place at the great table, crowded with books and manuscript, and wrote occasional reviews for both Meynell journals, as well as poems for *Merry England* in which appeared 'The Hound of Heaven' (July, 1890) and 'A Corymbus for Autumn' (March, 1891). In her memoir of her mother, Viola Meynell recalls: 'Francis Thompson—besides Coventry Patmore . . . was assisting our parents with the two papers, though in the case of Francis Thompson the help was not unassociated with a certain amount of hindrance. His excellent contributions were not produced to time, and he increased the inconvenience of his delays by chatting a great deal about them.'[1]

One of Thompson's articles, the review of General Booth's *In Darkest England*, called for a Catholic apostolate to the poor and wretched in the London slums, in terms which, in some ways, anticipated such modern French movements as the Jocists and the priest-workers. On reading this, the socially-minded Cardinal Manning, a friend of Meynell, summoned Francis Thompson to him, expecting from the tone of the article to find a man with the force and personality to inspire such a movement, and to translate into reality his own cherished plans for the amelioration of the lot of the English workers. He realized his grotesque mistake when he saw before him the delicate flushed, voluble poet, so manifestly out of touch with the realities around which he had spun passionate purple sentences. Thompson, too, realized the gulf between them. His poem on the 'Dead Cardinal of Westminster' of 1892, written as an obituary, has little to do with Manning, but much to do with his own sense of inadequacy.

The voluntary exile from family ties now had an adopted family—a mother-figure and a father-figure, and a family of young children, to whom he became devoted. Under Wilfrid Meynell's enthusiastic prompting he was writing as regularly as a person of his temperament could, although at times he was overwhelmed by the demands of life.

'I am more in a condition to sit down and go into hysterics like a girl than to write anything,' he tells Meynell. . . . 'I

[1] *Alice Meynell: A Memoir*, Cape, 1929, p. 104.

think I am fit for nothing; certainly not fit to be any longer the object of your too great kindness. Please understand that I entirely feel, and am perfectly resigned to the ending of an experiment which even your sweetness would never have burdened yourself with, if you could have foreseen the consequences.'

At other times, with his extraordinary shifts of mood, as unpredictable as the breezes, he was more cheerful and could say of himself, 'I have fits in which I see the black side of everything.'

In these days, his personality showed traits which at times exasperated even those who were drawn to him by his gentleness and manner of a lost child. Long withdrawn from the world of everyday things, and lacking the normal ways of social intercourse, Thompson had shaped his own private habits of thought and action. He did not so much fit into the Meynell menage as impinge upon it, sometimes with dislocating effect. He *would* talk about all kinds of trivialities while the others were working hard to meet inflexible dead-lines. Little tasks were devised to keep him silent and out of the hair of the others. But long spoken meditations on the respective merits of different kinds of pens and papers, commonplaces on anything that came into his head, reiterated until they were written into the articles of the others around the table, and frequent crises spun out of the loss of a rubber, a pencil or a note, proved a continual distraction. He was always mislaying the drafts of his articles, and his despairing cry, 'It's a penny exercise-book', would drive all thought of work from the minds of the Meynells until it was found. He seemed constitutionally unable to keep an appointment; if invited for a meal, he would arrive too late, or far too early, or on the wrong day; his excuses would be so elaborate, and so often repeated that they would provoke silent pleas for mercy. After a whole day's disruption of the harassed Meynells, he might produce a single paragraph of prose or a line or two of verse.

We might wonder how the Meynells endured him, for a more exasperating person to be foisted on the busy household could hardly be imagined. Yet, although in what they wrote of Thompson members of the family made little secret of his faults, they equally made no secret of their affection for him. The paradox of Thompson's character shows itself most clearly in his relations with this family. They recognized in him a core of innocence, of childlikeness, or perhaps childishness, and of gentleness for which they gladly forgave him much. 'During many years of friendship and almost daily companionship,' wrote Alice Meynell, 'it was evident to solicitous eyes that he was one of the most innocent of men.' This innocence was not simply passivity or meekness; he really had managed so to sunder himself from common life as to remain almost untainted by its malice and its brutalities; he had achieved a kind of detachment which included natural gentleness. We all build walls to keep out the too constant winds of cold reality; Thompson's were thicker than usual, with few chinks for the airs of actuality to penetrate.

He had only the faintest sense of social and personal obligations. 'Opium desocializes us,' records Jean Cocteau, 'and removes us from the community.' It is hard to defend Thompson's avoidance of basic obligations, which was different in character as well as intention from that of the religious who leaves all things to follow Christ. If he was incapable of malice, although not of testiness and pettishness, he seems also to have been incapable, for most of his life, of real regret for important things —his treatment of his father, for instance. This cannot be put down to reticence, since in poem after poem he bares his own sorrows to the world. At the same time, the testimony of those who best knew him, particularly forbearing though they were, cannot be lightly dismissed. Even the tough, sceptical Blunt was won over by his gentleness of manner, even those who, like Katharine Tynan, saw much that was pathetic and even comic in his character, found him fundamentally lovable. The Meynells entrusted their children to him; he took them skating and walking in the park; he was godfather to the newest arrival, Francis, in 1891, to whom he addressed 'To My Godchild'.

In the two years following Thompson's return from Storrington, Wilfrid Meynell, ecstatic about Thompson's poetry, was most active on the poet's behalf. He printed the pieces as fast as the poet could write them; he had reprints of the *Merry England* poems bound and sent round London. Copies reached Tennyson, who returned merely formal thanks, and Browning, who replied in 1889 with warm praise of the 'remarkable' poems:

'It is altogether extraordinary that a young man so naturally gifted should need incitement to do justice to his own
conspicuous ability by endeavouring to emerge from so un-
congenial a course of life as that which you describe. Surely
the least remunerating sort of "literary life" would offer
advantages incompatible with the hardest of all struggles for
existence, such as I take Mr. Thompson's to be. Pray assure
him, if he cares to know it, that I have a confident expectation
of his success, if he will but extricate himself—as by a strenuous effort he may—from all that must now embarrass him
terribly.'

Meynell was determined that others should know and love
Thompson's poems as he did. To the very end of his life—he died
in his ninety-seventh year in 1948—he was a tireless propa-
gandist for his protégé. Admirers of Thompson must always be
grateful to Meynell for his goodness to the poet; but it need not
follow that they must admit that he was the best adviser for
Thompson in the matter of his poems. His enthusiasm for all
that came from Storrington later proved an important factor in
blinding Thompson to the faults in his earlier work, in con-
firming him in his odd conglomerate style, and even in en-
couraging him to pour out ill-considered pieces. His own
daughter described him as a 'man more of feeling than of intellect, with little literary erudition beyond what might be hastily
improvised for the purpose of immediate journalism'. 'Author
himself', she continues, 'of much neat verse often turning on a
punning play of words, he might not have been eligible for the
almost-identification with Thompson which actually occurred.' [1]
Meynell's limited knowledge of poetry and his no less restricted
taste made him insensitive to the major flaws in Francis Thompson's work. It might not be unfair to a great-souled man—he
can afford the criticism—to suggest that some, at least, of his
zeal for Thompson's poetry was proprietorial. Thompson was
his discovery; and he remained fascinated by the wonder of it
all. He was completely unaware of what others described as
obscurities. To his last days, he derived unending delight from
the poetry which he read aloud on every occasion, to willing or

[1] Viola Meynell, *Francis Thompson and Wilfred Meynell*, Hollis & Carter,
1952, p. 128.

reluctant guests. No suspicion seems ever to have crossed his mind that much of the poetry was, in the literal sense, unspeakable.

In an anthology he edited in 1892, *The Child Set in the Midst*, he included four of Thompson's poems; this first publication in book form, the frequent pieces in *Merry England*, the circulated reprints, resulted in, bit by bit, Thompson's work becoming known and gaining admirers. At Palace Court, too, the poet met, although he did not become intimate with, several of the writers who were playing a significant part in what has been called 'the Catholic Literary Revival'. One of these was Katharine Tynan, the Irish poetess, who, while she was in London in 1889, inspired Thompson's poem, 'The Sere of the Leaf'. He also met several Capuchin friars from monasteries at Crawley in Sussex and at Pantasaph in Wales. Chief among these was Father Anselm Kenealy, who, in 1911, was appointed Archbishop of Simla. Father Anselm became one of the poet's very few close friends and left several interesting records of their association.

Between 1890 and 1892 Thompson spent brief periods of rest at Crawley, thanks to the generosity of Meynell and the friars. But he was not making the physical and mental recovery Meynell had hoped for. During this time, the Meynells were undergoing a particularly difficult period of financial and other worries attendant upon the growth of their family, and could ill carry the extra harassment of the cloudy-minded poet. To make matters worse, Meynell himself was far from well. But, more important in his eyes, he discovered that his protégé, whom he had so optimistically believed cured, was not. As he told Blunt, Thompson had reverted to opium shortly after his return from Storrington, and Meynell realized that many of the oddities of behaviour which so disrupted his household proceeded from the effects of the drug.

The short visits to Crawley seemed to do little for the poet's health or peace of mind. Although he spoke of London as 'that infectious web of sewer rats', he adapted to his feelings about country life some words of Touchstone: 'Truly, shepherd, in respect of itself, it is a good life; but in respect that it is a shepherd's life, it is naught. In respect that it is solitary, I like it very well; but in respect that it is private, it is a very vile life. Now in respect it is in the fields, it pleaseth me well; but in respect it is not in the city, it is tedious.' Accordingly, Meynell decided that Thompson would be better off for an extended period with the Capuchins, where he would be cut off from access to opium, and from memories of narcoticism which the sights of London might conjure up.

So, in February, 1892, Thompson was packed off to Pantasaph, in North Wales, where was located the mother-house of the English Province of the Capuchin Friars Minor. On the train journey he fell in with some Irish harvesters. One of them had an injured hand, filthily bandaged, which Thompson, who had had after all the bare rudiments of a medical training, insisted on washing and rebandaging in the most gentle, painstaking way, with his own handkerchief torn into strips. This, and his anxious concern for the fate of a canary whose cage was wrapped around with brown paper, left a deep impression of sweet simplicity in the mind of the Irish friend of Katharine Tynan who accompanied him.

At Pantasaph the poet stayed for a while as a guest in the Lodge Gates at Bishop's House, later, after a quarrel with his house-keeper there, in a cottage behind St. Mary's Monastery, and finally in Creccas Cottage, a stone dwelling with a roof of slate, standing in a large field, and looking towards the far distant peaks of the Snowdon Range. In these surroundings, removed from the temptation of opium, another great gush of poetry welled from him; this was, in fact, to be his last real surge of creative writing.

But, in the meantime, at the very beginning of the Pantasaph period, Wilfrid Meynell was pushing forward his long-cherished project of a volume of Thompson's poems. He was more eager for the book to appear than the poet was himself, who would have been quite content simply to go on exactly as he was, and who faced the labour involved in editing and proof-reading with no joy whatever. 'I find Lane has already announced the poems in his book-list, so I am bound to go through with them; else I would let them go to the devil. . . . Inwardly I suffer like old Nick; but the blessed mountain air keeps up my body, and for the rest—my Lady Pain and I are *au mieux*.'

He was much more concerned about his health than about the appearance of the book. 'The country here', he continues in

the same letter, 'is just beginning to get beautiful, and I am feeling the first quickening pulse of spring. Lord, it is good for me to
be here—very good. The clogged wheels in me are slowly
beginning to move.' Thus he was not at all certain about Meynell's project, lacking any genuine confidence in his poetic
powers. 'I send you two or three odd bits of verse, but I hardly
think you will find anything in them.' 'Your interest in the
volume is very dear to me. I cannot say I myself feel any elation
about it. I am past the time when such things brought me any
elation.' He was irritable during the correction of proofs, forwarded from John Lane through the Meynells, he felt depressed about the whole business; the book would almost certainly be, he said, his sole one. Comments like these reflect the
pains of another withdrawal period. And the fact is that
Thompson, for all his protests, did correct the proofs with care
and argued strenuously with the Meynells over the retention of
some of his odder words. As the corrected sheets came back from
Pantasaph, they were often sent back with further suggestions,
chiefly from Alice Meynell and from Coventry Patmore. Patmore, an intimate of the Meynells, had not yet met Thompson,
but Alice, to whom he was devoted, asked his advice on the
work of the new poet, and he gave it freely, decisively and
unequivocally.

Towards the end of 1893, the book appeared—*Poems* by
Francis Thompson, published by Elkin Matthews and John
Lane. A new poet was launched into the world of the nineties.

VI

This Vanished Day

HOWEVER dubious Francis Thompson may have been before *Poems* appeared as to the wisdom of publishing it, he had no doubt as to its quality once it was out. Richard Le Gallienne, at that time reader for John Lane, had recommended acceptance of the book, and also wrote the first review of it, for the *Daily Chronicle*, an appreciation both generous and perceptive. Yet Thompson was not wholly satisfied with the notice and told Wilfrid Meynell: 'I am actually disposed to rank myself higher than Mr. Le Gallienne's final sentence might seem to imply. I absolutely think that my poetry is "greater" than any work by a new poet which has appeared *since Rossetti.*'

By no means every critic agreed with him. Somewhat unfair charges were made that Thompson was merely the voice of a Catholic clique, whose appeal was limited to his co-religionists, and Andrew Lang voiced a fairly wide-spread opinion when he wrote in the *Contemporary Review*: 'The poetry seems to be hyperbolical rather than sublime; it seems to have more pose than passion.' Arthur Symons, too, had reservations. His review in the *Athenaeum* began: 'If Crashaw, Shelley, Donne, Marvell, Mr. Patmore and several other poets had not existed, Mr. Francis Thompson would be a poet of remarkable novelty', and went on to call him 'a cloudy visionary, a rapturous sentimentalist, in whom emotion means coloured words, and sight the opportunity for a bedazzlement'. Other critics were unhappy about the neologisms so frequent in the poems, the obscurity of many lines and the multicoloured disorder of the

67

This Vanished Day

imagery. Still, the reception was, in the main, generous; enthusiastic and warm praise for *Poems* was by no means confined to Catholic papers or to friends of the Meynells. H. D. Traill, in the *Nineteenth Century*, defended Thompson's baroque style: 'Mr. Thompson being really and truly a seventeenth century rhapsodist born out of due time, the sin of affectation would for him have lain in an attempt to express himself in the poetic manner of the present day.' John Davidson in the *Speaker* called him 'the latest, and perhaps the greatest, of English Roman Catholic poets of post-Reformation times'; and Graham R. Toman in *The Academy* said, 'For sheer beauty of thought, phrase and imagery, a great many of these poems could scarce be bettered; subtle with the fine subtlety of strength, remote yet intimate, austere and still sumptuous, fair with an unfamiliar excellence and sweet with an unearthly sweetness, this book is, as it were, the mystic rose of modern poetry.'

One of the most balanced, just and penetrating assessments of this first volume came from Coventry Patmore, in the *Fortnightly Review* for January, 1894. Although, as we have seen, Patmore had lent a hand in preparing the poems for publication, he was able to stand back from the volume and submit it to a clear-eyed scrutiny, except where his devotion to Alice Meynell impelled him to call 'Love in Dian's Lap' 'a series of poems which St. John of the Cross might have addressed to St. Theresa'. He praises Thompson's verse as equal, if not superior, to that of Crashaw 'in its peculiar beauties, as well as its particular defects'; he finds special interest in Thompson's handling of the 'irregular ode' form, in which Patmore says he feels a 'sort of proprietary interest'—of all modern experimentalists in this form, Thompson is the only one, he believes, 'who has, in some large measure, succeeded, notwithstanding his want of practice, and his occasional defects and redundancies of language'; he praises the 'great and passionate' 'Hound of Heaven'; the poetry, too, appeals to him because it explores 'the inexhaustible and hitherto almost unworked mine of Catholic philosophy', and because, if it is 'spiritual almost to a fault', the spirituality of which it gives evidence is a 'real ardour of life, and not the mere negation of life'.

All this sounds handsome enough, and while parts of it

68

perhaps reflect that basic kindness of Patmore which he often exercised towards new poets and something of his special generosity to a protégé of his beloved Meynells, most is unquestionably a characteristically honest and individual opinion. But at the heart of this review is a penetrating criticism of Thompson's methods and vision so exactly on the target that it must be quoted at length:[1]

'The masculine intellect, which is the first constituent of all poetry having any pretences to "greatness" and which has been so lamentably wanting in most of the poetry of the past generation, is as conspicuous and, alas, as predominant in Mr. Thompson's poetry as it is in that of Crashaw and Cowley. The feminine element, which is as essential to perfect poetry as a crust is to a pie, is in insufficient presence. Profound thought and far-fetched splendour of imagery, and nimble-witted discernment of those analogues which are the "roots" of the poet's language, abound; but in the feminine faculties of "taste", of emotion which must have music for its rendering, of shy moderation which never says quite so much as it means, of quickness to "scent the ridiculous from afar", of the dainty conscience which sets "decorum" far above all other duties and knows that in poetry the manner is much more important that the matter, since manner is beautiful in itself, whereas, without it, it is no matter where the matter may be since it fails to express itself with feminine *feeling* and perfection; in these qualities Mr. Thompson's poetry is as often deficient as is that of his two eminent predecessors. Even the barest sublimity cannot be adequately rendered in poetry without some measure of the chaste and timid reticence of womanhood. Mr. Thompson throws about him "handfuls of stars" and swings the earth as "a trinket from his wrist", but these are very cheap sublimities compared with Aeschylus's

Slow is the wrath of gods, but, in the end, *not weak*.

It is wonderful that, with such a truly splendid command

---

[1] It is perhaps significant that Everard Meynell, in quoting in his *Life of Francis Thompson* the greater part of Patmore's review (pp. 146–8), completely omitted the section here printed.

of language as is possessed by this poet, he should have thought it expedient to search the dictionary for words many of which are not only archaic, but really extinct and incapable of resurrection. . . . Only the very greatest poets have ever, so far as I recollect, succeeded in adding more than two or three new words to the language of English poetry, but Mr. Thompson's verse hatches them by the dozen, with the effect, in each case, of producing a shock of interruption, which spoils what might otherwise have been a delicate flow of thought and rhythm. One critic of note has condemned these inventions as "illiterate"; but this is quite unjust. Mr. Thompson is a good Latin and Greek scholar, and his linguistic freaks are only too "literate".'

The tact with which Patmore phrases this criticism and the words of praise with which he surrounds it do not conceal the fundamental nature of his reservations, nor the importance he attaches to the absence of control, taste and integration in the poems before him. Despite such criticism from Patmore and more than one delicately-stated admonition from Alice Meynell, it was undoubtedly in Catholic circles that Thompson later established his chief reputation. In 1898, Canon Sheehan complained that 'Francis Thompson who, with all his incongruities, ranks in English poetry with Shelley, and *only* beneath Shakespeare, has hardly had any recognition in Catholic circles'; but, in the twentieth century, the chief advocates of the poet have been Catholic writers, more especially priests, like Father Terence L. Connolly, Father T. H. Wright and Father John O'Connor, whose tone, in general, has been one of fulsome praise. While Thompson's reputation, once extravagantly high, has dropped so steadily in non-Catholic critical quarters that a couple of recent substantial histories of literature do not even mention his name, it has been maintained by certain Catholics. It is true that since the publication of Hopkins' poems in 1918, the emphasis in Catholic criticism has shifted sufficiently to lend some colour of truth to John Wain's waspish comment in a note on Hopkins in his *Preliminary Essays*: 'The vogue of Hopkins which followed on the publication of his poems in 1918 was, we may suppose, both a delight and a shock to his co-religionists. A delight because it enabled them to drop Francis Thompson as the official Roman Catholic poet of modern times (and it wasn't too soon to get out from under *that* structure), without feeling definitely committed to, say, Chesterton.' Yet Thompson still exercises such a powerful attraction over many of his fellow-Catholics that one of them can call him 'the Augustine of English song', compare him with Shakespeare, and say 'Thompson's approach to nature is all but infinitely above the wavering vision of Wordsworth'.[1]

I feel that this Catholic conviction of Thompson's greatness springs largely from non-literary causes. The first is the absence from the later Victorian scene of any significant poet who was challengingly Catholic—Patmore was there, to be sure, but he was an odd and faintly unorthodox character, with a habit of making anti-clerical jokes and of reading Swedenborg, not to mention his enthusiasm for the pleasures of matrimony; Alice Meynell was somewhat too austere; Lionel Johnson wrote infrequently on religious themes; Hopkins was, at this time, unpublished. To the Catholic minority, still somewhat self-conscious and apologetic, Thompson, who was a born Catholic at that, seemed a Heaven-sent genius from their own ranks, triumphantly demonstrating that Catholics could hold their own in literature.

A second and more important reason is that Thompson employs more often in his poetry than any of his contemporaries what we might call the furniture of Catholicism—the cult of the Virgin, the liturgy of the Church, the vessels of ritual, sacerdotal piety. A Catholic reading Thompson finds his attention caught by familiar landmarks; he recognizes religious signs and practices and ideas with which he has been acquainted since childhood. He walks from the secular landscape of the bulk of English poetry into a house that is home. He laughs at the ignorance of Sir Arthur Quiller-Couch who thought that 'monstrance' was one of the poet's freak coinages. He feels that, when critics profess to find Thompson's work obscure, it is their own lack of knowledge and not the poet's expression that is at fault; if academics will go to the trouble of studying Swedenborg to understand Blake more fully, or of occultism to comprehend Yeats, he says, why should they not

[1] Fr. Joseph Husslein, S.J., in the Preface to *Francis Thompson: In His Paths*, by Terence L. Connolly, Bruce, 1944, p. vii.

make themselves familiar with Catholic ritual and doctrine to
see what Thompson is getting at?

'In reading Francis Thompson's poetry, the Catholic has a
distinct advantage', asserts one Catholic critic.[1] Father Connolly goes further: 'In the literature I had been taught there
was no mention of what I particularly treasured—Our Lady,
the Incarnation, Christ's teaching and example, the Crucifixion, the Resurrection, and all the rest. But in Thompson's
poetry, I found all these—the fundamental truths of our common religious faith—expressed with an artistry that stimulated
and satisfied the imagination and the emotions, without
violence to the intellect and will.' [2]

All this is understandable enough; yet carried through logic-
ally, it begs the question of Thompson's absolute literary
quality and leads to the conclusion that he is essentially a
sectarian poet, valued for things in themselves very much worth
while, but having no necessary relation to literature at all. In
fact, much Catholic writing on the poet perpetuates the wide-
spread Victorian idea that the worth of a poem is to be judged
primarily by the quality of its subject.

Bound up with this is a strong sense of family pride; 'Thompson's genius shed a new glory on Catholicism', writes Father
Claude Williamson.[3] Hence one problem for a Catholic trying
to get at the essential poetic quality of Thompson's work is the
barrier erected by received Catholic judgment as to his superior
excellence. He recognizes that Thompson's use of Catholic ideas
and symbols is very different, in its sincerity, from, for instance,
Rossetti's purely aesthetic exploitation of their 'stunning'
aspects. But how intimately does Thompson's poetry touch the
hearts of all men; how does his poetry rate as poetry, not as
doctrine, beside the vision of Milton, Shakespeare, Chaucer,
Keats and Wordsworth? And, just as important, perhaps, how
truly and deeply Catholic, by comparison with Dante, or
Hopkins, for example, is this same poetry, once we get beyond
the liturgical trappings of the 'Ode to the Setting Sun', the
quotations from the Litany of the Blessed Virgin in 'Assumpta

[1] Francis Doogan: *The Catholicity of Francis Thompson*, Australian Catholic
Truth Society, Melbourne, n.d.
[2] Prologue to *Francis Thompson: In His Paths*, p. 3.
[3] 'Francis Thompson' in *Great Catholics*, Catholic Book Club, 1939, p. 462.

Maria' and those intimations too readily called 'mystical' in other poems? In sum, how far does the 'total meaning' of his poems do justice to the religious ideas underlying them?

In answering such questions, we cannot ignore his addiction to opium, on which I have already dwelt. This is frequently passed over lightly by Catholic and other critics, on the assumption that the drug played no significant part in his verse. Alice Meynell wrote to her husband about Everard Meynell's biography that it was 'just right in sincere feeling without too much of the illness which, as you know, I think ought not to be for the public'—a wish made, we can be sure, in all charity, but symptomatic of a desire to play down the place of opium in his life. Since we now know that almost all of Thompson's poetry was written when he was deprived of opium and undergoing not only the torments of withdrawal but also the pangs of the loss of a psychological prop, such questions arise as—how much of his poetry of 'asceticism' represents a voluntary acceptance of asceticism from religious motives, and how much is a rationalization of a physical state directly attributable to a long period of laudanum-taking?

My own view is that a considerable amount of his early poetry is only doubtfully religious, in that it contains religious sentiment diluted and tainted by the memories of opium-fantasies, as well as by his original neurotic instabilities, so that it becomes self-indulgent, confessional poetry, rather than a valid religious statement. In his successive books can be seen a constant struggle between his adult consciousness and his subliminal impulse to retreat back into his childhood or such a substitute for it as opium gave, between his growing awareness of the inadequacy of his grasp upon and his experience of his religion and his trust in remembered pieties, between his inclination to emotional self-indulgence and the promptings of his intelligence towards objective self-analysis. Here and there in the earlier poems there is a sense of timelessness, of the suspension of life and motion, a contemplative immersion in an unchanging vision, which suggests that at times an equilibrium was momentarily established between all these tensions. But, in the main, the first poems are shot through with the evidences of neurotic fantasies, unassimilated to his major poetic purposes, and beyond the reach of his religious faith.

At the same time, the existence of 'The Hound of Heaven' alone is sufficient to prove that, at some time during his years of destitution, Thompson underwent a profound religious experience which carried into his heart the sense of God's Providence, and which helped to stay him from despair and self-destruction. Although this experience awakened renewed fervour in him, it was not capable of the fullest realization until his later years, for Thompson required, although he knew it not, the example and the guidance of the Meynells and of Coventry Patmore before he matured spiritually.

If we read the *Poems* with the opium and Thompson's neurotic character in mind, it is hard to avoid the conclusion that he turned to poetry as a substitute for opium. 'Often verse written as I write it', he declared, 'is nothing less than a confessional, a confessional far more intimate than the sacerdotal one.' The 'Ode to the Setting Sun', the first fruit of his withdrawal from opium, has been described as 'the ecstatic, though veiled vision of faith' and 'the God-Man's reconcilement of pain and suffering and physical death with joy and life, temporal and eternal'.[1] Yet I doubt whether these themes predominate, and even whether the poem is actually about them at all. After a prelude, setting the scene in the Field of the Cross, where the poet sees the red sun as 'a bubble of fire' dropping slowly towards the hill and catching in a long beam the Figure on the Priory crucifix, while his sad heart vibrates to the 'wailful sweetness' of a violin, the ode begins by stressing the contrasts and affinities between the 'mystical twins', Death and Birth.

> And of these two the fairer thing is Death.

Thompson addresses the dying sun, whose 'Easter pomp' of rising is surpassed by the stately pageantry of its death, with a stately invocation to the power of this god that sustains and nourishes all things:

> Thou twi-form deity, nurse at once and sire!
> Thou genitor that all things nourishest!
> The earth was suckled at thy shining breast,
> And in her veins is quick thy milky fire.

[1] Connolly, op. cit., p. 29.

74

The long, slow, majestic dying of the sun suggests to him the impermanence and final annihilation of everything:

> Why have we longings of immortal pain,
> And all we long for mortal? Woe is me,
> And all our chants but chaplet some decay,
> As mine this vanishing—nay, vanished Day.

The single shaft through the encircling gloom which strikes on the crucifix turns his thoughts, so far couched in terms of classical mythology, to his religion. The sun becomes an image of Christ, he remembers the Resurrection, and takes momentary comfort in the Life through Death of which Christ is the great exemplar. In the 'After-Strain', the Cross is invoked as representing the price of pain that must be paid for poetry. Dolefully he accepts the burden, as the saints accepted it. In the final lines, he implores the Blessed Virgin for some tenderness to alleviate the 'Cross's vigorous austerity'.

A customary interpretation of this ode sees in it a romantic expression of the sacrifices the poet must accept for the sake of his vocation and a religious statement of faith in rebirth and regeneration. Yet the tone of the whole poem is not one of resurgent hope but of forlornness. Although some bitter pangful consolation is snatched at the end, the greater part of the poem is so much of a lament that the final lines have the appearance of a requirement of the Film Production Code. For what is it a lament? Surely it does not do violence to the poem to suggest that its pervasive melancholy directly expresses Thompson's dominant mood at the time; the physical and psychological pains of withdrawal and not the self-imposed austerities of the saint or the dedicated poet permeate it. Worship, faith and religious fervour have less place here than soul-sickness and misery. The religious conclusion is imposed almost as an afterthought on a poem which, for nearly its whole length, exudes a pagan melancholy. Even Father T. H. Wright, an admirer of Thompson, finds something odd about its religious experience. Part of it he calls 'a very doubtful interpretation of human life', and continues, 'We may feel strongly and even impatiently that Thompson interprets the fundamental life of a poet in too forlorn a strain. The Cross itself, as it is seen and experienced in this world, has elements of tenderness that need no supplementing by any less creations of the human imagination.'[1]

The emotional direction of the ode becomes plainer if we see the sun as a symbol of opium and the whole poem as a lament for the passing away of what had been for Thompson the sustainer of his personal universe.[2] Just as the deprivation of laudanum left him naked to the world with a cross he 'must bear alone'; by snatching from him that self-indulgent existence in which poetry is dreamed and need not be written ('What does one want with a tongue when one has silence'), so the sun, dying, robs the world of warmth and colour, leaving behind only 'a cold body'. Throughout the riot of imagery and the changing patterns of thought and feeling in the early part of the poem, one may trace the ebb and flow of fantasies encouraged by laudanum. Here is the synaesthetic experience of the addict, mingled with his increased sensitivity to sound:

> Thy visible music-blasts make deaf the sky,
> Thy cymbals clang to fire the Occident,
> Thou dost thy dying so triumphantly:
> I *see* the crimson blaring of thy shawms!;

here is the forced conceit of the dreamer, in which the sun can

> like a golden bee
> Sting the West to angry red;

here is the shifting imagery of the hazed consciousness:

> Friend of the forgers of earth,
> Mate of the earthquake and thunders volcanic,
> Clasped in the arms of the forces Titanic
> Which rock like a cradle the girth
> Of the ether-hung world.

What else, if not to the sense of dominance and self-completeness brought by opium, is Thompson referring in such lines as:

> Must ye fade—
> O old, essential candours, ye who made
> The earth a living and a radiant thing—
> And leave her corpse in our strained, cheated arms?

[1] *Francis Thompson and His Poetry*, Harrap, 1927, p. 83.
[2] I am indebted for this suggestion to an unpublished University of London Ph.D. thesis, by Dr. W. H. Pearson. 'A Comparative Study of Patmore, Hopkins and Francis Thompson' (1952).

When, at the end, he turns with bleak foreboding to his religion for consolation, he makes a gesture in the direction of resignation. He recognizes his spiritual weakness and emotional dependence; he acknowledges his limitations. But the dominant impression is not one of joy, but of loss, not of regeneration, but of death.

> Even so, O Cross! thine is the victory,
> Thy roots are fast within our fairest fields;
> Brightness may emanate in Heaven from Thee,
> Here thy dread symbol only shadow yields.

Throughout the poem runs an insistent note of self-pity, of almost masochistic indulgence. The flamboyant language suggests an attempt to compensate for lost fantasies, and the doleful tone leads us to feel that, while his sufferings were unquestionably real, they were physical and psychological, rather than spiritual.

In 'The Sere of the Leaf', also written at Storrington, we find further indications of Francis Thompson's attempt to make poetry a substitute for reality in default of drugs. The poem was inspired by his meeting with the Irish poetess, Katharine Tynan (Mrs. Hinkson), when she visited the Meynells in London in 1889. Her pleasant, kindly personality greatly impressed Thompson; he was even more struck by the joyous spirit and the content of her verse. Mrs. Hinkson had done much to make his poetry widely known before the appearance of *Poems*, by her reviews of individual poems in the *Irish Independent*. In 1892, he wrote to her: 'Not least among the alleviations of a not very appreciated lot I count that I should have had some of my poems praised in a few significant words by two poets—yourself and Mrs. Meynell.' [1] 'The Sere of the Leaf' expresses his inability to understand how a poet could be as joyful as she; he contrasts, almost with bitterness, certainly with an undertone of resentment, the love and contentment of her verse with the desolation and sorrow of his own. He quotes some lines of hers and shapes the metre of the stanza to fit them; they serve only to deepen his melancholy. Surely, he implies, a poet ought not to sing so happily; is not poetry the fount of suffering?

[1] *The Middle Years*, by Katharine Tynan, Constable, 1916, p. 14.

> The heart, a censered fire which fuming chants aspire,
>   Is fed with oozèd gums of precious pain;
> And unrest swings denser, denser the fragrance from that
>   censer,
> With the heart-strings for its quivering chain.

A profound sense of personal failure, and of weakness of character infects the poem, but as yet Thompson cannot get beyond this to a positive statement.

> I know not equipoise, only purgatorial joys,
>   Grief's singing to the soul's instrument,
> And forgetfulness which yet knoweth that it doth forget.

In the last line above the psychological craving for opium-oblivion is directly stated. Caught ' 'twixt the fires of heat and frost', he complains of his agony. When he says that he is glad for her peace and that he does not envy her, we may feel that he protests a shade too strenuously, since his conclusion is that he is one of the lesser poets, and that the most he can hope for is that the 'serèd leaves' of his verses

> May flit before deserted by the gust,
>   May touch some spirit's hair,
>   May cling one moment there,—
> She turns; they tumble down. Drift o'er them, dust!

While self-pity makes 'The Sere of the Leaf' a rather unsympathetic poem, it has a certain moving quality in its only half-intentional revelation of spiritual debility. Thompson himself recognized this, for when he sent the poem, with another, to Meynell, he wrote, 'If there be no saving grace of poetry in them they are damned; for I am painfully conscious that they display me, in every respect, at my morally weakest.'

It is probable that the other poem, to which Thompson referred when he said, 'The shorter of the two pieces especially is such a self-revelation, I feel, as even you have hardly had from me before,' was 'Daisy'. One of his best earlier poems, it finds its origin in a walk taken with a little girl in the hills at Storrington. For the first time in his works we meet a theme which was to give strength and individuality to later poems— the God-given innocence of the small child, to which something stubbornly unspoiled in Thompson responded. In the innocence of Daisy, he sees a reproach to his own counterfeit childhood, his attempt to retain, by artificial means, the unquestioning naïveté of infancy. He can find no consolation for his wounded heart in the purity of the child:

> The fairest things have fleetest end,
>   Their scent survives their close:
> But the rose's scent is bitterness
>   To him that loved the rose!

For his vision of life is clouded by his own misery, which suffuses the whole world with sadness; all he can win from the encounter is an aching sense of the transcience of all happiness, and, as with Katharine Tynan's poetry, puzzlement at the disparity between his mood and that of others.

> She left me marvelling why my soul
>   Was sad that she was glad;
> At all the sadness in the sweet,
>   The sweetness in the sad.

So he tries, as he did in the nursery, in his student days, and in the London slums, to wrench experience into a pattern determined by himself. Hence he ends with a platitudinous stanza which dilutes the effect of the whole poem:

> Nothing begins, and nothing ends,
>   That is not paid with moan;
> For we are born in other's pain,
>   And perish in our own.

Despite these lines, 'Daisy' has a poignance which even the moralizing scarcely impairs. Unquestionably imitative of Wordsworth, in subject, style, imagery, and perhaps in its moral, the poem still, in its frankness and simplicity, reflects the essential Thompson, which the gaudy verbiage of 'Ode to the Setting Sun' only serves to conceal.

The mood of 'Daisy' is developed in 'The Poppy', addressed to little Monica Meynell, and written perhaps a year later. The relationship between the poppy and Thompson's demon, opium, is obvious, and it is surely significant, in view of what was said of 'Ode to the Setting Sun', that here, in violent imagery, Thompson relates the flower both to the sun, and to wine, another of his symbols for oblivion:

79

With burnt mouth, red like a lion's, it drank
The blood of the sun as he slaughtered sank,
And dipped its cup in the purpurate shine
Where the eastern conduits ran with wine.

Till it grew lethargied with fierce bliss
And hot as a swinkèd gipsy is,
And drowned in sleepy savageries
With mouth wide a-pout for a sultry kiss—

the later stanza being about as complete a description of the narcoticized state as we might find anywhere in Thompson's poetry.

Much less direct than 'Daisy', and reverberating with echoes of Keats, 'The Poppy' speaks of another walk with a little girl, and this time, too, it laments the transcience of things. The child does not know the difference between love and amity:

You have loved me, Fair, three lives,—or days:
'Twill pass with the passing of my face,

and the poet sees in the poppy she plucks for him a symbol not merely of the passing away of affection, but also, as this 'withering flower of dreams', of his wasted days:

He knew the twenty shrivelled years—
No flower, but twenty shrivelled years.

While 'Daisy' is in great part, at least, about innocence, 'The Poppy' is about himself, the man deprived of light and hope. It is not the beauty of the child that concerns him, so much as the dismal fading of all love, beauty and consoling fantasy from his world. So he turns for desperate solace to the fact of his poetry, in stanzas which mingle memories of opium-dreams with the poet's vision and his faith in his immortality as a maker, and with a nagging awareness of the unreality of what his verses enshrine:

The sleep-flower sways in the wheat its head,
Heavy with dreams, as that with bread:
The goodly grain and the sun-flushed sleeper
The reaper reaps and Time the reaper.

I hang 'mid men my needless head,
And my fruit is dreams, as theirs is bread:

The goodly men and the sun-hazed sleeper
Time shall reap, but after the reaper
The world shall glean of me, me the sleeper.

.   .   .   .

Love! *I* fall into the claws of Time:
But lasts within a leavèd rhyme
All that the world of me esteems—
My withered dreams, my withered dreams.

Other poems written about the same time show that, despite
Thompson's tenacious hold on his religion, he also needed constantly some material thing beyond himself, which could be
loved without reciprocity. He found this in Alice Meynell, to
whom he addressed his sequence 'Love in Dian's Lap'. These
eleven poems have been praised as an expression of his 'intense
worship of the soul of Womanhood',[1] and as presenting a
Platonic love in dignified, spiritualized language. Here, it is
claimed, the poet, in a metaphysical concept of love stripped
of all sensuality, dreams of a spiritual and intellectual union,
with two souls fused beyond passion. Mrs. Meynell's intellect,
her poetic gifts, her 'dream-dispensing face', her soul, her
'passionless passion, wild tranquillities', her 'deathless beauty'
are all hymned. He lays his soul on hers

As maid's breast against breast of maid;

she is Diana herself, she is also, seemingly, the Blessed Virgin:

She that is Heaven's Queen
Her title borrows,
For that she, pitiful,
Beareth our sorrows.
So thou, *Regina mî*
Spes infirmorum;
With all our grieving crowned
Mater dolorum.

Reminiscences of Patmore are sown through the poem:

As lovers, banished from their lady's face,
And hopeless of her grace,
Fashion a ghostly sweetness in its place,

---

[1] 'Francis Thompson', by Albert A. Cock, *Dublin Review*, October, 1911,
p. 250.

Fondly adore
Some stealth-won cast attire she wore,
A kerchief, or a glove.

But how different from the realistic Patmore who joyed in the
physical pleasures of marriage, while at the same time celebrating its spiritual dimension, is Thompson's translation into a
bloodless abstraction of a healthy living woman, a 'pencilling
mamma' and happy wife, a sensitive poet and a highly intelligent and perceptive essayist.

For 'Love in Dian's Lap' is, in fact, a long string of ingenuous, but frigid compliments, barren conceits and emotional
absurdities. The compliments could hardly have been more
extravagant if Mrs. Meynell had been Sappho, Mary, Queen
of Scots, St. Teresa of Avila, and Isabella of Spain rolled up
into one. The whole work is forced, with the remote, strained
air of a commissioned occasional piece, as if Thompson,
anxious in some way to acknowledge the Meynells' kindness to
him, drove himself to compose a piece of special elaborateness,
which, while by no means devoid of sincerity, never really
pierces to the heart, or comes from it.

Yet, most of the criticisms which can be made of the Storrington and early London poems are stilled before 'The Hound of
Heaven', the best-known, if not the best, poem Thompson ever
wrote. Its popularity is sufficient proof that here he broke out
of the enchanted circle of self and reached the hearts of all men.
The origin of the title and the basic paradoxical idea of God
the pursuer rather than the pursued has been traced to many
sources—St. Augustine's *Confessions*, St. John of the Cross's
group of poems called 'Ecstasy of Contemplation', the *Spiritual
Exercises* of St. Ignatius, Silvio Pellico's 'Dio Amore' and
Shelley's 'Prometheus Unbound' among them. It remained for
E. H. W. Meyerstein, in a letter to the *Times Literary Supplement*,[1] to point to the source of the climax of the poem, where
the Divine Pursuer stands self-revealed, and of much of its
theme, in a passage in Shelley's 'Epipsychidion', which runs in
part:

[1] March 17, 1945. The connection between the two poems was independently observed by Arthur Little, S.J. See Chapter 10 of *The Nature of Art*,
Longmans, Green and Co., 1946, pp. 188–93.

Then from the caverns of my dreamy youth
I sprang, as one sandalled with plumes of fire,
And towards the lodestar of my one desire
I flitted like a dizzy moth, whose flight
Is as a dead leaf's in the owlet light . . .
When a voice said:—'O Thou of hearts the weakest,
The phantom is beside thee whom thou seekest.'
Then I—'where?'—the world's echo answered 'where?'
And in that silence and in my despair
I questioned every tongueless wind that flew
Over my tower of mourning, if it knew
Whither 'twas fled, this soul out of my soul . . .
And therefore I went forth, with hope and fear
And every gentle passion sick to death,
Feeding my course with expectation's breath,
Into the wintry forest of our life;
And struggling through its error with vain strife,
And stumbling in my weakness and my haste,
And half bewildered by new forms, I past
Seeking among those untaught foresters
If I could find one form resembling hers . . .
In many mortal forms I rashly sought
The shadow of the idol of my thought.
And some were fair—but beauty dies away;
Others were wise—but honeyed words betray:
And One was true—oh! why not true to me?
Then, as a hunted deer that could not flee,
I turned upon my thoughts and stood at bay,
Wounded and weak and panting.

The resemblance between Thompson's ode and 'Epipsychidion' is not so surprising when it is remembered that Thompson had always had a profound admiration for Shelley, and that he was writing his essay on the poet, in which 'Epipsychidion' is quoted, while also composing 'The Hound of Heaven'. The style of the ode, too, is as Father Little points out 'a more or less free imitation, more or less conscious, of what Thompson had persuaded himself was Shelley's style'. Apart from a considerable number of resemblances to 'The Hound of Heaven', the Shelley passage deals, as Thompson's poem does, with a cosmic flight in which the poet goes from one thing to another seeking tidings, in one case, of the object of his desire, in the other, of a haven. And the similarity between

When the voice said:—'O Thou of hearts the weakest,
The phantom is beside thee whom thou seekest.'

and

> Ah fondest, blindest, weakest,
> I am He Whom thou seekest!

cannot be dismissed as mere accident.

Nevertheless, whether 'The Hound of Heaven' was a deliberate borrowing from Shelley by a 'poor thief of Song' or owes its resemblance to unconscious memories, Thompson's poem is his own. Shelley is pursuing his 'Ideal Being', which turns out to be somewhat incongruously embodied in Emilia Viviani, and the high-flown language does not disguise the fundamental tawdriness of his erotic experience. But the intensity of Thompson's religious emotion, the vibrant sincerity of its expression, and its urgency give 'The Hound of Heaven' a depth not to be found in the romanticized affaire of Shelley. This was one case in which Thompson almost wholly assimilated borrowings into his own vision.

While the other earlier poems, 'A Corymbus for Autumn', for instance, deal in vague concepts, 'The Hound of Heaven' is, for Thompson, surprisingly concrete, with the imaginative pattern sharp and clear. In a sense, it is a stock-taking, epitomizing his emotional life up to the point when he achieved, through the power of his faith, a religious sublimation. The drug is not forgotten; indeed the familiar opening lines:

> I fled Him, down the nights and down the days;
>   I fled Him, down the arches of the years;
> I fled Him, down the labyrinthine ways
>   Of my own mind; and in the mist of tears
> I hid from Him, and under running laughter.
>   Up vistaed hopes I sped;
>   And shot, precipitated
> Adown Titanic glooms of chasmèd fears.

with their strange hallucinatory vistas, which have always suggested to me a canvas by John Martin, and the hint of hysteria and strain in 'running laughter' surely reflect Thompson's memory of his attempts to evade the real world in the embrace of laudanum, as do the grandiose visions of the planets in stanza two:

This Vanished Day

Across the margent of the world I fled,
And troubled the gold gateways of the stars,
Smiting for shelter on their clangèd bars;
    Fretted to dulcet jars
And silvern chatter the pale ports of the moon.

The flight of the soul recorded in the poem is a flight not only
from the Hound of Heaven, the transcendental reality, but
from mundane reality as well; when, at last, in exhaustion it
recognizes God as its pursuer, it is at the same time submitting
to the voice of conscience and the demands of common life.

In the examination of conscience which the poem in effect is,
Thompson acknowledges, first, that human sympathies have
been closed to him by his own fault, by his self-communing
habits and his unwillingness to make intimate contact with
others; then, too, that his cosmic fantasies were merely bolt-
holes, wherein he could not hide from 'this tremendous lover'.

He tells how he turned to children, hoping in their love to
reanimate his innocence, but found that he had lost their kind
of innocence for ever. Nature was his next refuge. Here, perhaps
more than elsewhere, the poem becomes inflated. Possibly
Thompson, without being really interested in Nature, wanted
another alternative to dramatize his loneliness. At any rate, the
references here are of the most general, literary kind, lacking
the exact observation of one who has really *looked* at the natural
world. Instead, he substitutes his favourite liturgical images:

I was heavy with the even,
When she lit her glimmering tapers
Round the day's dead sanctities,

and maternal metaphors, when he says of Nature, let her

Drop yon blue bosom-veil of sky, and show me
    The breasts o' her tenderness:
Never did any milk of hers once bless
    My thirsting mouth.

But, in his flight, even the drug fails him at the end, and his
narcotic visions and his poetry are revealed as empty self-
deception:

Yea, faileth now even dream
The dreamer, and the lute the lutanist;

85

> Even the linked fantasies, in whose blossomy twist
> I swung the earth a trinket at my wrist,
> Are yielding; cords of all too weak account
> For earth with heavy grief so overplussed.

Most commentators take these lines as referring simply to his imaginative resources and poetic gifts. If there is any doubt that Thompson was also thinking of laudanum as well as poetry, the references to *weeds* and *flowers* in the lines wondering if God is a jealous God, should remove it:

> Ah! is Thy love indeed
> A weed, albeit an amaranthine weed,
> Suffering no flowers except its own to mount?

Naked, defenceless, smitten to the knee, amidst the dust of the mounded years, he comes to that realization which must precede his recognition of the identity of his pursuer:

> Ah! must—
> Designer infinite!—
> Ah! must Thou char the wood ere Thou canst limn with it?

For the first time he accepts pain, not as a kind of ransom paid to poetry nor as a masochistic indulgence, but as having a divine purpose in it. Surveying his desolate life, with his heart

> as a broken fount
> Wherein tear-drippings stagnate. . . .

he moves to the wider vision of eternity announced by a mysterious trumpeter, who may be Christ or Death (probably the latter since he is 'cypress-crowned'). And as the trumpet sounds, he asks his last agonized question and utters his final desperate cry against the claims of reality:

> Whether man's heart or life it be which yields
> Thee harvest, must Thy harvest-fields
> Be dunged with rotten death?

It is then that the Voice surrounds him like a bursting sea, the footfall of the Hound halts by him and he sees his gloom as the shade of His hand outstretched caressingly. All that he sought was all that he fled from, the inflnite love and compassion of the Most High. He has put off pretence; he will accept what life has to give, sustained by the certainty of God's love and protection. With an inner coherence Thompson rarely achieved elsewhere, a firm hold on the main theme, and many passages which unforgettably crystallize the spiritual turmoils of a deeply sensitive soul, 'The Hound of Heaven' is a remarkable poetic achievement, a statement which strikes response in the hearts of many who do not accept its theology. But for Thompson himself, the fight was not over; the ideal of duty not established for good and all. The poem marks merely a resting-place, a resolution rather than a turning-point in his life.

'The Hound of Heaven' is torn from the painful experience of one who had experienced the very depths of spiritual abandonment. But, without its imaginative projection of actual psychological and emotional states, it would perhaps not have achieved its final poignant form. The two sides of Thompson's conflict are here in their clash, as in their distinction. It in no way impairs the universal truth of the poem to find bound up with his awareness of the Divine pursuit his sense of guilt at his wasted years and his treatment of his father, from which he was also fleeing. The God who confronts him at the end of the poem wears all the lineaments of a father who knows best, and whose actions have been wholly for his son's sake:

> All which I took from thee I did but take,
>> Not for thy harms,
> But just that thou might'st seek it in My arms.
>> All which thy child's mistake
> Fancies as lost, I have stored for thee at home:
>> Rise, clasp my hand, and come!

I must mention another poem belonging to the London period of 1891–2 to show another aspect of the temper of his early work. Thompson nourishing his abnormal sensitivity, indulging in secretive fantasies, fleeing from human obligations, inflicting misfortunes on himself and blaming Fate or the world for it, and prone to self-pity, is neither a particularly interesting nor an admirable figure. But in poems like 'A Fallen Yew' we see the stronger and more likeable side of his personality. One is tempted to regard the ideas on asceticism he expressed in his prose as rationalizations of his troubles, an attempt to give his neurosis stature, or to void his sense of guilt by projecting it on

to the Providential ordering of the universe. And it is likely that
so they began. But to leave it at that is to do an injustice to the
real innerness of Thompson's personality, to cut the Gordian
knot of his complex make-up; for he came to transcend self-
indulgence and to sink his temperamental miseries in a balanced,
religious theory of asceticism. He took years to achieve this
stability. What we have in 'A Fallen Yew' is an early intima-
tion of a slowly and painfully acquired attitude.

The starting-point of the poem is Thompson's contemplation
of an ancient yew-tree which used to grow at Ushaw:

> It seemed corrival of the world's great prime,
> Made to un-edge the scythe of Time,
> And last with stateliest rhyme.

Musing upon the antiquity of the tree, which seemed likely to
last beyond the reach of conjecture, and deeply moved by its
decay, its 'reverberations of mortality', he comes to the core of
the poem. Just as this noble tree has a secret heart, shielding it
against storms and the onslaught of years, and shut off even
from the exploration of boys and birds,

> But bird nor child might touch by any art
> Each other's or the tree's hid heart,
> A whole God's breadth apart:

so in man there is a hidden, unplumbable mystery, the essence
of his particular personality, his deep-hid secret self.

Even in the most intimate of all relationships—that of
marriage—the partners can never make themselves free of each
other's inmost heart. The 'heart's heart' resists human love as
it resists hate. For this is the part of man God has reserved for
Himself alone:

> Yea, in that ultimate heart's occult abode
> To lie as in an oubliette of God,
> Or in a bower untrod,

> Built by a secret Lover for His Spouse;—
> Sole choice is this your life allows,
> Sad tree, whose perishing boughs
> So few birds house!

This is good psychology. Small wonder, then, that the final

stanzas of the poem, from the time the image of marriage is introduced, are strongly reminiscent of Patmore, who treated precisely the theme of 'A Fallen Yew' in several poems in *The Angel in the House*—'Why, having won her, do I woo?' for instance.

> The sweetest wife on sweetest marriage-day—
> Their souls at grapple in mid-way,
> Sweet to her sweet may say:

recalls 'The Azalea' and 'Built by a secret Lover for His Spouse' looks back to 'To the Body':

> Little, sequestered pleasure-house
> For God and for His Spouse;

although Patmore would hardly have allowed himself the extravagance of 'as in an oubliette of God'.

Yet Thompson does give the concept an individual colouring. For Patmore, love, even at its most exalted, is felt to be imperfect and the 'ultimate heart' remains inviolate because all human love is a shadow of the love between God and the soul; but Thompson uses the analogy of married love to define the nature of the human personality, and identify the depths wherein resides man's awareness of God. As in 'The Hound of Heaven', Thompson is universalizing his own characteristics— in this case, his difficulty in responding to human affections and his cherished secretiveness. The poem does not rank with 'The Hound of Heaven', partly because the conclusion is too plainly a private lament, narrowing the vision and reducing the quality of the feeling, and partly because there are some clumsy archaisms and affectations like

> Its keys are at the cincture hung of God;
> Its gates are trepidant to His nod;
> By Him its floors are trod.

For all that 'A Fallen Yew' impresses with the purity of its statement. Like the tree it celebrates, it has an inner core of strength and a philosophic calm; unlike other early poems, too, its images have a cogency and aptness which indicate the sincerity of the poet's feeling.

The poems we have been considering are among the chief

fruit of Thompson's stay at Storrington and just after. In these and others written at the same time—'To the Dead Cardinal of Westminster', 'A Corymbus for Autumn' and 'To My God-child'—the poet charts his tormented, grief-stricken soul—his inner tumult, his struggle through the labyrinth of drugs towards God, his awareness of his withered past, his need to accept common responsibilities, his doubts and his certainties about his poetic vocation, his groping, with stumbling steps, towards asceticism, and the clash in his spirit between his tenacious desire to hold fast to his inner independence and his genuine affection for the Meynells. I have stressed the 'confessional' aspects of the poems, to which Thompson himself admitted, and the light they throw upon the configurations of his lacerated soul. What of their poetic quality? For in poetry, whatever the value of its psychological and biographical elements, the way a thing is said determines what in fact is said. A closer look at Thompson's poetic technique in *Poems* should take us some way towards understanding why his reputation has fluctuated so much.

VII

An Alien Tongue, of Alien Things

FROM the first reviews of *Poems* down to the present day, there have been widely different opinions about Thompson's style. The admirers of his early poems were enraptured by what seemed to them a magnificent display of language, a special richness of rhythms and textures, and dazzling tapestries of thickly-woven images. The *Edinburgh Review* referred to his 'powerful and truly poetic use of metaphor'; the *Speaker* praised his 'domination over language'; Arnold Bennett committed himself to the statement that 'Francis Thompson has a richer natural genius, a finer poetical equipment, than any poet save Shakespeare'; J. L. Garvin found in his first volume a kinship with Marlowe, saying, 'It seemed to reveal the same "high astounding terms", the same vast imagery; the same *amour de l'impossible*; the soul striking the sublime stars, the intolerable passion for beauty.'

Others were less enthusiastic. Coventry Patmore's and Arthur Symons' reservations on Thompson's manner have already been quoted; Sir Arthur Quiller-Couch, too, was annoyed by Thompson's vocabulary—listing words 'not easily allowed by anyone possessing a sense of the history of the language' and E. K. Chambers went much further in the *Academy*, speaking of 'the habitual perversity which prompts him so often, instead of searching fairly for the appropriate—the right—word, to foist in some makeshift which is alike flashy and ineffective' and of his 'ugly linguistic monstrosities, blue roses'. As the years have gone by, it is the opinion of Chambers rather than that of J. L. Garvin which has gained ascendancy, until a contemporary Catholic critic can go so far as to contrast the freshness and virility of D. H. Lawrence's language with that of Thompson in his most famous poem. 'The *Hound of Heaven* may, as a distinguished preacher once argued,' writes Martin Turnell, 'be an excellent "retreat book" but the soundness of its theology or the "majesty" of its central idea does not concern the critic. What does concern him is that the language of the poem is tired, effete, stale.'[1]

In almost all the long poems Thompson wrote, his language has been tarnished by changes of taste during half a century; it was, even to begin with, tired and effete. This is the style which has been described as the 'Thompsonian conglomerate' —a vocabulary stuffed with archaisms, like 'shawm', 'swink', 'devirginate', 'eld', 'ostent', 'lustihed'; neologisms like 'supportlessly', 'sciential', 'coerule', 'immeditatably', 'impitiable', 'dulcitude', 'roseal', 'wassailous', 'frore'; with Latinisms—'large compacting hand', 'aspirant soul', 'Sublimed the illuminous and volute abundance', 'With such Hesperian fulgence', 'Lay in an oozy pool of its own deliquious light', 'the trepidant air', 'thy conflagrate fancies' and

> Some, with languors of waved arms,
> Fluctuous oared their flexile way;
> Some were borne half resupine
> On the aerial hyaline;

and with exotic inversions, strained locutions and capricious coinages producing lines like these:

> Who in most dusk and vidual curch,

> who set
> Upon her brow the day-fall's carcanet,

> Who queened her front with the enrondured moon?

> Uneuphrasied with tears, the hierarchical
> Vision lies unoccult.

[1] *Poetry and Crisis*, Sands, 1938, pp. 77–8.

                a grisly jaw, whose verges soon,
Slowly and ominously filled* by the oncoming plenilune,
Supportlessly congest with fire* and suddenly spit forth
    the moon.

    Far off a lily-cluster poised in sun
      Dispread its gracile curls of light.

Alice Meynell herself remonstrated with him, especially over his favourite '-less' termination, which he used recklessly in words like 'tameless', 'shunless', 'rebukeless', 'mateless', 'moveless': 'The Bible has "unquenchable", ' she writes, 'and I don't think it could have "quenchless". Lowell has "exhaustless" somewhere. I think one can strictly hold "less" to mean "minus" or "without" and with these the verb is impossible. I remember refusing to be taught a setting of some words of Praed's that had "tameless" for "untamable", so you see it is an old objection with me.'

She did, however, defend his Latinisms: 'Obviously there are Latinisms and Latinisms! . . . in F. T. the majestic Latin word is forged hot on the anvil of the artificer. No Old English in the making could be readier or closer.' Other friends urged him to moderate his verbal exuberance in the interests of clarity; even Wilfrid Meynell found in 'Ode to the Setting Sun' a 'violence of diction' which deformed it. And from the later version of this poem Thompson eliminated some archaic words and changed some phrases, such as 'Thy visioned music-blasts' to 'Thy visible music-blasts', but these were minor alterations, and he was always quick to defend his predilection for odd words. 'As for "immeditatably" it is in all respects the one and only right word for the line', he writes to the Meynells; 'as regards the exact shade of meaning and feeling, and as regards the rhythmical movement it gives to the line', and in an essay: 'To write plainly on a fine subject is to set a jewel in wood. . . . The true abuse of "fine language" is rich diction applied to a plain subject, or lofty words to weak ideas.'

In answer to criticism, his friends pointed out that many of his words had precedents in Elizabethan poetry. This is as much beside the point as the fact that an occasional Thompsonian coinage like 'labyrinthine' has achieved common currency; the objection is not to the occasional use of an archaism or strange coinage, but to the profuse pouring out of inkhorn terms. In Thompson's poetry, unusual words do not come as a sudden delight, caprice or illumination, but proliferate until they ensnare the feet and blot out the sun. 'He is that strange phenomenon,' wrote Arthur Symons, 'a verbal intelligence. He thinks in words, he receives his emotions and sensations from words, and the rapture he certainly attains is a rapture of the disembodied word. . . . Styles he has, but not style.' And Lionel Johnson wrote to Katharine Tynan of his fellow-Catholic's style: 'He has done more to harm the English language than the worst American newspapers: *Corruptio optimi pessima.* Has the opulent, prodigal manner of the seventeenth century; a profusion of great imagery, sometimes excessive and false; and another opulence and profusion, that of Shelley in his lyric choruses.'

Curiously enough—or perhaps not so curious if we remember Thompson's lively intelligence—in his essays and notebooks are many criticisms of the practices of other poets, which apply with at least equal force to his own manner. One note reads thus:

'There are word-tasters and word-swillers. Unfortunately the two are confounded. Because the tasteless many among writers indulge in orgies of "strong" and "picturesque" language unrecking of fitness and delicate adjustment of meaning, a hue and cry goes out against the few whom they ignorantly imitate, the few whose love of language goes down to the sensitive roots of words, the few who never bang on a strong word like a tin kettle to deafen the ears of the groundlings, but use it because it is the one word which is the exact vehicle for a strong thing; because it is not *a* strong word but *the* strong word culled carefully from many strong words. These are connoisseurs in words. The others are drunkards in words. Like the dram drinker, they have swallowed language till their palate has lost all distinction but that of coarse stimulus. Is it intoxicant enough? Is it hot in the mouth? Whether it be the best, the right word, they care nought, so it blisters the tongue.'

It is clear from this statement that Thompson considered himself a 'word-taster', a 'connoisseur in words'; yet most of his early poetry shows him to have been a 'word-swiller', a 'drunkard in words'.

Did he have a theory of style, as Wordsworth did, as Keats, Rossetti, Hopkins did? Much of what he has to say about rhythm is by no means without interest; for instance, some remarks in a letter to Katharine Tynan about the metre of 'The Making of Viola': 'It is . . . founded on the bold application of a metrical principle which has lain dormant since the decay of the early alliterative metre. . . . The true law is that you take a metre (the more received and definite the better) and then vary it by the omission of syllables, leaving the lines so treated to be read into given length by pause, and by dwelling on the syllables preceding or following the *hiatus*.' But this, like most else Thompson wrote on metrics, is merely a simplified restatement of one of the principles Coventry Patmore had set forth in his *Essay on English Metrical Law* and practised in his *Unknown Eros* odes. Thompson's comments on poetry and vocabulary, save for his etymological notes, which show a sound classical knowledge, are of the most general and unoriginal kind. As Everard Meynell admits: 'He was at no pains to coin or collect, nor even to possess a theory.'

Why, then, the flood of freakish words, the eccentric, bookish vocabulary? We may find three main reasons behind Thompson's choice of words—first, the nature of his vision, second, the state of the English language in his time, and, third, his immaturity as a man and a poet.

We have seen that Thompson's vision was compounded of several things—his inner innocence, his guilt about his wasted years, his fear of reality, his memories of his opium dreams, his religious faith, his love for the 'unknown She'. Deprival of the drug released not only a host of pent-up emotions and subjective visionings, but also the need to use words as a substitute for opium. From youth, he had a certain verbal facility, but he had not hammered out a personal style by trial and error. He was thirty before he began to write poetry seriously and consistently. But he had since childhood read voraciously in the English, French, Greek and Latin poets, and, as he had a tenacious memory, if not always an accurate one (the original quotations in his 'Shelley' essay were remarkably extensive but garbled), when he came to write poetry, his lines were clamorous with echoes of other men's work. It is hardly less surprising that his style should be 'literary', in the sense that it smells not of men, but of books. The manner of 'A Corymbus for Autumn' and 'Ode to the Setting Sun', for instance, is pieced out of several other manners, sewn together with exotic coinages and odd Latinisms, like a clever adolescent playing tricks with newly acquired words, or a quiz-kid astonishing adults with his knowledge of the dictionary. The result is a spurious magnificence impressive mainly to those who have not read much poetry.

It was not that Thompson knew no better. It seems rather to me that his lack of contact with real life, his innocence about men and nature, his lack of interest in the external world of things drove him to a second-hand literary vocabulary. He was not seeking words for things he knew; but using words in detachment, as Symons saw, from things. His knowledge of nature is very limited. Although his admirers claim him as a great poet of Nature, his poems do not bear this out, his references being of the vague, 'poetic' kind, or showing a tasteless extravagance:

> Or the butterfly sunset claps its wings
> With flitter alit on the swinging blossom.

> In the new-sucked milk of the sun's bosom
> Is dabbled the mouth of the daisy-blossom.

> And beings that, under night's swart pinion,
> Make every wave upon the harbour bars
> A beaten yolk of stars.

At times, it is true, if very infrequently, we find touches of that specific observation and exact detail with which Hopkins, Tennyson, Wordsworth and Coleridge link their vision to the concrete world.

> Or rooks in spreading gyres like broken smoke.;

> The long, broad grasses underneath
> Are warted with rain like a toad's knobbed back.

But these are uncharacteristic. More often than not, Thompson takes an image from someone else's poetry and inflates it so that it loses its precision. In *Sister Songs* he writes:

An Alien Tongue, of Alien Things

> And, glimmering to eclipse,
> The long laburnum drips
> Its honey of wild flame, its jocund spilth of fire,

but although the laburnum was one tree the Londoner Thompson could hardly help knowing, his image is not struck from life, but is a spun-out variation on Tennyson's concise, exact

> Laburnums, dropping-wells of fire.

Where Thompson succeeds is in a certain *fin-de-siècle* prodigality, reminiscent of Swinburne, an intoxicated swirl of colourful words, which the mid-twentieth century tends to regard as hiding rather than projecting poetic feeling:

> before the mountainous shock
> The rankèd gods dislock,
> Scared to their skies; wide o'er rout-trampled night
> Flew spurned the pebbled stars; those splendours then
> Had tempested on earth, star upon star
> Mounded in ruin, if a larger war
> Had quaked Olympus and cold-fearing men.

This strange vocabulary has little in common with Doughty's conscious attempt at a new Elizabethan manner, or with Hopkins' dynamic medium bending and straining under feeling, but kept firmly in place by a high poetic intelligence. Thompson wanted at the same time to confess and to conceal himself from the world; he wanted to speak of real things, but he was not sure that he had real things to speak about. So he turns inevitably to the less real words, the ones with vaguer outlines, covering his emotions with a kind of literary haze, using metaphors as similes, inflating and repeating, rarely achieving poetic tautness.

His translations from Victor Hugo's 'Feuilles d'Automne' rather give the game away; Thompson makes Hugo's flamboyant passages even more flamboyant, and blows up his simplicities into Thompsonian gorgeousness. For instance,

> un jour qu'en rêve
> Ma pensée abattit son vol sur une grève.

becomes

> One day at least, whereon my thought, enlicensèd to muse,
> Had dropped its wing above the bleachèd margin of the ooze.

and

> Et je me demandai pourquoi l'on est ici,
> Quel peut être après tout le bout de tout ceci.

is inflated as

> And I make question of me, to what issues are we here,
> Whither should tend the thwarting threads of all this
> ravelled gear.

Hugo's poem, despite occasional rhetoric, is in the main direct
and simple; Thompson's version, full of words like 'trepidates',
'investuring', 'fanfaronnade', 'destrier', 'rumorous', 'fluctuous',
is as roundabout as it is pompous.

Not only in vocabulary do his early poems smell of books,
but also in the unspeakable nature of most of his lines. The vices
which infest Thompson's poems—inflation, verbalism, hollow
magnificences—can also be charged against Swinburne, another
refugee from reality, but Swinburne's poetry is usually musical,
in rhythm and in phrase, and can be spoken fluently. Not so
Thompson's whose poetry is probably the least recitable of any
of his age. With his eye trained to print and his ear not tuned to
others' voices, and hearing over years the hissing, booming,
reverberant sounds from laudanum-caves, he seemed not to
have appreciated the rhythmical awkwardness of lines like
these:

> Thou as a lion roar'st, O Sun.

> A passionless statue stands

> With plumes night-tinctured englobed and cinctured* of Saints,
> his guided steps held on
> To where on the far crystalline pale* of that transtellar Heaven
> there shone
> The immutable crocean dawn* effusing from the Father's Throne

> But if mere unappeasèd cicatrices
> Might get them lawful ease.

> But joy only lurks retirèd
> In the dim gloaming of thine irid.

or the odd sound of words and phrases like 'cluck'dst', 'perpetual-burnishable', 'vestal-vesture', 'foist'st', 'sigh-suggesting', 'vaporous shroudage', 'who medicinest sickness', 'a moiety in the Paoli's seams Statelily builded their Venetian name'.

These are not the infrequent noddings of a master of words; clotted consonants halt the tongue everywhere and whole nests of wretched sibilants hiss in line after line of his poems like vipers spun out of opium-smoke. His frequently strained rhymes, uncertain rhythms, abrupt shifts of style, and the sudden injection of uneuphonic lines into his laboured odes indicate that Thompson's ear was startlingly defective. He would often select a rhythm quite unsuitable for his subject, that, for instance, of 'To the Dead Cardinal of Westminster', used presumably only because Marvell did, where we encounter such oddities as

> I will not perturbate
> Thy Paradisal state
> With praise
> Of thy dead days;

> To the new-heavened say,
> 'Spirit, thou wert fine clay';
> This do
> Thy praise who knew;

or the jingling thump-thump rhythms of 'The Lily of the King' or the absurd starred lines of 'A Judgment in Heaven', supposed to be an imitation of Old English alliterative metre.

In respect, then, of vocabulary and style, Thompson has little in common with the seventeenth-century Metaphysical Poets, with whom enthusiastic contemporaries compared him, but shows the state of the nineteenth-century poetic vocabulary when the original Romantic inspiration and the succeeding aesthetic one had run to seed. The Romantics' exploitation of connotations and their stress upon secondary meanings gave the poetry at the beginning of the century a new freshness and ambience. But with the proliferation of inferior poets and the fading of the original Romantic impulse, the connection between connotation and denotation became gradually looser, and associations rather than meanings were given greater emphasis in poetry, resulting in diffuseness and in the use of 'poetic' words to put the reader into a 'poetic' frame of mind. That precision which is the heart of poetry fades, and well-worn counters of diction begin to appear, even in a superior poet like Elizabeth Barrett Browning, as poeticizing tricks. The aesthetic poets who succeeded the Romantics skilfully exploited the vague suggestiveness of feeling encouraged by such poetic attitudes to language, and at the same time, recognizing the danger of mere verbalism, sought to sharpen their expression by reviving archaic words. Rossetti, for instance, was always on the look-out for 'stunners'.

No serious Victorian poet could remain unaware of the problem of the poetic vocabulary; there were three main ways in which a poet of the century could prevent himself from falling into diffuse, vague, poetic diction—the first was to recharge language with a new personal energy as Browning did when he liberated himself from Shelley's influence or as Hopkins did with his inscaping; the second was by a careful simplicity, like that of Thomas Hardy or of William Barnes in his dialect poems; the third was by injecting new life into the current poetic diction through importations of new words. D. G. Rossetti's attempts to enlarge the stock of 'poetic' words, and indeed his whole conception of the art of poetry had a powerful effect on Thompson. His regard for the pre-Raphaelite leader is shown in his poem on the anniversary of Rossetti's death, where these lines occur:

> He taught our English art to burn
>   With colours from diviner skies,
> He taught our English art to gaze
>   On Nature with a learner's eyes:
> That hills which look into the heaven
>   Have their fair bases on the earth;
> God paints his most angelic hues
>   On vapours of a terrene birth.

In Rossetti's fake-liturgical splendours and carefully mediaevalized vocabulary Thompson found inspiration for his own borrowings and coinages; unhappily, he came too late; the language for poetry had deteriorated still further since Rossetti's day, and what in Rossetti had had something of the attraction of novelty and of a sophisticated game becomes in Thompson tired and naïve. Working less to a theory than by instinct and influence, Thompson tried to create a special language for poetry as far removed as he could make it from the ordinary vocabulary of prose. It is true that he claimed that it is 'the infantries of language, so to speak, which must make up the mass of a poet's force; i.e. common diction of the many in every age; the numerous terms of prose, apart from special poetic diction', but even this statement suggests that for him the 'special poetic diction' was something embedded in poetry like currants in a cake. He looks to words to do his thinking and feeling for him; he exploits the shock value of unusual words. Where there is a choice, he nearly always chooses the more exotic and sensational word.

Perhaps he is aiming at a timeless style, formed out of bits from the Elizabethans, Chaucer and the Metaphysicals pieced out with neologisms and Latinisms. But, since, in his more elaborate pieces, he seldom saw or felt the thing itself, poem after poem becomes a glass-case exposing dead and stuffed word-specimens. Deficient in self-criticism and burdened with a clouded and pain-racked vision, he needed above all a mentor, a person of sensitive taste who could bring pressure to bear on him to modify his practice. Alice Meynell, as we have seen, did remonstrate somewhat; so, to a less degree, did Wilfrid Meynell. Yet Meynell's limited literary sensitivity and his excited encouragement of Thompson's rapid writing tended to confirm the poet in his practices. Eager to please, or to appear to please his benefactor, Thompson continued to foam out his hyperboles, grotesqueries and tawdry linguistic bubbles.

One careful analyst of Thompson's style, F. B. Tolles, has suggested that it was not that Thompson deliberately imitated Rossetti's use of words, so much that he was 'forced by the circumstances of his situation at the end of the tradition of nineteenth-century poetry to push this theory of language to extremes which Rossetti never envisaged'.[1] Some of his poems, says Mr. Tolles, show that, writing under different conditions, Thompson might have been a genuinely great poet. 'But he was hampered in his mystical flights by a vocabulary inherited from the poets who had preceded him. He never succeeded in freeing himself from these impedimenta, and only occasionally was the poetical impulse enough to enable him to rise in spite of them.'[2]

[1] 'The Praetorian Cohorts', *English Studies*, April, 1940, p. 56.
[2] Ibid., p. 63.

In a sense this is true. Yet Hardy and Housman, not to mention Lionel Johnson, Alice Meynell and several others, were, in the same circumstances, writing a simple, clear, direct poetry. And, as Mr. Tolles does not recognize, there was another Thompson, he who could write 'Daisy', 'Contemplation', 'The Poppy', 'A Fallen Yew' and most of 'The Hound of Heaven'. It is more reasonable to attribute the freakishness of Thompson's odes to laudanum and temperament, rather than to any conscious literary theory, and to see in them the part of Thompson which used words not to fix reality but to evade it, diffusing meaning to avoid facing the truth at the heart of meaning, and indulging in a nursery game of charades.

The resemblances to Crashaw and the Metaphysicals which Mégroz, for instance, has stressed prove to be of the most superficial kind. Thompson is like, say, Donne and Herbert only on the principle of 'salmon in both'—the three poets write about religion, or like Crashaw, in that the language of both poets is often ecstatically verbose. What there is of the metaphysical manner in Thompson is almost wholly borrowed. While the seventeenth-century poets were concerned with the exact rendering of ideas and emotions, with the use of unusual analogies to create a special mood or attitude, with the search for the quiddity of the thing, in Thompson's case it is not a matter of inscape at all; he is striving to project his feelings most of the time without really giving anything away. Hence he must garnish the facts with coloured lights; he must swathe the emotion in dyed muslin. Alice Meynell becomes a marble statue; opium is the sun, which is a 'beaming flood', a butterfly, a lion, a brazing bowl, a dying dragon, the Host at Benediction, a nursing mother, a twi-form deity, a bee stinging the West, Christ on the Cross, a flame-chorded psalterion, and much else, the healthy Meynell children become elves, sprites and diaphanous nymphs; the stars become the marbles for little angels to play with, and the planets balls to roll idly underfoot.

In fact, as Osbert Burdett and Paul Elmer More observed, Thompson is a typical decadent poet in the literary sense—his language is artificial and affected, sensation concerns him more than emotion, his images, in their bookishness, operate at a couple of removes from life; and the general tone of his early poetry is morbid, spiritually inert, in the minor key. Need we be surprised that Thompson's favourite 'sandalled'—'Thy naked feet unsandallèd', 'In sandalled shadow of the Triune feet'—and lines like

> The silver-stolèd damsels of the sea

should combine in the last verse of Oscar Wilde's 'The Harlot's House':

> And down the long and silent street,
> The dawn, with silver-sandalled feet,
> Crept like a frightened girl,

nor that Oscar Wilde on hearing a reading of *Sister Songs* should say: 'Why can't I write poetry like that? That is what I've wanted to do all my life.'

Although the whirl of words, the Bacchantes' dance of images, give an impression of dynamism, the main temper of Thompson's poetry is static, with more than a touch of fatalism in it. The poet who wrote so many lines like these:

> Woe is me,
> And all our chants but chaplet some decay,
> As mine this vanishing—nay, vanished Day.

was not expressing the mood of Donne, Crashaw, Marvell or Herbert; but the mood of his age, a melancholy that was both individual and social, a weariness of spirit as the last sands of the century ran out. In one of his early essays, 'Moestitiae Encomium', which might have been written by many of the contributors to *The Yellow Book* and *The Savoy*, Thompson explicitly recognized his kinship with the men of the Nineties:

'I know her [Sadness], for I am of the age, and the age is hers. Alas for the nineteenth century, with so much pleasure, and so little joy; so much learning, and so little wisdom; so much effort, and so little fruition; so many philosophers, and such little philosophy; so many seers, and such little vision; so many prophets, and such little foresight; so many teachers, and such an infinite wild vortex of doubt! the one divine thing left to us is Sadness. Even our virtues take their stamp; the intimacy of our loves is born of despair; our very gentleness to our children is because we know how short their time. "Eat," we say, "eat, drink, and be merry; for tomorrow ye are men." '

If Thompson's poetry often seems artificial and tired, it as frequently seems second-hand. It would be wearisome to list the echoes, borrowings, paraphrases and half-rememberings of a host of earlier poets which bespatter Thompson's pages. Critic after critic has pointed to, for instance, the clear marks of Rossetti in 'Dream Tryst', 'The Making of Viola' and 'To My Godchild', of Shelley's 'Epipsychidion' in 'Love in Dian's Lap' and 'The Hound of Heaven', of Patmore in many poems such as 'By Reason of Thy Law' and 'The Dread of Height', of Crashaw in *Sister Songs* and 'Little Jesus'; of Wordsworth in 'Daisy' and 'The Poppy', of Alice Meynell in *Sister Songs* and 'The Cloud's Swan Song', of Victor Hugo in 'Orient Ode', to name but a very few of the poets Thompson has ransacked.

His inability to distinguish between fantasy and poetic truth based on reality is almost certainly the chief reason for his falling back upon the ideas of others. Sometimes the resemblance is one of image; as between Southwell's

> Did Christ manure thy heart to breed him briers?
> Or doth it need this unaccustomed soyle
> With hellish dung to fertile heaven's desires?

and Thompson's

> Whether man's heart or life it be which yields
> Thee harvest, must Thy harvest-fields
> Be dunged with rotten death?;

sometimes it is an unacknowledged quotation, like 'the beachèd margent of the ooze' reproducing 'A Midsummer Night's Dream's' 'the beachèd margent of the sea' or Coleridge's 'the Lampads Seven' repeated by Thompson at the end of 'To My Godchild'; sometimes it is a paraphrase, wherein Shelley's 'the republic of the stars' becomes the 'Populacy of Heaven' or Patmore's

> But like the bard, who freely sings
> In strictest bonds of rhyme and rule,
> And finds in them, not bonds, but wings.

is rendered

> Right poet! who thy rightness to approve,
> Having all liberty, didst keep all measure,
> . . . .
> Find gay variety no license could devise!;

sometimes it is a close imitation of another poet's typical style, like the Keatsian pastiche of the long passage in 'A Corymbus for Autumn' beginning 'For other saw we, other indeed', or the equally close copy of Wordsworth's 'Tintern Abbey' in the central lines of 'Contemplation'; and sometimes it is, to modern ears, a ludicrously exact echo of a now familiar piece, as when Kipling's 'Mandalay' obtrudes incongruously into 'The Mistress of Vision':

> So fearfully the sun doth sound,
> Clanging up beyond Cathay,
> For the great earthquaking sunrise rolling up beyond Cathay.

When in 'Assumpta Maria', Thompson calls himself 'poor Thief of Song', he is referring to the fact that the poem is based closely on the office of the Blessed Virgin, but his declaration may very aptly be extended to many more of his poems.

What then of his imagery? Has this a freshness and originality which would compensate for his other failings? Alice Meynell herself, for all her tenderness to Thompson's work, felt constrained to say that some of his poems were 'piled so high in imagery so beautiful as almost to persuade us that imagery is the end and goal of poetry. But Thompson himself was soon to learn that these ceremonies of the imagination are chiefly ways of approach, and that there are barer realities beyond, and nearer to the centre of poetry itself.' Her criticism is valid, but has wider implications than she allows. For much of Thompson's imagery is wilful and capricious. Mrs. Meynell also wrote of his 'terrible or tender trick of likening great things to small'. Rather than being 'terrible or tender', this trick, as Patmore saw, had the effect of degrading the larger referent. Thompson, at the centre of his fantasy-universe, swinging the earth like a censer or a trinket, seeing the stars as egg-yolk, or the sun as an angry bee, is shrinking the cosmos to the dimensions of his own dreams. 'The universe', as he says in the passage already quoted from 'Shelley', 'is his box of toys.'

His generous use of liturgical imagery is an important reason for his success with Catholic readers. The many references to the Mass, to Benediction, to other ceremonies, and to the furniture of the Church are impressive to those who share Thompson's faith, and few can resist the elaborate Benediction image that opens his 'Orient Ode':

> Lo, in the sanctuaried East,
> Day, a dedicated priest
> In all his robes pontifical exprest,
> Lifteth slowly, lifteth sweetly,
> From out its Orient tabernacle drawn,
> Yon orbèd sacrament confest
> Which sprinkles benediction through the dawn;
> And when the grave procession's ceased,
> The earth with due illustrious rite
> Blessed,—ere the frail fingers featly
> Of twilight, violet-cassocked acolyte,
> His sacerdotal stoles unvest—
> Sets, for high close of the mysterious feast,
> The sun in august exposition meetly
> Within the flaming monstrance of the West.

This is well worked out, with a consistency rare in Thompson, yet, if we stand back from the image for a moment and divest it of some of its directly religious appeal, we will find that his use of the Benediction service is fanciful rather than imaginative. Does he really see the sunrise as sacramental? The rest of the poem belies this, for little is in fact added to our ideas of the sun or the Benediction service by it. Whereas Patmore's 'Arbor Vitae' does present an effective metaphor of the Church—the gnarled, ancient, moss-encrusted tree, with life and power of regeneration at the heart, Thompson does not fuse the two referents. He sees ritual less as a means than as an end in itself, so that the reconciliation of the sun with the consecrated Host is only superficially achieved. Neither the adoration of God in the bread nor of the Creator through the sun is illuminated by the uneasy juxtaposition, which, in fact, leans towards a non-Christian pantheism. The general impression the whole poem leaves is of wilful indulgence in an attractive fancy, not of a poetic statement shaped by its ostensible or actual subject. In fact, although Thompson had none of the epic pretensions of the author of *Festus*, much of his liturgical poetry shows a startling resemblance to the verse of the Spasmodics, who also present vague, cosmic vistas in inflated, repetitive language, grandiosely use all space as their stage and deal in large-sounding 'poetic' images.

Looked at closely, Thompson's imagery in his odes turns out to be a jumble of inappropriate or barely appropriate figures. There are undeniably many fine lines and exciting images; such as these from 'The Hound of Heaven':

> The long savannahs of the blue

> The pulp so bitter, how shall taste the rind?

> And now my heart is as a broken fount
> Wherein tear-drippings stagnate, spilt down ever
> From the dank thoughts that shiver
> Upon the sighful branches of my mind.

Yet, as a rule, he is carried on from image to image with scant regard for their congruity. It is almost a process of free association in metaphor suggesting the phantasmagoric parade of a laudanum-dream or the idle fancies of a mind giving itself up to a dissolving shadow-show or a film negative on which several images have been superimposed. Mégroz defends Thompson's odes as a kind of Dionysian chanting; an odd argument in support of one who wrote: 'It is false that highest or supremest poetry is stripped of figure. Purely emotional poetry at its height is bare of imagery, not poetry of supremest flight. . . . Supreme emotion is not supreme poetry.' The objection to much of Thompson's imagery is that it lacks direction, and provides a series of illustrations by a virtuoso rather than creates a poetic experience. Take, for instance, these lines from *Sister Songs:*

> Thou rushest down in every stream
> Whose passion frets my spirit's deepening gorge,
> Unhood'st mine eyas-heart, and fliest my dream,
> Thou swing'st the hammers of my forge;
> As the innocent moon, that nothing does but shine,
> Moves all the labouring surges of the world.

In six lines, the child he is addressing is flotsam on or

something dissolved in a river, a falconer, a blacksmith who is the moon who lets slip the hawk as she moves the tides as she swings the hammers. This muddle of images and the inappropriate word 'frets' show lack of poetic control, which is typical of almost all his longer poems.

So far I have done little more than point to the faults in Thompson's poetry, the rich harvest of embarrassment a critical reader can garner from his pages. What has been said in this chapter might seem to reduce him to the level of a pitiful neurotic voiding all his problems and his uncertainties in a torrent of ill-considered words. If this were all, Thompson's poetry would be hardly more worthy of examination than the scribblings of a psychopathic patient encouraged, by way of therapy, to project his troubles on to paper. But there remain, among his early poems, the stubborn facts of 'Daisy', 'A Fallen Yew', 'The Poppy', and other works of a striking purity of statement, and 'The Hound of Heaven' which, although by no means free from fustian and excess, has an admirable integration and progressive movement.

There were, in fact, two poets in Thompson; and just as the contradictions in his character proceed from a clash between the weak-willed and the insistently innocent sides of him, so the two types of poetry he wrote show on the one hand the escapist, evasive, egocentric Thompson, and on the other the deeply religious man conscious of the claims of life, of duty, of others. The second Thompson was the truly poetic one; the other a talented adolescent aping the manners of his favourite poets. But the adolescent had his legs firmly around the throat of the man, and it called for years of struggle and pain before their grip could be broken. In the poems named above, the more rigorous self-examination shows Thompson approaching reality, timidly perhaps, rationalizing, moralizing, shrinking back easily, yet aware of a context to his own life, and aware that his first thirty years had led him down a *cul-de-sac*. In more than one place, he acknowledges his own duality. In 'An Anthem of Earth', for instance, he describes his own early poetry in the phrase

an inexhaustible
Wassail of orgiac imageries,

and he opens 'Retrospect' thus:

> Alas, and I have sung
> Much song of matters vain,
> And a heaven-sweetened tongue
> Turned to unprofiting strain
> Of vacant things, which though
> Even so, they be, and thoroughly so,
> It is no boot at all for thee to know,
> But babble and false pain.

From the beginning, buried beneath the over-praised first poems, beneath the mellifluous phrases, and the dazzling exhibitionism of the colliding conceits, lay a genuine poetic talent. In his heart of hearts, the core of the yew, Thompson realized that in fact he was not hymning God and His ways with the world, but projecting his own disturbances, Nietzsche-like, upon the universe. At Pantasaph, he seems to have been approaching the understanding that, in his earlier poems, a dominant mood was one of nostalgia for the oblivious security of infancy. He now laments incessantly the passing of things; as when, in 'Absence', the death of 'maiden May' brings nothing but sorrow:

> Sweet shall have its sorrow,
> The rainbow its rain,
> Loving have its leaving,
> And bliss is of pain
> So fain,
> Ah, is she bliss or pain?

The world is a prison; life is a prison; dreams are withered; all things decay; all beauty passes. Not yet had Thompson come to the point where he could praise death and decay because they liberate the spirit. Yet he is, at Pantasaph, beginning to feel the crumbling about him of his cloudy towers of dream. In sum, when Thompson published his first volume he had not, despite the resolute stock-taking of 'The Hound of Heaven', resolved the conflict between the two sides of himself; but he had advanced some way towards recognizing the existence of that conflict. Scattered among the lush, empty, over-coloured poems, and occasionally flashing from behind the cold conceits and frigid hyperboles were intimations of a more responsible Thompson, the true poet.

VIII

Sad Soul of Sovereign Song

WE left Thompson at Pantasaph, correcting the proofs of *Poems*. Here he was to stay for almost five years, deprived of laudanum, recovering as much health as he ever would, writing poetry, striding over the Welsh hills, and living in close contact with the Capuchin friars of the local monastery. Thompson's relationship with the Community proved to be one of the most salutary influences in his life, a turning-point in the progress of his soul. Not only did his health and spirits markedly improve under the friendly encouragement of the bearded, sandalled friars, but he also, in his conversations with them and with the Catholic visitors to the monastery, came closer to the heart of the saint after whom he was named. In voluble discussions at Pantasaph, Thompson faced challenges to his undeveloped ideas about Catholicism which left him more understanding of its mystique and dissatisfied with his own earlier liturgical debauches.

His chief friend among the friars was Father Anselm E. J. Kenealy, whom he had met earlier at the Meynells. Just before Thompson came to Pantasaph, Father Anselm, after some arduous years as Lector of Philosophy, had been appointed editor of the *Franciscan Annals*, and had comparative leisure. It was he who was appointed to keep a special eye on the poet, and, by visiting him several times daily, to make sure that he had no access to laudaum. The friar took a special liking to Thompson, and went for prodigious walks with him, sometimes in silence, sometimes discussing 'all things in heaven and in infernis'. The Archbishop's several reminiscences of Thompson, written thirty or forty years after the event, although doubtless coloured by hind-sight and by the nostalgia of the old, are valuable as giving an impression of the poet at this time:

'Francis Thompson was not much of a man to look at. Slightly under middle height, his face was redeemed from the commonplace by a fine forehead and a pair of splendid eyes. . . . He was gentle of manner and during all the years I knew him I never once heard a harsh word fall from his lips. Though unimpressive in figure he was a wonder when he opened his mouth to talk. His language was virile and flowing. He would, indeed, to his intimate friends, both speak and write at times with a phraseological pomp that was hardly justified by the subject.'[1]

Thompson had much the same impact on the Hon. Everard Fielding, who with a friend called on the poet at Pantasaph, at five one evening, and found him still in bed, called again at 6.30, with no better luck, then wrote a note inviting the poet to breakfast at 9.30 p.m. He came, and

'instead of parables in polysyllables and a riot of imagery, we found simplicity and modesty and a manner which would have been commonplace if it had not been so sincere. But the charm and interest of his talk grew with the night, and it was already dawn when . . . we escorted him back across the snow to his untimely lunch. He told us, I remember, of his poetic development, and of how, until recently, he had fancied that the end of poetry was reached in the stringing together of ingenious images, an art in which, he somewhat naïvely confessed, he knew himself to excel; but that now he knew it should reach further, and he hoped for an improvement in his future work.'

It was while at Pantasaph in 1894 that Thompson was taken to Chester by Father Anselm to be photographed for the Meynells. This is the most formal adult likeness of the poet in existence. With unwonted neatness of suit, wing collar and cravat, and with beard and large, curved, Kaiser Bill moustache very neatly trimmed, the thin pale-faced poet, the upper part of his countenance that of a youth of about eighteen, looks

[1] 'Francis Thompson', *Capuchin Annual*, 1933, p. 42.

solemnly away from the camera with great sad eyes. The derelict of the streets has, in external appearance at least, been made
over, for this occasion, into the respectable literary gent.

Prompted by Father Anselm and another friar, Father
Alphonsus, a particular admirer of Patmore's odes, Thompson
wrote a great deal of prose and poetry for the *Franciscan Annals*,
from 1893 to the very year of his death. But he was not always
as alive and placid as Father Anselm's account would suggest.
The reception given to *Poems* plunged him into alternating
moods of elation and gloom. His joy at the good reviews is
reflected in his letters to Wilfrid Meynell, and his depression at
the bad ones in long one-sided arguments in his notebooks.
Now and again, a perceptive comment reveals an intellectual
sharpness contradicting the confusion of his poems. For instance,
in a letter to Meynell, objecting to the comparison of his poems
with those of Matthew Arnold, he writes:

'It is not merely that I have studied no poet less; it is that
I should have thought we were in the sharpest contrast. His
characteristic fineness lies in that very form and restraint to
which I so seldom attain; his characteristic drawback in the
lack of that full stream which I am seldom without. The one
needs and becomes strict banks—for he could not fill wider
ones; the other too readily overflows all banks.'

Yet, although he was enjoying his association with the friars,
and expanding his sensibilities, he was anything but at peace.
He wrote to Wilfrid Meynell, just before *Poems* was issued, 'I
never since I knew you felt so low-hearted and empty of all
belief in myself. I could find it in my heart to pitch my book
into the fire; and I shall be thoroughly glad to get it off to you,
for my heart sinks at the sight or thought of it.' Mrs. Blackburn,
friend of the Meynells who assisted Father Anselm in the production of the *Franciscan Annals*, wrote to the family in London:

'I wish he would show some kind of human elation at his
unprecedented success, but he seems to take it all in a dull
mechanical sort of way which is distressing—I feel he is in
some way or other getting into the old habit, and a fortnight
ago I spoke to him about it, for not I alone had noticed the
change but others also. However, he has assured Father An-

Francis Thompson
in 1894

selm solemnly that he is not taking opium, but he is certainly taking something. . . . He isn't doing a stroke of work and stops in bed the best part of the day, and lately he falls asleep when he comes to see me in the way he used to do at Palace Court.'

Whether or not, despite Father Anselm's vigilance, he had managed to get access to laudanum again, or whether his depression was a reaction after the effort expended in getting *Poems* ready for the press, Thompson began to be haunted by fears that his poetic gift was fading. 'I have been "all in a tremble" because I had written nothing of late. I am constantly expecting to wake up some morning and find that my Daemon has abandoned me. I hardly think I *could* be very vain of my literary gift; for I so keenly feel that it is beyond my power to command, and may at any moment be taken from me.'

It was about this time that Coventry Patmore entered decisively into Thompson's life. In 1894, Patmore, who was a member of the Third Order of St. Francis, lay auxiliaries of the Franciscans who follow a modified rule, came to visit the friars at Pantasaph. It seems likely that the Meynells, anxious about Thompson's emotional state, had asked Patmore to cast an appraising eye over the younger man. In any case, together in Wales, the two men rapidly developed a close friendship. Patmore, then a man of seventy-one, leonine, proud, celebrated, at the height of his intellectual powers, had always followed his own line, equally unaffected by the popular reception of *The Angel in the House* and the widespread neglect of *The Unknown Eros*. A convert to Catholicism after the death of his first wife, he had soaked himself in Catholic mysticism and theology, and sifted many esoteric ideas from these sources, and from Swedenborg, through the meshes of his own highly individual mind. At first sight, he would seem to have been the least likely person to understand and respond to Francis Thompson, if only because Patmore's insistence on the place of the body in the divine plan and his constant hymning of the dignity of sexual love were in such contrast to Thompson's 'Uranian' idea of love. While for Patmore the relationship between human love and divine love is a reciprocal one, for Thompson human love has significance only in relation to divine love.

Then, too, while Thompson found abstract notions of God, Love, Spirit and Infinity, attractive, Patmore abhorred them:

> The wedded light and heat
> Winnowing the witless space
> Without a let
> What are they until they beat
> Again the sod, and there beget,
> Perchance, the violet?

Thompson was fascinated by the ceremonial trappings of his religion; Patmore was interested less in ritual than in the spiritual truths it embodied; Thompson's knowledge of Catholicism was just beginning to develop; Patmore had studied St. Thomas Aquinas, St. John of the Cross, St. Augustine and the Fathers, and was expert in mystical lore; Thompson was a docilely accepting Catholic, deferential to the priesthood; Patmore had a touch of waggish anti-clericalism in his make-up and liked few things better than making jests at the expense of popular pieties. Yet they also shared much—principally a common devotion to Alice Meynell, in different ways, according to their temperaments, and a sense of being excluded from the innermost heart of this busy wife and mother. 'My heart goes forth to you as it goes to no other man; for are we not singularly visited by a great common delight, and a great common sorrow? Is not this to be one in Christ?' Patmore once wrote to Thompson. Both, too, were earnest Catholics, united in admiration for the Franciscan way of life. They both knew and loved the poets of the seventeenth century, whose temper is felt much more powerfully in Patmore's poetry than in Thompson's.

Thompson, always seeking somebody to look up to, and imitate, was rapt with Patmore's wisdom. He had had his doubts about Patmore's philosophy. When given a collection of the older poet's essays, *Religio Poetae*, to review, he was dubious about its orthodoxy until Father Anselm, who, as Patmore said, 'went all lengths with me in honour of the marriage embrace', reassured him. The result was one of Thompson's best prose pieces, 'A Poet's Religion' (*Merry England*, September, 1893), in which he shows a genuine appreciation of Patmore's style: 'He desires exposition, not the softer graces. Indeed, his subject matter is such, that the cultivation for beauty's sake would but obscure what is in itself difficult enough. The beauty of precision is the only legitimate beauty in such a case.'

In Thompson's early poems, the influence of Patmore was one of the many to which he submitted, consciously or otherwise. That he could apologize in his Preface to *Sister Songs* for an 'unconscious plagiarism' from Patmore's 'St. Valentine's Day' which is not really a plagiarism at all, and be apparently oblivious of the countless borrowings from and echoes of Patmore elsewhere in his work suggests that a tenacious memory rather than a plagiarizing instinct was responsible for the rag-bag quality of much that he wrote. From the time the two poets came together at Pantasaph, Patmore's influence on the younger one was prodigious. 'What I put forth as a bud he blew on and it blossomed. The contact of our ideas was dynamic'; Thompson, wrote in a notebook: 'he reverberated my idea with such and so many echoes that it returned to me greater than I gave it forth. He opened it as you would open an oyster, or placed it under a microscope, and showed me what it contained.' To Patmore himself he declared: 'You are the only man with whom I can talk at all. With all others it is a matter of playing an intermittent chord or so, as an accompaniment to *their* talk. . . . Yours is the conversation of a man who has trodden before me the way which for years I trod alone, and often desperate, seeing no guiding parallel among modern poets to my aims and experience.' In what he called 'the basic silence of our love', Thompson found a completeness of understanding he had never before experienced with anyone else. When Patmore died he recorded, for his own eyes alone, 'It remains, a personal (and wonderful) memory that to me sometimes athwart the shifting clouds of converse, was revealed by glimpses the direct vision of that oceanic vast of intellect.'

On his side, Patmore, perhaps flattered by the respect of Thompson, became greatly attached to the younger man. Describing an early encounter to his wife, he said: 'All I saw in him was pleasant and attractive—so I asked him to come for some Sunday to Lymington, which he joyfully promised to do.' Thompson was to become a frequent visitor to The Lodge, Patmore's home at Lymington, in the years just before the latter's death. Patmore's little son, Francis, was not very impressed by his father's guest:

'Francis Thompson often stayed with us. Great poet though he was, I fear I had but a poor idea of him, a weakly little man, with untidy red hair and unkempt beard, he had a peculiar dread of dogs, and as he could not hide his terror of our retriever Nelson, I regret to say that my only feeling for him was unmixed contempt. But as my father delighted to feed the dog on huge quantities of raw meat, till it became the terror of the district, Thompson may be excused.'

But the two poets, the short, thin, bearded one and the tall, lanky, crane-like seer, with his mane of white hair and bushy silver moustache, were ideal companions. Not only did they walk together—both were great striders—and keep silence together, but at Pantasaph and at Lymington, they shared animated conversation. Apart they exchanged long letters in which Thompson asks his master to elucidate points of arcane symbolism, a rather profitless correspondence, verbose and plodding on Thompson's part, courteous and suggestive on Patmore's.

It is difficult to over-estimate the impact of the older poet upon the younger. It may well be that Thompson, realizing the limitations of Wilfrid Meynell as a literary adviser, turned with especial relief to the experienced and sensitively critical Patmore. Certainly the poems written at Pantasaph after 1892 are saturated with Patmore's style and ideas. Sometimes there are verbal echoes of *The Angel in the House* and *The Unknown Eros*, as in

> Lo, God's two worlds immense
> Of spirit and of sense,
>   Wed
>   In this narrow bed;
>
> Yea, and the midge's hymn
> Answers the seraphim
>   Athwart
>   Thy body's court!

or

> But thou, who knowest the hidden thing
> Thou hast instructed me to sing,
>   Teach Love the way to be
>   A new Virginity!

At others, whole poems are organized as imitations of Patmore's thought, style and metre, such as 'By Reason of Thy Law', 'The Dread of Height' and 'From the Night of Forebeing'. It is true that Thompson had early experimented in the 'free ode' form, and that he left in his notebooks remarks about its structure, indicating that he had speculated about the principles involved. He claimed that he had arrived at something like Patmore's form independently, although he admitted that the older poet's influence operated quite early: ' "The Ode to the Setting Sun" was published before I had seen any of Mr. Patmore's work; and a comparison of the two poems will therefore show exactly the extent to which the later poem was affected by that great poet's practice. The ode metre of *New Poems* is, with this exception, completely based on the principles which Mr. Patmore may virtually be said to have discovered.'

In fact what Thompson wrote about metrics simply paraphrases Patmore's ideas, as when he says: 'It is quantity which gives the law—is the masculine element—in classic verse; it is accent in English. In English, quantity takes the feminine or subordinate place, as accent does in classic verse.' He even takes up as his own such typical Patmorean phrases as 'so-called irregular metre' and 'temporal variations of metre responsive to the emotions, like the fluctuations of human respiration'.

It was not, however, for matters of technique, theory or theme that Thompson was chiefly indebted to Patmore, but for the revelation of a new vision of reality, or rather, it would be truer to say, for the reinforcing of that deeper instinct for truth in Thompson which had shyly shown itself in poems like 'A Fallen Yew', but had been all but suffocated beneath laudanum and atrophy of spirit, in which, to adapt a line from his own 'A Narrow Vessel', 'his own self-will made void his own self's will'. The mental and spiritual stimulus of the friars, a restful life free from opium, the friendship of Patmore—all combined to lead Thompson towards values he had stubbornly refused to look at, to see that poetry and religion were much more than escape-lanes, to understand the central role of the Incarnation in Christian philosophy, to realize that love is no abstract thing, but lives only in relation to some concrete reality. For Patmore, the Incarnation was the great central fact of man's existence; the Blessed Virgin was for him

> Our only saviour from an abstract Christ;

and man may now 'see the disc of Divinity quite clearly through the smoked glass of humanity, but not otherwise'.

Although Thompson was, of course, well aware of the doctrine of the Incarnation, it was Patmore who taught him to realize it in himself, to see God through the tangible, and not through escapist dreams. Had he not met Patmore, it is unlikely that he could ever have written:

> Therefore I do regret
> That with religion vain,
> And misconceivèd pain,
> I have my music bent
> To waste on bootless things its skiey-gendered rain.

But before Patmore's influence worked its leaven, Thompson had published another volume of poems belonging to his early days of rehabilitation. This was *Sister Songs*, composed largely in Kensington Gardens in the spring of 1891 and pencilled out in the inevitable penny exercise-books. Thus, although published in 1895, it belongs to the period of 'The Hound of Heaven' and 'A Fallen Yew' and bears all the marks of his earlier manner. Thompson was not satisfied with *Sister Songs*; by the time it came out, he had largely outgrown the kind of impulse that prompted it. He had left the poem on the Meynells' mantelpiece as a Christmas gift, with a note which said: 'If intensity of labour could make it good, good it would be. One way or the other, it will be an effectual test of a theme on which I have never yet written; if from it I have failed to draw poetry, I may as well take down my sign.' Yet in the 'Inscription' he added to the revised poem just before its publication there is a fairly broad hint that he thought rather meanly of it. He depicts himself watching others leave their gifts, then

> Last stole this one,
> With timid glance, of watching eyes adread,
> And dropped his frightened flower when all were gone;
> And where the frail flower fell, it witherèd.

> But yet methinks the high souls smiled thereon;
> As when a child, upstraining at your knees
> Some fond and fancied nothing, says, 'I give you these'.

After its poor reception by critics and public alike, he had even more serious doubts about its value. To Patmore, he wrote: 'My own ill-destined volume has appeared and even Lane has evidently realized that it ought not to have appeared. I have seen a review in the *Chronicle*—by Le Gallienne, I presume. By no means enthusiastic, and mainly just in its non-enthusiasm. I am apathetic about the book, as a bad business which I cannot mind, and wash my hands of.' Somewhat later, writing again to Patmore about his third book of poems, he says: 'This should have been my second book if W. M. had not frustrated my careful writing by committing me to the publication of my last ill-starred volume—which has sold only 349 copies in twelve months.' This is one of the very few instances of testiness against his benefactor, and indicates that Meynell had brought pressure to bear upon Thompson to publish work the poet knew to be inferior, so as to cash in on the praise generally accorded *Poems*.

Yet, despite Thompson's misgivings and the poor reception given to *Sister Songs*, the poem is one of his most interesting works, not so much as a literary achievement, as showing his ambivalence and the personal problems he faced as a man and a poet. Originally he had intended to call it 'Amphicypellon' (a two-handled cup in Homer, signifying the double nature of the poem) a title which recalls Shelley, as indeed the whole work does. When he changed the title in deference to Meynell's wishes, he retained the sub-title of 'An Offering to Two Sisters'. For the poem was written ostensibly for Monica and Madeline, the little Meynell girls. Although the children played tricks on the poet and were much less impressed by him than their parents were, they gave him their tender trust, walking with him in Kensington Gardens and playing around him, so bringing to the racked and soul-sick man joy and innocent beauty which soothed him in the early days of his rescue. These are the children whose affection he dramatizes in 'The Hound of Heaven' as one of his refuges from the Divine hunter.

Sister Songs is his longest poem, with a Proem and an epilogue and two lengthy parts, the first addressed to Madeline

under the name of 'Sylvia', the second to Monica, the elder
girl. Almost all that could be said against *Poems* could be said
more strongly of this work. E. K. Chambers found it full of
'literary wantonness' and 'habitual perversity'. 'There is more
in the making of a great poet than the instinct to sing', he wrote
in the *Academy*. 'The instinct for style; for the selection, the
reticences, the renunciations that all art demands: this is good
for something too. And it is the want of this, or rather the disregard of this, that leads Mr. Thompson into his worst indis-
cretions.' Still, behind the over-ornate language, the intricate
convolutions of imagery, the baroque ornaments and bravura
of detail, there is much poignancy and delicate feeling not quite
concealed by the exotic façade.

Sister Songs, in a sense, parallels 'The Hound of Heaven'; it
is an ambitious poetic rhapsody in which Thompson attempts
to record his spiritual development, his intimations of nature,
his awareness of the problems of writing poetry and of the
impermanence of worldly things, and a melancholy which, he
finds, pervades all creation.

The first part, to 'Sylvia', is the less successful. Here the
Thompsonian conglomerate piles up in formidable clusters:

> Or a fine sorrow, lovely to behold,
> Would sweep them as the sun and wind's joined flood
> Sweeps a greening-sapphire sea;
> Or they would glow enamouredly
> Illustrious sanguine, like a grape of blood;
> Or with mantling poetry
> Curd to the tincture which the opal hath,
> Like rainbows thawing in a moonbeam bath;

rhymes are often strained and ugly—'fancy' and 'pansy',
'haunt' and 'palpitant', 'sown' and 'brown', for instance;
there is a long, embarrassingly coy passage about elves; there
are grotesque lapses of taste—'their pretty, pretty prating those
citherns sure upraise'—and there are innumerable echoes and
unassimilated bits pillaged from other poets—from Rossetti,
Shelley, Crashaw, Coleridge, Wordsworth, and Keats, as in

> If Even burst yon globèd yellow grape
> (Which is the sun to mortals' sealèd sight)
> Against her stained mouth.

At the same time, the Proem and Part One, despite a slight tinge of desolation;

> So heavenly flutes made murmurous plain
> To heavenly viols, that again
> —Aching with music—wailed back pain;
> Regals release their notes, which rise
> Welling, like tears from heart to eyes;
> And the harp thrills with thronging sighs,

shows the poet in a more relaxed and placid mood. The fancy that opens the poem is artificial and shop-soiled—the powers of Spring do homage to the child, adopt her and guarantee her future. But in parts the piece dances with a rare gaiety and tripping joy, and, mingled with the usual grandiose vagueness are one or two sharply realized vignettes:

> I know in the lane, by the hedgerow track,
> The long, broad grasses underneath
> Are warted with rain like a toad's knobbed back.

Towards the end comes the well-known passage in which he recalls, in contrast to the joys of the present, the 'nightmare time which still doth haunt my dreams'.

> I had endured through watches of the night
>   The abashless inquisition of each star,
> Yea, was the outcast mark
>   Of all those heavenly passers' scrutiny;
>   Stood bound and helplessly
> For Time to shoot his barbèd minutes at me;
> Suffered the trampling hoofs of every hour
>   In night's slow-wheelèd car;
> Until the tardy dawn dragged me at length
> From under those dread wheels; and, bled of my strength,
>   I waited the inevitable last.

Then follow the lines concerning the prostitute's charity which I have quoted earlier. The whole passage is instinct with feeling, and such precise touches as Time's 'barbèd minutes', which Sir Shane Leslie has identified as representing the arrowhanded clock-face in Charing Cross Station, balance the artificializing of the role of the street-walker as 'a flower fallen from the budded coronal of Spring'. Such a mixture of styles and feelings

is typical of Part One; for all its tawdriness and pompous peri-
phrases, Thompson comes close to celebrating the innocent
purity of young girlhood. In kissing the gentle child, he feels
himself to be, for an instant, in touch again with the 'subtle
sanctities' of infantine innocence.

Part Two is much longer, more complex and more darkly
tinged with melancholy. In nearly all his early poems about
childhood, we find his longing to return to the security of his
own infancy, even to go back beyond consciousness to the eye-
less comfort of the womb, in conflict with his intellectual awareness that such a return is impossible. So, in sad nostalgia, he
envies the child her joy, and rails against the fate that prevents
him from sharing it. In Part One, because 'Sylvia' is the younger,
he gets somewhat beyond this mood; but in Part Two, addressing Monica, the elder child, growing out of infancy, he plunges
deeply into it.

In a psychological study of Thompson,[1] Ella Freeman
Sharpe, pressing hard on a rigoristic Freudian interpretation of
the poems, lists many lines which show, she claims, an infantile
fixation on the poet's part, notably references to the female
breast, to milk, and to suckling. We need not confine the interpretation of Thompson's poems to the level of infantile sexu-
ality, or to find them stuffed with 'virginal and prostitute
fantasies' to recognize a nostalgia for the security of infancy in
such images from *Sister Songs* as these:

> Authentic cestus of two girdling arms.
>
> Stay is heat's cradle, it is rocked therein.
>
> Gentle Lady! she smiles sweetest
> Just ere she clasps us to her breast.
>
> When—as a nymph's carven head sweet water drips,
> For others oozing so the cool delight
> Which cannot steep her stiffened mouth of stone—
> Thy nescient lips repeat maternal strains.

Monica, 'elder nursling of the nest' is the occasion, rather
than the subject, of the poem; for Thompson is again writing
principally about himself. The three themes he explores are the

[1] 'Francis Thompson—A Psychoanalytical Study', *British Journal of
Medical Psychology*, Vol. 5, 1925, pp. 329-44.

nature of poetic inspiration, ideal womanhood and the sad burden of change and maturity. The first, a subject he was to dwell upon increasingly as he found his gift fading away, finds expression here chiefly in a sense of uncertainty about his ability to communicate with others:

> I who can scarcely speak my fellows' speech,
> Love their love, or mine own love to them teach;
> A bastard barred from their inheritance.

and about his power to control his flow of poetry:

> And ah, we poets, I misdoubt
> Are little more than thou!
> We speak a lesson taught we know not how,
> And what it is that from us flows
> The hearer better than the utterer knows.

He is sensible, too, that he is not really addressing the child at all—she would not comprehend a fraction of what he is saying—but talking through her to her parents. Hence the desire to please the elder Meynells gives much of the poem the appearance of a series of 'poetic turns', and helps account for the conceits and sterile ingenuities of the poem.

Some of Thompson's admirers see in his emphasis upon the ephemeral nature of beauty and the transcience of earthly things evidence of his religious sensibility. This may be true of other poems. But here the context and the sentiments are predominantly pagan rather than Christian. Even his beloved ecclesiastical imagery is used sparingly, although we get a typical sun-opium-liturgy image in

> The day is lingered out:
> In slow wreaths folden
> Around yon censer, spherèd, golden,
> Vague Vesper's fumes aspire.

Decadent symbols heap up high, and there is much typical laudanum-imagery, the swirl of colours, the confusion of sound, the synaesthesia, the circling of half-seen forms, the clash of images I have noted in earlier poems. His mind, he admits at one stage, is

> A shadow-world wherethrough the shadows wind
> Of all the loved and lovely of my kind.

Speaking ostensibly to Monica, Thompson enunciates his concept of ideal Woman. She is to be worshipped, but not possessed;

> Ever I knew me Beauty's eremite.

It is his destiny to remain solitary, cut off from woman's love, since he is dedicated to poetry, and the poet needs the inspiration of ideal womanhood:

> Therefore must my song-bower lone be
> That my tone be
> Fresh with dewy pain alway.

At times, it is difficult to be sure when he is addressing the mother through the child, and when he is, unconsciously, speaking directly to Alice Meynell. The sight of the ingenuous child stirs him deeply, for the spontaneous, uncalculated love she has given him is one of the chief things that have brought him back to life

> As the innocent moon, that nothing does but shine
> Moves all the labouring surges of the world.

For, in the child, sex is only in the soul; she knows nothing of the actuality of sex that sleeps within her. But, since all beauty and innocence pass, she must submit, too, to 'tyrannous time', which will bring her to 'Woman's fateful-fair allure'.

This leads him to consider the relationship between soul and body, in terms revealing less the Thomist view of man as a body-soul, than an awkward compromise with Shelleyan Platonism. The soul, for him, is

> Born of full stature, lineal to control;
> And yet a pigmy's yoke must undergo.

This question much concerned Patmore, who was fascinated by the idea of the canalizing of the soul's powers in the body and by the paradox of the Incarnation in which God the Limitless imposed the limits of corporeal form upon Himself. Thompson dutifully paraphrases Patmore's odes, sometimes directly quoting from 'Legem Tuam Dilexi':

> The splendent sun no splendour can display
> Till on gross things he dash his broken ray,
> From cloud and tree and flower re-tossed in prismy spray.

> Did not obstruction's vessel hem it in
> Force were not force, would spill itself in vain;
> We know the Titan by his champèd chain.

and, like his master, he finds the reconciliation of soul and body in the Incarnation:

> supreme
> For Spirit subject was to clay,
> And Law from its own servants learned a law.

But he rebels against this great doctrine as he has rebelled against life itself:

> So is all power, as soul in thee, increased!
> But, knowing this, in knowledge's despite
> I fret against the law severe that stains
> Thy spirit with eclipse.

Must everything submit to the law of the growth of the spirit in harmony with the body? Why cannot the pure innocence of inspiration remain unconscious? Monica, reciting her mother's verse, her lips 'murmurous with music not their own', becomes for him analogous to the poet, subject to a power beyond his control:

> The poet is not lord
> Of the next syllable may come
> With the returning pendulum;
> And what he plans today in song
> Tomorrow sings it in another tongue.

He rationalizes his own past and loneliness as part of his poetic destiny:

> I thank the once accursèd star
> Which did me teach
> To make of Silence my familiar,
> Who hath the rich reversion of thy speech,
> Since the most charming sounds thy thought can wear,
> Cast off, fall to that pale attendant's share.

And finally he meditates, at wearisome length, on Monica's future and imagines the lover who, one day,

> shall dip his hand to drink
> In that still water of thy soul.

Such a one will know how to penetrate to the secrets of her heart, and, after the poet's death, will recognize and respond to the knowledge-in-love that the poem enshrines. Again Thompson asks the tutelary spirits to protect Monica from evil, hoping for her a happier future than he, as a poet, can aspire to. He takes consolation from the fact that, although the child he knows soon must vanish in the woman, she will remain ever gay and innocent in his poem.

As with so many of his poems, the sun sets as *Sister Songs* ends; the memory of opium is still with him. In the 'Inscription' he describes himself modestly adding his gift to the family pile. What did he really think of the poem? Towards the end, he asserts its immortality:

I have caught you fast for ever in a tangle of sweet rhymes.

Yet, as we have seen, in the 'Inscription', the work becomes a frail flower withering as soon as dropped. It is idle to expect consistency of mood from him, even in the same poem, yet the odd confusion of artificiality and sincerity in *Sister Songs*, as much as his uncertainty about the quality of the poem itself, reflects the dual nature of the piece—to please the Meynells by an ostensible address to their children, and, at the same time, to work out a coherent personal attitude towards his talent, love, sex and children. For all the seeming gaiety of parts, the poem leaves finally a sad impression. Thompson cannot take pleasure in the fact that children grow to adulthood and lose their mindless innocence.

The temper is the same as that of 'To Daisies', where, stripped of baroque trappings, the theme of *Sister Songs* shows itself nakedly. Here the 'silted memories' of his heart are vexed by the sight of the women who once were children. He appeals to them in self-pity:

Hide your sweet selves! I cannot bear it.
For when ye break the cloven earth
With your young laughter and endearment,
No blossomy carillon 'tis of mirth
To me; I see my slaughtered joy
Bursting its cerement.

Under the maddening elaborations, then, of *Sister Songs*, Thompson is questioning the nature of his muse, and struggling with searing doubts as to what constitutes truth. Throughout the poem, too, runs his 'Uranian' idea of love, the sterile non-sexual emotion which is celibate, not for God's sake, as that of a religious is, but largely because of neurotic frustration.

Few modern readers of this sprawling poem will agree with Mégroz that it 'contains the finest metaphysical poetry of nature ever written in English until Thompson himself produced still finer'. But there are some striking passages in which he passes beyond the merely personal projection of a stubborn infantilism and the mother-child relationship used as an image of his relationship to God, and broadens this out to epitomize the union between soul and body. However, in *Sister Songs*, any religious statement seems less significant than the poignancy of a starved virility; for the 'withered flower' of his poem, like the 'withered dreams' of 'Daisy' may indeed be a subconscious sexual symbol, such as was hinted at in the earlier 'Daphne':

> You plucked the boughed verse the poet bears—
> It shudders and bleeds as it snaps from the tree.
> A love-banning love, did the god but know it,
> Which barks the man about with the poet,
> And muffles his heart of mortality!
>
> Yet I translate—ward of song's gate!—
> Perchance all ill this mystery.
> We both are struck with the selfsome quarrel;
> We grasp the maiden, and clasp the laurel—
> Do we weep or we laugh more, *Phoebe mî?*

This is a good point at which to say something about Thompson's other poems of childhood. It was noted quite early, by K. Rooker, that the real subject of these pieces is the poet himself: 'La méthode de Wordsworth est celle de la psychologie objective, tandis que chez Thompson les poèmes consacrés à l'enfance sont par excellence personnels', and, also, by Floris Delattre that their dominant tone is one of melancholy: 'L'affection charmée que Thompson a vouée aux enfants est plus sobre, plus grave, plus idéaliste souvent. Il les considère d'abord avec un retour douloureux sur son passé.' These poems show a genuine love for children and for their innocence and, although they tend to ignore original sin, a sense of Christ-like goodness in the child. There are, too, many moving passages recognizing the parallel between the childhood vision and that of the poet.

Yet Thompson views the child, as he views all else, with a divided mind and heart. First, he identifies himself with the child, and in doing so, he wants at the same time both to return to the haven of the nursing embrace and to flee from it. Secondly, the child is exploited as a kind of persona from behind which the poet muses on death, his state of soul and his poetic problems. Unlike Blake he is unable to identify himself emotionally with the heart of a child, and, in singing of innocence, to be a child. He could never forget that he was no longer an infant, hence he uses the children, weaving fantasies of elves about them to hide the fact that he is a man incongruously wearing the garments of the nursery. For instance, 'To My Godchild' is obviously worked up for the occasion; it is a freakish amalgam of whimsy and seriousness, thickly coated with Thompsonian exoticisms. It is impossible to imagine this piece beginning:

> This labouring, vast, Tellurian galleon,
> Riding at anchor off the orient sun,
> Had broken its cable, and stood out to space
> Down some frore Arctic of the aerial ways.

being directed *to* any child; nor, in fact, is it written *about* any child. 'It is an address to a potential fellow-poet rather than a child', says Mégroz. In fact, it is self-pityingly about himself and his verse, with a recognition of the tension in his innermost being:

> When you have compassed all weak I began;
> Diviner poet, and ah! diviner man;
> The man at feud with the perduring child
> In you before Song's altar nobly reconciled;
> From the wise heavens I half shall smile to see
> How little a world, which owned you, needed me.

In the war between the 'man' and the 'perduring child', Thompson apparently expects the child to conquer, since he counsels his godchild to

> Look for me in the nurseries of Heaven.

The entire poem looks as if it had been organized to lead to this final line (which, incidentally, appears on Thompson's tombstone) especially as its language shows no trace of affection whatever for the infant Francis, nor does Thompson pay any attention, as we would expect a Catholic godfather to, to the spiritual link established by baptism between him and his godchild.

The case is similar with 'To Monica Thought Dying', in which he anticipates the child's death, even calling her 'my dead, my dead', so that he may lash himself with his own fear of death:

> How can you deem what death
> Impitiably saith
> To me, who listening wake
> For your poor sake?

Instead of thinking what death would have meant to the child herself, he uses words spoken by her in her delirium to force an analogy between the poet babbling in his own despite and 'dreadful Death' speaking through the child only 'dreadful childish babble'. He even chides the sick girl for betraying him to death by showing him to be so deeply moved by her trivial words:

> Why have you done me this
> Most unsustainable wrong
> And into Death's control
> Betrayed the secret places of my soul?

The best-known of his poems about children is 'Little Jesus', inspired by a Christmas crib at Pantasaph in 1892. In this poem there is no melancholy self-indulgence, but instead Victorian nursery sentimentality, and a Christopher-Robin-ish approach which conjures up visions of prissy night-gowned children exchanging confidences after Nanny has put out the light. Some of the whimsies are embarrassingly coy:

> And didst Thou play in Heaven with all
> The angels that were not too tall,
> With stars for marbles? Did the things
> Play *Can you see me?* through their wings?

Even in such a context, Thompson cannot resist the temptation to fling planets around from his cosmic box of toys.

Yet, although 'Little Jesus' is disfigured by the poet's adolescent mawkishness, it is not completely spoiled by it. In effectiveness, depth of insight and feeling it cannot compare with Patmore's 'The Toys', where we find actual human truth and spiritual delicacy instead of Thompson's cuteness; but 'Little Jesus' has a certain old-fashioned charm and sensibility which show, as clearly as anything he wrote, the gentle sweetness, and even the touching helplessness of his personality which made the Meynells love him, for all his exasperating weaknesses.

> So, a little Child, come down
> And hear a child's tongue like Thy own;
> Take me by the hand and walk,
> And listen to my baby-talk.
> To Thy Father show my prayer
> (He will look, Thou art so fair)
> And say: 'O Father, I, Thy Son,
> Bring the prayer of a little one.'
>
> And He will smile, that children's tongue
> Has not changed since Thou wast young!

IX

The Region Elenore

IN 1896, Thompson was deeply shaken by two deaths. The
first was that of his father, whom he had not seen since
McMaster arranged for the Christmas visit in 1886. They did,
however, communicate from time to time, and it is recorded
that the elder Thompson was both amused and gratified when
his son's first book was praised, although he confessed that he
found the poems largely incomprehensible. In 1893, Francis
had heard that Charles was at Rhyl, and he made the effort,
unusual for him, of journeying over to see his father, only to
find that he had left a few days before. In April, 1896, learning
from his sister Mary that Charles was dying, he set out from
Pantasaph for Ashton, borrowing a sovereign for the fare from
one of the friars, but again arrived too late. Charles Thompson
died on April 9, in his seventy-third year. Francis attended
the funeral, mourning not only the death, but also his own
irreclaimable acts.

As we have seen, he later castigated himself to Blunt as 'in
every way an unsatisfactory son', and there can be no doubt
that he never really forgave himself not only for the equivoca-
tions and idleness of his student years, but for his failure to
clasp his father's hand before he died. One joy lightened the
sorrow of this visit to Ashton. Francis saw his beloved sister,
now a nun, 'looking the merest girl still, and sweeter than ever.
She did not look a day older than ten years ago.' But she, on
her part, found the poet very changed and worn, older than
his portrait. Despite the pleasure this reunion gave Francis he did not linger at Ashton, for there was no love at

all lost between him and his stepmother, but returned to Pantasaph.

The second blow came on November 26, when Coventry Patmore, his second father, died at Lymington. The bonds between the two men had grown steadily stronger during their three years of intimacy. To Patmore, Thompson, a very spasmodic correspondent, wrote more frequently than to anybody else. He discussed his past work and his forthcoming book, *New Poems*, with his friend, sent him poems for comment ('I think you know that I esteem it more honoured to be condemned by an austere than approved by a lax judgment'), and wrote to him of *Religio Poetae*, 'Your little book stands by a stream of current literature like Cleopatra's Needle by the dirt-eating Thames.' Patmore, for his part, told Thompson: 'You dissipate my solitude and melancholy as no other, but one, can.' The two met for the last time when Thompson paid a visit to London in the middle of 1896. Immediately after his return to Lymington, Patmore wrote:

> 'You were looking so unwell when we parted that, not having heard from you, I am somewhat alarmed. Pray let me have a post-card.
>
> If, at any time, you find yourself seriously ill, and do not find the attendance, food, &c. sufficiently good, tell me and I will go to Pantasaph to take care of you for any time you might find me useful. It would be a great pleasure and honour to serve you in any way.'

Coming as it did from a man himself on the point of death, this letter gives the lie to a widespread impression of Patmore as lofty, proud and self-centred, and shows, too, the depth of his affection for Thompson.

Four months later, when the sad news of Patmore's passing came to Pantasaph, Thompson was plunged into a limbo of gloom. His agony of loss knew no bounds. In high-pitched phrases he wrote of his grief to Mrs. Patmore: 'There has passed away the greatest genius of the century, and from me a friend whose like I shall not see again; one so close to my own soul that the distance of years between us was hardly felt, nor could the distance of miles separate us. . . . My friend is dead, and I had but one such friend.' He had already written 'A

Captain of Song', on Sargent's portrait of Patmore, to be printed in *New Poems*; when Patmore died, Thompson used it as an obituary piece in the *Athenaeum*, on December 5, 1896. But, in his notebooks, there are many fragments of prose and verse prompted by his sorrow. Indifferent, or worse, as poetry, the verse is drenched in grief; yet, through the sadness shines a profound gratitude to Patmore for forcing him to re-examine his poetry and his attitude towards life:

> Take thou this book!
> Thou didst not read it, living, O my dear!
> Take it then, dead. My Judge, who only knew
> Thereof the inmost true:
> But now that inmost voice is none to hear,
> That voice which, too late coming, found—thy bier.
> It turneth a dumb look
> On men of a strange language, most forsook,
> And babbles a vain thing,
> An isolate speech, no man interpreting.
> O writ for thee, who wouldst not stay to hear,
> Be then this book
> A secret 'twixt my soul and thy dead ear!

Elsewhere, he wrote:

> You, only, spoke the tongue I spake
>   And my poor song is thus born dumb:
> Alas! why did you me forsake,
>   And this poor child of mine, born dumb?
> And this poor child we both did make,
>   You father, I as mother?

The reference to parenthood is especially significant in view of what was said earlier about Thompson's infantile imagery. He casts himself for the feminine role, thus symbolizing his passivity before the dynamism of experience. Patmore is both husband and father, who completes Thompson's feminine sensibility with the masculine force of intellect, and also acts as a substitute for his lost parents.

With the elder poet, Thompson enjoyed a relationship more intimate and formative than his friendship with Wilfrid Meynell. Anxious as he was to please Meynell, he felt in his heart of hearts that the journalist, a naturally robust and resilient personality, could never really understand his problems as a man, a Catholic and a poet as fully as Patmore could. 'A Captain of Song', rhetorical and excessive though it is, is largely free from the whipped-up feeling of the poems addressed to Alice Meynell and her children. Thompson had some doubts about printing the poem in the *Athenaeum*—'To dwell on the harsher side of his character now has an ungracious air', he wrote to Meynell. Yet it does recognize and pay tribute to an aspect of Patmore's character few of his contemporaries saw— the stern discipline with which he carried out 'a weary life's campaign' against himself:

> You shall mark well
> The mighty cruelties which arm and mar
> That countenance of control,
> With minatory warnings of a soul
> That hath to its own selfhood been most fell.

It would be going too far to claim that Thompson took over all Patmore's ideas or that, leaving de Quincey behind, he set out to remodel himself on the older poet's example. (It is hard enough to visualize one wife for Thompson, much less three!) The dedication of *New Poems* is an acknowledgement of "il miglior fabbro" that reveals no special awareness of indebtedness:

> Lo, my book thinks to look Time's leaguer down,
> Under the banner of your spread renown!
> Or if these levies of impuissant rhyme
> Fall to the overthrow of assaulting Time,
> Yet this one page shall fend oblivious shame,
> Armed with your crested and prevailing Name.

Yet the poems in the book, as well as Thompson's later prose, show that Patmore's counsel of curbing of extravagance in his review of *Poems*, his example of freedom in control in poetry, his constant preaching that true poetry is that from which eccentricities are purged and that has 'interior finish', the importance he attached to the 'point of rest' in art—all of these things, carried to Thompson by their own urgency, but driven into his heart by his affection for Patmore, gave a new purpose and depth to his writing. Aided by Patmore's precepts and example, he faced the challenges of life more resolutely than he had ever done before, even when they seemed to prompt him to discard his poetry as an adequate substitute for spiritual truth.

It may have been Patmore's immense good sense on the subject of the love between the sexes that led Thompson to reach out tentatively towards the love of a woman. Among the Meynells' literary friends was Mrs. Hamilton King, a poet and essayist, and a disciple of Mazzini. One of her daughters, Katherine Douglas King, had some literary ability and contributed stories to *Merry England*. She was a girl of generous heart and spontaneous humanitarian sympathies, who especially loved children. She often played with the Meynell youngsters, and spent much time in voluntary service at a little East End hospital in Leonard Street for incurable and dying children. From Pantasaph, Thompson wrote to tell Meynell of his admiration for the idealism in Katie King's *Merry England* stories, adding a comment strongly flavoured with Patmore, but also indicating that he is now sensitive to faults in his own poetry: 'Her weak point is a feminine tendency to pile up the agony, heaping one emotional touch upon another, until the accumulated effect is overstrung. Some French novelists gain pathos by accumulated touches. But then the touches are carefully minor and unimpressive singly: so that the pathos gains on you imperceptibly as a mist. Where the artist's tendency is to work by poignant detail there should be reserve and selection in quantity.'

On one of his visits from Pantasaph to Palace Court, Thompson met Miss King, and was charmed by her naturalness, vivacity and goodness. She seems also to have been drawn to Thompson, although to what degree beyond that of spontaneous amity, it is impossible to know. At any rate, he believed that she had a special feeling for him, and preened himself to Patmore with a vanity that would be engaging in an adolescent, but is somewhat pathetic in a man of thirty-six: 'I have come to London for a month. . . . Am already engaged to go to George Meredith's for a day, while a girl I have met wants me to visit her; which is pretty fair for the very evening one reaches town.'

It was not long before he was writing poems to Katie, addressed ostensibly to a 'friend', but full of the ardour of a lover. Chief among these was the sequence of five sonnets published under the title 'Ad Amicam', in one of which he asks her:

> O friend, who mak'st the mis-spent word of 'friend'
> Sweet as the low note that a summer dove
> Fondles in her warm throat! And shall it end
> Because so swift on friend and friend broke love?

But there were many other poems to her which remained in his notebooks and on papers unseen by any eyes save his and hers until after his death. In one of these Thompson tells Katie that she has replaced Mrs. Meynell in his affection:

> The dearer must I rate
> Thee, then, that to her most canst be a more,
> Out-marvelling marvel.

Mrs. King, an invalid, but scrupulously careful of her daughter's reputation, and with Thompson's past history in mind, wrote to him to protest gently against the implications of the poems and letters he had written to Katie. Whatever hope Thompson may have had before Mrs. King's letter, he took fright, and replied in terms that made it plain he had no intention of pursuing the courtship. Mrs. King accepted his reply as an honest and honourable one, saying: 'It is not in her nature to love you; but I see no reason why some other good woman should not;—yet perhaps you are most fitted to live and die solitary, and in the love only of the highest Lover, whom you yourself in your supreme moments feel to have espoused you to himself. The solitary life has many advantages.'

True enough, but small consolation, in these circumstances, for Thompson, who had to endure the intervention of Mrs. King at the same time as Patmore died. He put his grief at the change in his relationship with Katie in a sonnet never intended for publication:

> So now, give o'er; for you are lost, I see,
> And this poor babe was dead even [in] its birth,
> Which I had thought a young Joy born to me,
> Who had no child but Sorrow; and with mirth
> I gazed upon its face, nor knew it dead,
> And in my madness vowed that it did smile;

I said: 'Dear Soul, learn laughter, leave thy shed
Sore tears, put off thy mourning weeds a while.
This is our child a space, even though it die
Hereafter; laugh a season, though it be
Thy tears are but sad jewels thou put'st by,
One day to wear again.' Very wan she
Tried, doubting, unused smiles; then bowed her head:—
'Much tears have made thee blind: this, too, is dead!'

Katie, who seems to have been as sensible as she was affectionate, continued to correspond with Thompson as with a dear
friend. He visited her and her charges at the hospital at least
once. She was delighted to see him and to 'see for myself from
your face and know from your ready hand-clasp that we are
friends—not "again", but "still" and I hope always'. In April,
1900, she announced in a kindly letter that she was soon to
marry Godfrey Burr, the vicar of Rushall. In less than a year
after the wedding she had died in child-birth.

However closely Thompson found Katie King corresponded
to his ideal of womanhood, she did not love him, as a woman a
man, but responded to his need for understanding and affection
with instinctive kindness and the sympathy of true friendship.
It may be doubted whether, even had she come to love him
as he seemed to wish, he would have been capable of a formal
courtship and marriage. It is almost as if the poet, reaching
out for a normal life, felt he *ought* to love her. As soon as her
mother put his affection to the test, he drew back, protesting
that his poems had been misconstrued.

The only other woman with whom Thompson made any
kind of normal love-contact was a young girl, Maggie Brien,
whom he met at Pantasaph. While at his last residence there,
Creccas Cottage, with the Catholic Briens, he found himself
attracted to the adolescent girl of the family. Yet it was an odd
infatuation, fantastical and unreal, more like his attachment
to the Vatican Melpomene than like his feeling for Katie King.
In his description of the girl to Wilfrid Meynell, there is a not
wholly pleasant touch of Barrie-esque whimsy:

'I rather fancy she thinks me one of the most admirable of
mortals; and I firmly believe her to be one of the most daintily
supernatural of fairies. And now I am in a fever lest (after the

usual manner of fairies) her kinsfolk should steal her from me. Result—I haven't slept for two nights, and I fear I shall not recover myself until I am resolved whether my glimpses of her are to be interdicted or not. Of course in some ways she is sure to vanish; elves always do, and my elves in particular.'

Maggie Brien is the girl of 'A Narrow Vessel', the group of poems which Thompson subtitled 'a little dramatic sequence on the aspect of primitive girl-nature towards a love beyond its capacities'; here the poet almost hates the girl because, by being herself, she made him fall in love with her, and was unable, or unwilling, to give him love in return. His elf turned out to be a teasing sylph; the relationship between them was shy, adolescent, unsatisfactory, and ended with evasion on both sides, and Thompson's realization that, however much he tried, he could not combine in love the sexual feelings of a man and the emotions of a child, and so could make no real contact with the girl. There is just the faintest trace of the misfortunes of Ruskin and Hazlitt in this abortive affair. But, when the poet returned to London, Maggie kept his photograph in her room at Creccas Cottage until her death a year after his own.

The last three years at Pantasaph, then, were the most 'normal' of Thompson's adult life. Deprived of laudanum, for most of the time, at least, and becoming reconciled to its absence, growing in mind and spirit by contact with Patmore and the friars, venturing upon tentative love-affairs, seeing much of his friends, the Meynells, writing prose and poetry copiously, some of it new in character and of a finer quality than before, and reading the proofs for *New Poems*, the reclaimed derelict enjoyed more tranquillity than he had known since infancy. Patmore's death, at the very dawning of a new sense of purpose for Thompson, snatched nearly all his peace away. His mentor and friend was gone:

> No, for this thing the world grows dark—the great
> Is dead, and all the little are alive!

he lamented. The future was a desolate waste shrouded with black clouds. In the meantime, *New Poems*, which he had intended to lay at the feet of his living master, was published, in 1897.

For this book, he had written a note, which was later cancelled: 'Of words I have coined or revived I have judged fit to retain but few; and not more than two or three will be found in this book. I shall also be found, I hope, to have modified much the excessive loading both of diction and imagery which disfigured my former work.' Although this note does credit to his maturing power of self-criticism, it is as well he did not print it, since he had greatly underestimated the number of freakish words and images the poems contained. Frederick B. Tolles found that out of 183 rare, archaic and obsolete words used in the poems as a whole, 88 appear in *New Poems*; and, out of 134 words coined by him, 76 are in the same volume. His last book is, in fact, a very mixed collection of poems written in his old, flamboyant style, like the stupefyingly ornate 'Anthem of Earth', some in an intermediate style like 'The After Woman', and several in a more homogeneous, simpler style like 'The Mistress of Vision' and 'Contemplation'.

Much more clearly than in *Sister Songs* are the two Thompsons to be seen here—the weak-willed dreamer obsessed with escape into oblivion or childhood, and the religious man with a powerful basic integrity and a will struggling to break through the ramparts of temperament and circumstance. Almost all the better poems grouped together under the heading 'Sight and Insight' were written after he met Patmore. The technical advances and the more disciplined style reflect the combined influence of Patmore and Alice Meynell, both of whom not only gave him precedents in their own verse, but also made many suggestions on the proofs of the poems, which Thompson sometimes accepted, and sometimes rejected.

The extent to which Patmore's example had sunk into his heart is seen from some notes he made for a letter to Patmore after reading *The Unknown Eros*—a letter, apparently, like so many others, never sent:

'So far as our language is concerned, you have invented a new literary form and none of your *Academic* followers handles it with such habitual assuredness of mastery. These brief notes of impression are easily and unforcedly right and there is the end of it. The thing is seen and felt; the perception and feeling are transmitted to the reader; no more, for there needs no more. Nor needs there that I say more. When we see an object with clear definition under a microscope, we know the glass is by a first-rate maker. Here are things seen— and I have seen them.'

Pervasive though Patmore's influence is throughout *New Poems*, the pieces therein reveal, also, a new dimension of Thompson's own talent. He felt himself that he had something fresh to impart on the nature of vision, and that he had achieved, too, something perhaps of the ineffable quality of Patmore's odes, for he says to Wilfrid Meynell when his book is in its final stages: 'It will be a book as long as the *Unknown Eros*.' The title gave him much worry, before he pitched upon a neutral one, and some of his tentative suggestions indicate the importance he attached to the different note sounded in the book— *Songs of the Inner Life*, *Night Before Light*, and *The Dawn Before the Day-Star*.

The transformation is announced in the astonishing poem, one of his most individual achievements, which opens the volume, 'The Mistress of Vision'. Its place at the head of the book is not accidental, for it dramatizes Thompson's forsaking the manner and mood of his earlier poetry and his acceptance of a different concept of reality. Much more than those poems greeted by the critics as 'Metaphysical' in character, 'The Mistress of Vision' fuses thought and feeling in the Metaphysical way. The section, 'Sight and Insight', of which 'The Mistress of Vision' forms part, has as its epigraph a quotation from the Book of Wisdom: 'Wisdom is easily seen by them that love her, and is found by them that seek her. To think therefore upon her is perfect understanding', and at least one element in the composition of the Mistress of Vision herself is Wisdom.

The poem opens with the description of a mysterious garden:

> Secret was the garden;
> Set i' the pathless awe
> Where no star its breath can draw.
> Life, that is its warden
> Sits behind the fosse of death. Mine eyes saw not, and I saw.

Within this 'mazeful wonder', all things are suspended in trance, the birds hang a-dream, the sun swings like a thurible, and, at the garden's heart, in the Land of Luthany, is the Lady of fair weeping, whose sorrowful song the poet would capture in verse. He finds his powers unequal to the task, but he presses on towards the Land of Luthany, the tract of Elenore, and hears the Lady's voice telling him that sureness and depth in song are found only through suffering:

> Pierce thy heart to find the key;
> With thee take
> Only what none else would keep;
> Learn to dream when thou dost wake,
> Learn to wake when thou dost sleep.
> Learn to water joy with tears,
> Learn from fears to vanquish fears;
> To hope, for thou dar'st not despair,
> Exult, for that thou dar'st not grieve;
> Plough thou the rock until it bear;
> Know for thou else couldst not believe;
> Lose, that the lost thou mayst receive;
> Die, for none other way canst live.
> When heaven and earth lay down their veil,
> And that apocalypse turns thee pale;
> When thy seeing blindeth thee
> To what thy fellow-mortals see;
> When their sight to thee is sightless;
> Their living, death; their light, most lightless;
> Search no more—

Pass the gate of Luthany, tread the region Elenore.

What is the garden and who is the Lady? There have been many exegeses of this haunting poem. Father O'Connor has written a commentary which identifies the Mistress of Vision with the Blessed Virgin, the Land of Luthany with the realm of Grace and the region Elenore with the Paradise of God. The essence of the Lady's advice he sees as an awareness of the difference between self-inflicted, self-indulgent pain, and pain accepted for God's sake, through grace. For Ella Freeman Sharpe, the Lady has affinities with the pitiless Goddess Pain, the 'pale Ashtaroth who rul'st my life' in Thompson's poem 'Laus Amara Doloris', while she finds in the description of the garden and the realms a quality of static ecstasy based upon infantile experience, not upon adult sexual maturity, and claims that the garden itself represents the oblivious suspense of the womb. For Frederick Page, the Lady combines Wisdom, Persephone, Beatrice, Alice Meynell, everyone's 'mistress of vision', and, finally, 'Ascetical Theology'.

I feel that all of these elements are held in suspension in the poem. Although any exclusively religious interpretation must strain some parts of the poem and ignore others (the Blessed Virgin hardly conforms to Thompson's description of the Lady), the image of the censer and two powerful stanzas on the Crucifixion which break into the static first part, and that portion of the Lady's advice which reflects the tenets of Ascetical Theology, show that the poem does have a religious dimension. But there is also here a pervasive sense of trance, of suspended time. The religious element does not make the piece abstract, for it is more than a dream of Paradise, and more, too, than the 'Gospel of stark renunciation' a commentator calls it.

'The Mistress of Vision' is an intensely personal, keenly felt statement which allegorizes Thompson's life, and brings together, in contrast, not only his two ways of looking at experience, but also, almost in epitome, his two kinds of poetry. It looks back to 'The Hound of Heaven' in stanza xxiv:

> And as a necromancer
> Raises from the rose-ash
> The ghost of the rose;
> My heart so made answer
> To her voice's silver plash—
> Stirred in reddening flash,
> And from out its mortal ruins the purpureal phantom blows;

to the 'Ode to the Setting Sun' in its image of the sun as 'a silver thurible . . . fuming clouds of golden fire', to his pillagings from other poets in the unfortunate Kipling echo; but it looks forward to his more personal poetry not only in its tone but also in the purgation of its vocabulary. Apart from an occasional fancy word, here is a style shaped to its purpose, free from capricious embellishment. And he anticipates his great poem 'In No Strange Land' in the lines:

> That thou canst not stir a flower
> Without troubling of a star.

Several critics have found clear traces of Coleridge in the piece. Sir Arthur Quiller-Couch said that it reminded him of 'Kubla Khan', and indeed, such lines as

> Lend me, O lend me
> The terrors of that sound
> That its music may attend me,
> Wrap my chant in thunders round,
> While I tell the ancient secrets in that Lady's singing found.

indicate a direct relationship. Whether or not 'Kubla Khan' was written directly under the influence of opium, and Elisabeth Schneider seems to have shown that it was not, Coleridge's poem surely contains memories of opium visions, as does 'The Mistress of Vision'.

In Thompson's mysterious garden are the bogus sense of timelessness, and the suspension of sound and sense characteristic of opium. But this time Thompson does not rest here, nor does he look back at it in longing; the real timelessness of poetic and religious contemplation grows mysteriously out of the narcoticized mood. He is not merely remembering with regret his evasions of responsibility; he is using the memory of drug-induced states to portray a dubious poetic vision, a world of retreat, which he then explicitly rejects, as Rimbaud rejected his early hallucinations. As he moves to the centre of the true vision, he receives the message of a new life and responsibility, which he takes to his heart. His discovery of this inner validity reminds us of Patmore's words to the Blessed Virgin towards the end of his life:

> When clear my Songs of Lady's graces rang
> And little guess'd I 'twas of thee I sang!

For the Lady's words, quoted above, indicate that Thompson means to bear suffering and loneliness for God's sake, not as a kind of poetic talisman or a neurotic self-indulgence. Accept God's will, accept the imperative of strenuous suffering, accept the ideal of the ascetic, that is your way to virtue, says the voice, and if you will be a poet, look into your own hurt heart, learn to plumb the anguish of reality, not the chasms of dreams. Instead of cherished morbidity, here is a stern renewal of the resolve taken earlier in 'The Hound of Heaven', to cease flying from obligation, and to seek in the religious transformation of experience material for a now sternly controlled poetry. In 'The Mistress of Vision' is dramatized the breaking through of the real Francis Thompson, the gentle soul who kept his fundamental innocence.

The form of the poem is not perfect; the climax, for instance, is weak:

> When she shall unwind
> All those wiles she wound about me,
> Tears shall break from out me,
> That I cannot find
> Music in the holy poets to my wistful want, I doubt me!

Nor is the transition from the narcotic ecstasy to the imperative of wisdom prepared for; the latter breaks in abruptly in stanza xx, almost as if Thompson had begun a poem of stasis, and then completed it with a new inspiration. Yet that this is not so is seen from the strange combination in the early part of laudanum surrender with a hushed expectation that might almost be Keats' negative capability. And such a combination is, in fact, the remarkable feature of the poems in the book which was to be his last.

X

In a Little Peace

THE concept of the poet patiently awaiting upon the dynamic of inspiration, as Patmore had tirelessly counselled, is the subject of the next poem in 'Sight and Insight', 'Contemplation', another of Thompson's more unexpected flights. It begins with a description of a mood of Nature, the earth stretched out 'in a lull of power' after rain, a picture more exactly realized than is usual with him:

> field, water, tree, were still,
> Nor was there any purpose in the calm-browed hill.

> The hill which sometimes visibly is
> Wrought with unresting energies,
> Looked idly; from the musing wood,
> And every rock, a life renewed
> Exhaled like an unconscious thought
> When poets, dreaming unperplexed,
> Dream that they dream of naught.

He relates this aspect of Nature to himself as a poet, seeing in both a docility and wise passiveness, which, while seeming absolutely tranquil, are actually charged with enormous reserves of power:

> In poets floating like a water-flower
> Upon the bosom of the glassy hour,
> In skies that no man sees to move,
> Lurks untumultuous vortices of power
> For joy too native, and for agitation
> Too instant, too entire for sense thereof.

We are reminded at once of Patmore's

> But for compulsion of strong grace
> The pebble in the road
> Would straight explode
> And fill the ghastly boundlessness of space.

No longer does the description of tranquillity carry overtones of narcoticism; even the infantile response barely, lightly obtrudes. Thompson has a new humility before Nature; he has ceased to be the nursery ring-master; here, too, is a new conception of the poet—no longer one who projects his own fantasies upon the universe, nor a juggler of stars:

> His heart's a drop-well of tranquillity,
> His mind more still is than the limbs of fear.
> . . . .
> He round the solemn centre of his soul
> Wheels like a dervish, while his being is
> Streamed with the set of the world's harmonies.

And out of this calm meditation upon inward power he draws an affirmative message of renewed courage and inspiration.

The attitude here is Patmorean in that it is neither ascetic nor transcendental. Thompson looks deep into a living reality that has become for him both intimate and subtle, and finds in it an immanent cosmic power. But he is able to do this only when he genuinely feels that in what seems to be death is the germ of new life. Is 'Contemplation', then, a parallel to the mystic's prayer of quiet? Scarcely, for although Thompson would certainly intellectually identify the force that works in and through Nature with God, there is hardly anything of a personal God in this poem. It might almost have been written by a pantheist; the mood is that of Wordsworth in 'Tintern Abbey', and, in fact, Wordsworth's lines are echoed here:

> To human things he grows a desolation,
> And is made a habitation
> For the fluctuous universe
> To lave with unimpeded motion.
> He scarcely frets the atmosphere
> With breathing, and his body shares
> The immobility of rocks.

Nowhere more insistently than in 'By Reason of Thy Law' and 'The Dread of Height' in *New Poems* is Patmore's influence seen. Alice Meynell, indeed, speaking of the volume as a whole, said: 'The influence of Coventry Patmore's Odes is somewhat too evident; there is more likeness than there should be between poet and poet in "The Dread of Height", for example.' Both of Thompson's poems incorporate fragments of particular *Unknown Eros* pieces, and in style mix Patmore's particular rhetoric with Thompsonian exoticism. However, neither poem attains the logical and emotional tautness of a Patmorean ode.

In 'The Dread of Height', with its blend of Thompson's early manner:

> Lo, sweet music, sweetest music,
> From distances of distance drifting its lone flight,
> Down the arcane where Night would perish in night,
> Like a god's loosened locks slips undulously.

and of Patmore's later one:

>   make
> Of extreme sad a rod to mete
> The incredible excess of unsensed sweet,
> And mystic wall of strange felicity,

we feel again the reverberations of the unresolved struggle between Thompson's emotional and linguistic self-indulgence, and his new resolve to tighten his hold on his style as well as in things. The pure vision of Heaven, he claims in the poem, is so dauntingly far beyond his reach that despair at his own unworthiness may cause him to sin:

> And lacking thus thine arms, then may
> Most hapless I
> Turn utterly to love of basest rate;
> For low they fall whose fall is from the sky.

In part, the poem is a prayer for grace to sustain him in his resolve not to surrender to his earlier self. It is an expression of 'fear of the abyss'—a horrified evulsion against his past life seen now with eyes sharpened by a deepened religious sense; it is also another despairing protest against the burden of his talent and the sensitivity that makes him prey to moral dilemmas:

> Ah, for a heart less native to high heaven,
> A hooded eye, for jesses and restraint,
> Or for a will accipitrine to pursue!

Towards the end he records his main spiritual crisis. The poet is in conflict with the religious man; he feels now that what he has previously written is empty and yet he lacks the confidence to encompass the new vision:

> My soul with anguish and recoil
> Doth like a city in an earthquake rock,
> As at my feet the abyss is cloven then,
> With deeper menace than for other men,
> Of my potential cousinship with mire;
> That all my conquered skies do grow a hollow mock,
> My fearful powers retire,
> No longer strong,
> Reversing the shook banners of their song.

Equally revealing is the 'Orient Ode', about which he wrote to Patmore in 1894:

> 'I shall send you with this, or later, a small poem of my own; not for its literary merit, but because, without such a disclaimer, I fear you would think I had been the first to find your book "d——d good to steal from". As a matter of fact, it was written soon after Easter, and was suggested by passages in the liturgies of Holy Saturday. . . . With superfluous caution, I intended much of it to be sealed; but your book has mainly broken the seals I had put upon it. There is quite enough in it of yours, without the additional presumption that I had hastened to make immediate use of your last book.'

Yet, for all this, the 'Ode' is largely a reversal to the style of the 'Ode to the Setting Sun', a long luxuriant piece full of swirling words and clotted, well-nigh unintelligible lines, and with passages that recall the laudanum-prompted synaesthesia of the earlier poems:

> My fingers thou hast taught to con
> Thy flame-chorded psalterion.

On the other hand, Thompson's increased control over language is seen in several tauter sections and in generally firmer command over the lines, which, as in Patmore's odes, fluctuate more nearly in accordance with the varying emotions.

The ingenious opening comparison, between the elevation of the Host at Benediction and the progress of the sun, already quoted, is developed in a protracted description of the sun's function. It is the health-giving assaulter of darkness, the puissant lover of the earth, the child of aboriginal Light, the giver of Life, and Beauty, and Desire; it is the inspirer of the poet, it is a lion. Then in a terrific incantation, whose intoxicating appeal to his contemporaries it is not hard to understand. Thompson praises the sun's quickening power, its maleness and its potency, and returning at the end to the image with which he began, sees it as a symbol of Christ in His immanence, pervading the universe with sustaining life:

> When men shall say to thee: Lo! Christ is here,
> When men shall say to thee: Lo! Christ is there,
> Believe them: yea, and this—then art thou seer,
> When all thy crying clear
> Is but—Lo here! lo there! ah me, lo everywhere!

Despite the Shelleyesque kaleidoscopic imagery, the 'Orient Ode' has a real unity of purpose. Yet, to me, its total effect, even on its own baroque level, is unsatisfactory. There is too much of the earlier Thompson's hypnotized fascination with the sun, and hence, apparently, with the 'inspirations' of opium. Again, while the parallel with Benediction is skilful, it smacks of contrivance, even to a Catholic familiar with the ceremony. More seriously, the whole emotional direction of the poem tends away from its presumed subject—Christ. While it is clear that Thompson intends to compare the life-giving power of the sun with the transformation of human nature by the grace of Christ, the main poetic emphasis falls on the sun itself. The poet seems less a Christian on his knees before the consecrated Host than a sun-worshipper hymning the potency of his god. Thompson's indulgence in the personal emotive associations the sun has for him get in the way of his full realization of the religious element. He recognized this himself since, Everard Meynell tells us: 'Not long after it was written, he cancels even the "Orient Ode", and recants "his bright sciental idolatry" even though he had religiously adapted it to the greater glory of God before it was half confessed. . . . What profiteth it a man, he asks in effect, if he gain the whole sun but lose the true Orient—Christ?'

The same unequal war is waged in 'An Anthem of Earth', an immense, complex piece in irregular unrhymed lines. Nothing else in *New Poems* so closely resembles the works of the 'Spasmodics' in its verbosity, clouds of rhetoric and cosmic attitudinizing. Yet quite early on, he stands aside from his own practice and comments critically upon it:

> Then what use knew I of thy solemn robes
> But as a child to play with them?

Ostensibly an address to the earth as 'Orient Ode' is to the sun, the 'Anthem' is actually another melancholy stock-taking, a desperate attempt to find some personal justification for being, through a haze of self-mistrust. He feels that his poetic powers are failing, and that it is perhaps better for him to be silent:

> Though I the Orient never more shall feel
> Break like a clash of cymbals, and my heart
> Clang through my shaken body like a gong. . . .
>   ruled lips
>   Befit a votaress Muse.

Here and there Thompson puts on his playboy-of-the-western-stars costume again, echoing his 'Shelley' essay, for instance:

> He dogs the secret footsteps of the heavens,
> Sifts in his hands the stars, weighs them as gold-dust,

and even translates a passage of the essay into verse:

>   it discovers
> Life in putridity, vigour in decay;
> Dissolution even, and disintegration,
> Which in our dull thoughts symbolize disorder.

But the poem is the record of a relentless pursuit of Death as peace; despite the assurance of regeneration, it is not resurrection Thompson seeks at the end of the poem, but oblivion, a surrender like that of the child at the breast:

>   Now, mortal-sonlike,
> I thou hast suckled, Mother, I at last
> Shall sustenant be to thee. Here I untrammel,

In a Little Peace

Here I pluck loose the body's cerementing,
And break the tomb of life; here I shake off
The bur o' the world, man's congregation shun,
And to the antique order of the dead
I take the tongueless vows: my cell is set
Here in thy bosom; my little trouble is ended
In a little peace.

The Proemion sees man as an 'efflux' of the rocks and fields, and the Anthem proper pretends to set forth man's life in relation to the earth. But it is really Thompson's own life, rather than that of mankind, that is being portrayed. Refrains at the beginning and end of each section epitomize the stages of his awareness—'In nescientness, in nescientness', 'In a little joy, in a little joy', 'In a little thought', 'In a little strength', 'In a little sight', 'In a little dust', 'In a little peace'. 'In nescientness' introduces the idea of man's dependence upon the earth; yet the main reference is to Thompson's sense of dependence, and his nostalgia for the unthinkingness of the infant. 'In a little joy' carries us into his youthful world of fantasies, his dreams and poetic visionings:

I brake through thy doors of sunset,
Ran before the hooves of sunrise,
Shook thy matron tresses down in fancies
Wild and wilful
As a poet's hand could twine them.

'In a little thought' he speaks of the demands knowledge makes upon the man, and the struggle between the adult awareness of growth and decay, and man's ambitions and dreams. Confronting the demands of maturity, he wakes 'disgarmented of glory'. 'In a little strength', he endures the 'shunless fardel of the world', for he feels his poetic gift dissolving like his dreams; what is there left for him but to accept 'the monstrous Temple's moveless caryatid'? And yet, he believes that, through suffering, he has come to a vision of the spiritual order of the universe that links all things to the Creator:

Uneuphrasied with tears, the hierarchical
Vision lies unoccult, rank under rank
Through all create down-wheeling, from the Throne
Even to the bases of the pregnant ooze,

'In a little sight', the scientist is confident that he, too, knows the answers. Whatever maturity has taken from Thompson, it has at least kept him from this presumption. He recognizes that there is something beyond analysable phenomena, for man cannot even understand himself:

> Who the chart shall draw
> Of the strange courts and vaulty labyrinths. . . .
> Wherein I wander darkling, of myself?

'In a little dust', earth reclaims men and devours great and small. 'In a little peace' it will also eat Thompson. He looks back to days when he was unwitting of death; now it shows itself as 'Pontifical Death', his only chance of oblivious rest. In an unexpectedly concrete image, he calls it

> Death, wherewith's fined
> The muddy wine of life; that earth doth purge
> Of her plethora of man; Death, that doth flush
> The cumbered gutters of humanity.

And so at the end he reaches out for the ending of his 'little trouble' in a little peace.

In this poem, Death, like the earth, is many things, reckless of contradiction—king of nothing, being's drone-pipe, a rainstorm, a purgative, a smoked glass, a bridge, a Bishop, and so on. And, without much conviction, Thompson claims it as the entrance to eternal life 'true Fount of Youth'—without conviction, because the entire poem is steeped in melancholy. Despite one or two glowing Christian references, it is almost completely barren of sustaining religious feeling. It is hard to reconcile the claim that Thompson is essentially and always a religious poet with this lengthy neo-pagan threnody on earth and death.

The alternation between hope and despair which marks many poems in the volume is felt especially in 'From the Night of Forebeing'. The ode is obviously Patmorean, both in its restating of Patmore's idea that true freedom is to be found only in the voluntary acceptance of limitations, and also in verbal echoes so close as barely to escape the charge of plagiarism:

> the wings
> Hear I not in praevenient winnowings
> Of coming songs, that lift my hair and stir it?

Yet the poem is, in the main, Thompson's own, if only in its reading of the signs of the seasons in personal terms; and it leaves a different impression from 'An Anthem of Earth', written perhaps as much as two years earlier, for here the attitude is one of stoical endurance:

> Not without fortitude I wait
> The dark majestical ensuit
> Of destiny, nor peevish rate
> Calm-knowledged Fate.

Despite some verbal irresponsibility, this is one of the few poems in which Thompson celebrates Nature directly. It is somewhat amusing to find anticipations of Roy Campbell in

> Vault, O young winds, vault in your tricksome courses
> Upon the snowy steeds that reinless use
> In coerule pampas of the heaven to run;

while other passages are almost Wordsworthian in their insight.

In Spring, the poet looks back upon his days of poetic fruitfulness and sees himself now plunged into a winter, which excludes poetic creativeness:

> Soul, brain, and pulses dead,
> The mind no further by the warm sense fed,
> The soul weak-stirring in the arid mind.

At the same time, counterpointing his mood with that of the Christian season of Easter, he feels beneath the winter of his desolation the faint stirrings of his approaching Spring. (The poem, clearly, has its inspiration in Patmore's magnificent ode 'Winter'.) He counsels patience to himself, in the hope of a resurrection not only to a mature joy, but also to a fresh world of poetic inspiration. Then he would be like Patmore

> who looks past
> To slow much sweet from little instant sour
> And in the first does always see the last.

As a poem, 'From the Night of Forebeing' barely rises above

the confessional level; under its nature imagery and flashes of real poetry, it deals rather too narrowly with 'What am I going to write about now that I can no longer take interest in my earlier subjects?' And again it exploits rather than assimilates religious material, for the passages from the Easter liturgy on which it claims to be based are buried beneath the statement of personal problems.

In *New Poems*, Alice Meynell is again praised in several pieces of hyperbolic devotion, under the title 'Ultima', either lamenting her indifference in the tones of a distraught troubadour, or singing her qualities. Thompson thought so little of these poems that he told his publisher in November, 1896, that he preferred that his indifferent translations, rather than 'Ultima', be retained in the volume. 'I do not at all mind leaving out the section "Ultima" ', he wrote. However, in the midst of the arid conceits addressed to 'My Lady the Tyraness', there are occasional passages which catch the attention with their incisive realism. For instance, in 'A Holocaust':

> O God! Thou knowest if this heart of flesh
> Quivers like broken entrails, when the wheel
> Rolleth some dog in middle street, or fresh
> Fruit when ye tear it bleeding from the peel.

And in 'Ultimum', he passes beyond his formalized devotion to the reality behind Alice Meynell, and recognizes explicitly that she has been only a temporary resting-place on the way to a higher goal:

> And, Lady, thus I dare to say,
> Not all with you is passed away!
> Beyond your star, still, still the stars are bright;
> Beyond your highness, still I follow height;
> Sole I go forth, yet still to my sad view,
> Beyond your trueness, Lady, Truth stands true.

But it is in 'A Narrow Vessel' and 'The Cloud's Swan-Song' that the face of the new Thompson can be most plainly seen. The first is a sequence of eight poems prompted by his abortive relationship with Maggie Brien, and revealing Thompson's emotional inadequacy in love. There is no reason to doubt the psychological truth of the episode described. The girl is furious with the man because he has persuaded her to give him a lock of her hair, and because she thus no longer feels mistress of herself:

> To hear him praise my eyes' brown gleams
>   Was native, soft delight;
> But now it usurpation seems,
>   Because I've given him right.

She feels inadequate to receive his love. After they kiss she is overcome with revulsion, for she fears love as much as she desires it. In the poet's eyes, she is like a child unable to cope with adult passion, and pettishly asking back for what she has given:

> She did not love to love, but hated him
>   For making her to love; and so her whim
>   From passion taught misprision to begin.

The epilogue explains that the poems form an allegory of the relation between God and the soul. To me, this appears an attempt to lend extra significance to a record of a frustrated love-affair. Human and divine loves are not integrated as they are in *The Unknown Eros*; and the epilogue reads like the moral to a fable without which the story is already complete. Thompson strenuously defended the symbolical character of the sequence against someone who claimed that the epilogue turned it into an unreal allegory.

'He could not understand', wrote Thompson, 'that all human love was to me a symbol of divine love; nay, that human love was in my eyes a piteous failure unless as an image of the supreme Love which gave meaning and reality to its seeming insanity. . . . Though God asks of the soul but to love him what it may, and is ready to give an increased love for a poor little, the soul feels that this infinite love demands naturally its whole self, that if it begin to love God it may not stop short of all that it has to yield. . . . One is always less generous of love than the other.'

Although this sounds rather like Patmore's preaching, the resemblance is superficial. For Patmore, love is dynamic; in his view, each sex complements the other, uniting on an equal plane. Thompson, however, does not move upwards from the love between man and woman to the love between God and the soul, to whom all souls are feminine. He recognizes the immense disparity between God and his creature, and, as in 'The Hound of Heaven', conceives of the Creator's love for man as that of a father for a son. It is not to question the validity of this analogy to recognize it as a principle that breaks down when extended to sexual love. In Thompson's description of the love between the two in 'A Narrow Vessel', there is much of the quality of an infantile suspension, what Miss Sharpe calls 'a static ecstasy, instead of a dynamic ecstasy', based, as she sees it, 'upon infantile experience, not upon adult sexual experience'. The kiss produces 'enchanted movelessness' and 'impassioned calmness'. It is a 'film of trance between two stirrings' wherein

> the wild train of life
> Reeled by and left us stranded on a hush.
> This moment is a statue unto Love
> Carved from a fair white silence.

Such lines recall at once the student Thompson entranced before the cast of Melpomene; Maggie is loved *because* she cannot return the poet's love.

Many of Thompson's poems, as we have seen, deal with his own poetry. He was, says Everard Meynell, 'the laureate of his own verse'. Was there ever another poet who devoted so many lines to lamenting the difficulty of writing poetry, the problems of capturing the inner life in its purity, and the anxiety bred by a diminished store of subjects? His changed attitude towards his earlier poetry provoked poem after poem in his last volume wrestling with the question of what he should write about now. Even in pieces that deal with other topics, we encounter lines like these:

> For ever the songs I sing are sad with the songs I never sing,
> Sad are sung songs, but how more sad are the songs we dare not
> sing!

It is in 'The Cloud's Swan-Song' that Thompson most plainly shows that he knew his poetic inspiration was drying up. Here he mourns his loneliness; feeling that not only is he cut off from humanity, but that the joy he once took in poetry has deserted him:

In a Little Peace

Like grey clouds one by one my songs upsoar
Over my soul's cold peaks; and one by one
They loose their little rain, and are no more;
And whether well or ill, to tell me there is none.

For 'tis an alien tongue, of alien things,
From all men's care, how miserably apart!
Even my friends say: 'Of what is this he sings?'
And barren is my song, and barren is my heart.

When Patmore used the phrase 'an alien tongue', he was
lamenting that men did not understand what he had written;
when Thompson uses it, he is regretting that he has said nothing
that relates to the concerns of men.

Musing upon his spiritual and emotional suffering, he associ-
ates himself with Keats and Shelley, both of whom died before
their inspiration failed: 'Life longer had been life too long.'
But he, alas, is barren, sick, void of poetic impulse:

Now, with starved brain, sick body, patience galled
With fardels even to wincing.

A passing cloud catches his attention; he considers how it
obeys 'the uncomprehended wills' of heaven's winds, draws
sustenance from the subject earth it seems to scorn and waits
patiently and long in shadow and oblivious cold for a little
light. The cloud becomes for Thompson, as it was for Shelley,
a symbol of the

Right poet! who Thy rightness to approve,
Having all liberty, didst keep all measure,
And with a firmament for ranging, move
But at heaven's uncomprehended pleasure.

Clearly he is thinking again of Patmore, whose advice ever was
not to 'force the note' but to wait upon inspiration; the behaviour of the cloud is that of the poet who does not write for
the sake of writing, but who waits until he has something to
say, and Thompson contrasts his own state with that of such a
poet:

How far am I from heavenly liberty,
That play at policy with change and fate,
Who should my soul from foreign broils keep free,
In the fast-guarded frontiers of its single state!

Could I face firm the Is and with To-be
Trust Heaven; to Heaven commit the deed, and do;
In power contained, calm in infirmity,
And fit myself to change with virtue ever new;

Thou hadst not shamed me, cousin of the sky,
Thou wandering kinsman, that didst sweetly live
Unnoted, and unnoted sweetly die,
Weeping more gracious song than any I can weave;

Which these gross-tissued words so sorely wrong.
Thou hast taught me on powerlessness a power;
To make song wait on life, not life on song;
To hold sweet not too sweet, and bread for bread, though sour.

The veils of self-deception have now been flung aside;
Thompson knows that the hope for his poetry as well as for his
soul lies in his grasping fast the concrete now, the Is, and
trusting to God for the rest, and that only by seeking in the
very core of his heart for his own unsoiled individuality can
he survive as a poet. 'To make song wait on life, not life on
song' states more explicitly than anything else in his verse that
life matters more than poetry, and that his own life has before
been largely shrouded in profitless fantasies.

Even more strongly than in the obituary verses on Patmore
'The Cloud's Swan-Song' pays tribute to the authority and
formative influence of the elder poet. Patmore had compelled
Thompson to stare directly in the face of reality; he taught
him to be humble before experience and not arrogantly to
distort it. In this poem, Thompson makes his most thorough
emotional, spiritual and artistic stock-taking. However much
his friends encouraged him, he knew that he was at the virtual
end of his poetic career; just before *New Poems* was launched,
he wrote to Wilfrid Meynell; 'From the higher standpoint I
have gained, I think, in art and chastity of style, but have
equally lost in fire and glow. 'Tis time I was silent. This book
carries me quite as far as my dwindling strength will allow;
and if I wrote further in poetry, I should write down my own
fame.'

XI

The Sinking Sun

WHEN *New Poems* came out in 1897 it met with a response so
hostile as to provoke the suspicion of anti-Catholic prejudice.
'*Poems* was judged upon its merits,' writes Father Terence L.
Connolly, 'but by the time *New Poems* appeared, it was generally known that Thompson was not only a Roman Catholic
and the son of parents who were converts, but he had even
gone to a monastery to write his poems! As a consequence,
New Poems was very differently received.' It seems to me more
likely that some of the critics had been taking another look at
the earlier volumes and, once the initial reaction to their
seeming individuality had worn off, had become sharply aware
of their deficiencies. Consequently, *New Poems*, which actually
contains more purer poetry, suffered somewhat unfairly from
this revulsion, as, with more justice, Mr. Colin Wilson's second
book did not so long ago. 'A dictionary of obsolete English
suffering from a fierce fit of delirium tremens', 'a very artificial
and unnecessary and inelegant way of expressing very ordinary
truths', 'barbarous jargon', 'formless, purposeless and mindless', 'wordy hugger-mugger of ecclesiastical metaphor', 'sanc-
timonious hyperbole'—these and similar phrases abound in the
reviews, while a not unsympathetic critic, Paul Elmer More,
wrote: 'Even in this, the residue from which all the dross of his
work has supposedly been drawn off, there is still so much to
harass the ear and tease the mind—uncouth words that simulate
oracular frenzy, jagged edges of rhymes, harsh inversions, and
gaping ellipses; so often his tortured language sounds like the
beating on the ground of wings that cannot rise.'

Some spoke more kindly of the book; William Archer, Arthur Quiller-Couch and J. L. Garvin, for instance, found substantial virtues in it. But Thompson's star had set. The great original genius hailed only four short years before was now generally regarded as a freak talent manipulating outrageous conceits and tearing the petals from other men's flowers. The public was indifferent to the new volume, and its sales were miserable. If Thompson had had any doubts about his loss of 'fire and glow', the reception given to *New Poems* must have removed them. In the last ten years of his life, he was to write a mere handful of poems, almost all of them tired, inferior, and repetitive.

One reason for the drying-up of the river of poetry in him was, obviously, the new vision of life and truth which made it impossible for him to continue 'to play at policy with change and fate'. With his old gods dead, he had looked to Patmore for inspiration. But Patmore died. Had he lived a few more years, it is likely that he would have led Thompson gradually to complete confidence in his new way. Again, Thompson's deepening knowledge of his religion made him doubt the supreme value he had, with at least half of his mind, attached to poetry. Further, as we have seen, nearly all his poetry was produced when he was not taking opium. But, after he returned to London, he resumed his draughts of laudanum, and continued this right up to his death.

Why did he return to the drug? He had not taken it, or had taken it at very rare intervals, for about five years, and may be presumed to have broken off the habit as far as one could who had been so long dependent upon it. Yet, when he no longer had poetry as a means of projecting his lonely inner self, the remembered comforts of laudanum must have offered themselves to him with renewed force. What friend, too, could so console him for the loss of his dear Patmore as opium could? There was, too, the growing burden of the lung disease which was to kill him. The privations of his half-starved, half-naked nights in the bitter London streets had left permanent marks on a never robust constitution, and drove him to what he knew would alleviate his pain and weakness. Very likely laudanum gave him an extra year or two of life.

Whatever we may feel about Thompson's addiction in

earlier years, it is hard to be censorious about it in later days, especially as he seems to have rationed his doses after his return from Pantasaph; certainly he never sank to such depths as he did in his pre-Meynell years. He did not tell his friend that he had reverted, and Meynell, whatever his suspicions, did not ask him, understanding, in charity, the motives that had led to his regression. It was only when Thompson was virtually on the point of death that the word 'opium' was spoken between them.

Patmore's death brought Thompson to the Metropolis again; he had greater need now than before of Meynell's kindness. For the years that remained to him, he lived in London, at various addresses, mostly near the Edgware and Harrow Roads, moving restlessly from lodging to lodging, with a battalion of anonymous landladies, some tolerant, some exasperated, as his guardians. Immediately after his return from Pantasaph, he stayed for a time with the Meynells at Palace Court; later he would spend many of his days there, by night wandering the London streets or drowsing before a public-house fire. At Palace Court, he became, as Viola Meynell describes him in her biography of her mother, 'the utterly dependent friend— the gentle, late, voluble, flushing, dozing visitor of every day'. He caused the family more than one despairing moment; one's admiration for their patience grows as the record unfolds of appointments missed, days mistaken, meals congealing, engagements broken and the lengthy self-justifications in letters of puzzled, half-resentful expostulation.

The Meynell household, still busily engaged in multitudinous journalistic activities, could not often afford to accept the 'help' Thompson was eager to give. Wilfrid, still fascinated by Thompson's poetry, nursed him along, praised his verse, tolerated his eccentricities, and found him work as a book-reviewer. It was to Alice Meynell, again, however, now that Patmore was no more, that Francis transferred the weight of his dependent affection. His love for her was expressed not in speech or action, but privately, in his notebooks:

'I thought I owed it to her whom I loved more than my love of her finally to unroot that love, to pluck away the last fibres of it, that I might be beyond treachery to my resolved duty. And at this second effort I finished what the first had left incomplete. The initial agony had really been decisive, and to complete the process needed only resolution. But it left that lady still the first, the one veritable, full-orbed and apocalyptic love of my life.'

Yet, despite all these protestations of ineradicable devotion, he could not, on the social level, even do Alice Meynell the courtesy of keeping appointments with her. He was quite capable of arriving at Palace Court on Tuesday for a Monday engagement or of coming five or six hours late for dinner. The complete unreality of his relationship with Mrs. Meynell, expressed in wordy, breast-beating letters of abject apology for social neglects and of Platonic worship, mixed with extravagant Christian terms (he even ends a letter, 'Ahi! soavissima Madonna Alice, avete pieta di me!'), contrasts as strongly with Patmore's meticulously courteous treatment of her as Patmore's philosophy of love contrasts with Thompson's. Writing after his death, Alice Meynell generously emphasized Thompson's lovable qualities: 'As he was one of the most innocent of men, he was also one of the finest-tempered', she said. 'I affirm of Francis Thompson that he had natural good spirits, and was more mirthful than many a man of cheerful, of social, or even of humorous reputation.'

But, in fact, she suffered more than one experience with him which drove her to the edge of her very considerable patience. Katharine Tynan, for instance, records a visit Thompson and Mrs. Meynell paid her in 1895, 'when lunch, fixed for 1.30, awaited the visitors till 3.30. Mrs. Meynell arrived almost in tears. She could never bear any lack of courtesy. Francis Thompson, she explained, would not get up, although the gayest of little radiant girls had threatened him with the cold water jug.'[1]

The Meynell youngsters' attitude towards the poet was rather more down-to-earth than his to them. In his poems he always idealized them as elfish embodiments of joy and innocence; and he believed that they were especially devoted to him. Yet, in later life, Viola wrote: 'He was not the visitor at

[1] *The Middle Years*, Constable, 1916, p. 135.

the sound of whose special knock the Palace Court children raced down the stairs to be the first to open the door; he is not remembered as ever being sought by them or causing the smallest stir of that expectation which children easily feel.'

They used to play tricks on him in an affectionate way, but with a clear recognition of his oddity. Whenever he was due for a luncheon appointment, they would call him from his refuge between the sheets at 8 o'clock and would continue energetically with their summonses at five-minute intervals, so that there might be a reasonable chance of his stirring by midday. His many lost campaigns against accidie are commemorated on the placard he placed on his bedroom wall:

> At the Last Trump thou wilt arise Betimes!
> Up; for when thou wouldst not, thou wilt shortly sleep long.
> The worm is even now weaving thy body its night-shift.
> Love slept not a-saving thee. Love calls thee.
> Rise, and seek Him early. Ask, and receive.

Even for his beloved children he could not change his dreaming ways. The eldest daughter, Monica, had been his special favourite, she it was to whom he had written 'The Poppy', and to whom he once declared: 'Never, my dear, doubt I love you. And if I have the chance to show it I will do.' In his own copy of *Poems* he sewed a lock of the hair of Monica, Viola, Francis and Olivia over the poem addressed to each child. Yet he could not even remember the time of Monica's wedding, and, arriving too early at the church, he left in the belief that the ceremony was over, repenting his error later in a lengthy letter of apology. Surely one does not have to be a Freudian to find in such happenings evidence of a subconscious rejection of the facts before him.

With the second Meynell son, Everard, Thompson established one of his few close friendships. The gifted young man, an art-student turned bookseller, and founder of the noted Serendipity Shop, which dealt in rare books, had responded sensitively to the poet, and, after his death, wrote a fine just biography of his friend. Thompson used to visit Everard frequently at the shop in Westbourne Grove, where he would talk endlessly about their common passion, cricket, sit for a portrait and a life-mask and waste Everard's never-begrudged time with chatter.

Thompson's volubility, which alternated with abstracted silences, was something that called for fortitude in the hearer. Wilfrid Whitten recalled: 'Thompson cared nothing for the world's comment, and though he would talk with radiant interest, on many things, it was always with a certain sunny separateness, as though he issued out of unseen chambers of thought requiring nothing, but able and willing to interest himself in the thing to which his attention was drawn.'

'And his talk when he was in mundane mood, a mood that did not interest him!' writes C. Lewis Hind. 'He would labour a minor point until our heads swam, pausing politely when the general conversation turned to another topic, and, at the first opportunity, break in to tell us for the tenth time something that was not worth telling once.' Everard Meynell, too, describes a typical late-night parting with him:

'It was after an evening divided between silence and explanations that, wondering how well he covered the fires of his imagination, one went to the door to help with hat and coat. Some final repetition, unblushingly proclaimed with "As I said before" would still longer delay his return to himself; but once he had begun to go down the steps . . . he would find himself face to face again with the realities of life that he chose to keep private, and be loudly talking to himself in a style more meaningful and threatening than any speech of his in company.'

Thompson, in fact, seemed to be so completely and humourlessly detached from the concerns of others that he was quite unwitting of incongruity, as when, during a family Shakespeare reading, he broke in upon Desdemona's death-scene with the loud lament: 'Here's a go, Mrs. Meynell. I've lost my *Athenaeum* cheque!'

The wordy arabesques he wove around trifles, his making a crisis out of choosing one of two alternative addresses or finding a stamp, were the attempts of someone trying hard to cling to visible realities; perhaps, too, his flow of words was a substitute for the verbal release he could no longer find in poetry. Yet he found the simplest things in life a difficulty, He had become a pipe-smoker, and his attempts to light the tobacco, and, once having lit it, to keep it so, was for him a highly complicated process which he never appears to have mastered. Sarath Kumar Ghosh, an Indian, in whose novel *The Prince of Destiny* Thompson figures as a character, describes the process thus: 'He took out his pipe, a huge briar, struck a match, gave just one puff, held the match over the bowl till his fingers were nearly burnt, threw away the match, struck another, also gave a single puff, relapsed into thought—and so on, with several matches. Afterwards Wingate picked up the burnt matches, and counted them. "Just fourteen!" he said gleefully to Barath.'

As he moved in his withdrawn way through the streets of London, disaster constantly lay in wait for him. On one occasion he was bowled over by a hansom cab and had to be taken to a hospital in Queen's Square to have a cut on his head dressed. On another occasion, his habit of smoking, or rather of striking matches, in bed, brought trouble when he set the curtains of his lodging-room alight and upset his lamp while trying to extinguish them. The room was almost completely gutted. When Thompson told Lewis Hind of the affair, Hind said, 'But, Francis, did you not rouse your landlady?' And Thompson's reply, typical of his naïve self-concern, was, 'My dear Hind, a house on fire is no place for tarrying.' It is no wonder that Katharine Tynan found him humourless, but the cause of humour in others.

In these later years, then, all the oddities of Thompson's temperament came to the surface. His will seemed to have become torpid again; he suffered, too, from spells of extreme physical exhaustion, although this did not become plain to the Meynells until a couple of years before his death. Yet all who knew him, amused though they often were by his unpracticality and exasperated by his social irresponsibility, found in him qualities of ingenuousness and gentleness which went far to balance the more trying features of his character.

Katharine Tynan describes him at this period:

'An odd figure in a drawing-room presided over by the most exquisite of women, short, untidy, in a suit of ugly, yellowish tweed, with the unfailing pipe, a pipe of the grimiest, clutched in his fingers when it was not between his lips. The lower part of the face was poor, the mouth and chin covered by a short beard; but the brow was splendid, and there was the width between the eyes that never goes with insignificance. The expression was simple and cordial; indeed, a simpler soul never lived.'

Alice Meynell argued that his garrulousness was something impossible to a melancholy man: 'No soul oppressed by sadness is busy, as he was, with unnecessary words', and she commemorates his laugh: 'It is a pleasure to remember Francis Thompson's laugh, a laugh readier than a girl's, and it is impossible to remember him, with any real recall, and not to hear it in the mind again.'

In the late nineties, Thompson had reached a stage of stoical inner acceptance of his condition, in which he adjusted himself as fully as one of his temperament ever could to life about him, sustained by the never-flagging interest of the Meynells. His contacts with the literary life of the period were slight. Apart from Patmore, Katharine Tynan and W. S. Blunt, he met, through the Meynells, Aubrey de Vere, the regal Irish poet, W. E. Henley and George Meredith. Meredith, who had become one of Alice Meynell's most devoted admirers, once invited her and Thompson to spend a night at Box Hill. Thompson found himself ill-at-ease in the luxuriant natural setting of Meredith's home, and no real contact was established between the two men. Meredith had serious reservations about Thompson's poetry, and, in his convoluted way, chaffed him about its inequalities. He invented a landlady for Thompson, named Amelia Applejohn, and imagined the poet composing sonnets to her and calling her in from her baking to listen to them. One is baffled to conceive what kind of conversation could have passed between the author of 'Modern Love' and 'The Woods of Westermain' and the author of 'The Hound of Heaven' and 'Orient Ode', between the subtle, witty, involved novelist, and the poet of melancholy and ecstatic reverie. It is more than likely that whatever both said on this occasion was directed past the person addressed to the common object of their affections.

With Henley it was different. He had not cared much either for Thompson's poetry, nor for some of his critical pronouncements, but came to see virtue in both. E. V. Lucas and Lewis

Hind took Thompson to visit the old man, arriving two hours late after waiting for the poet. Hind described the encounter thus: 'I shall never forget one afternoon when he sat at Henley's feet, literally, on a footstool, in the house at Muswell Hill, and Henley talked, and Thompson talked, and the younger poet unleashed his magnificent admiration, and the elder poet, amusement and pleasure mingling in his giant face, purred.' This suggests that Thompson could put himself out where such an abiding interest as literature was concerned, for, in print, he was rather less enthusiastic about Henley as a poet.

Perhaps the most tantalizing account of Thompson's glancing contact with his fellow-poets of the nineties is that given by Lewis Hind in his book of reminiscences, *Naphtali*, of a night at the Rhymers' Club held at Dr. John Todhunter's in Bedford Park:

'Most of the poets talked most of the time with articulated precision about quantitative equivalents, and, with the exception of courteous Dr. Todhunter, no one seemed to notice the guest of the evening—Francis Thompson. We—that is, Vernon Blackburn and I—had brought him there by special request. I wish the meeting had been held at that "pub between two stage-doors". Bedford Park seemed to awe those tame young poets. Francis Thompson sat next to Ernest Dowson, but I did not see them speak to one another. The Nineties poets were often like that—remote, shy, aloof. Ernest Dowson frequented "cabmen's shelters" as a "sensation"; such harbourages were natural to Francis Thompson. Oh, and Lionel Johnson was another at the Rhymers' Club meeting; another silent man. His twitching face was always watching and smiling. And I think Arthur Symons was there, too.'

I should greatly like to know all that these four did not, on that unique occasion, say to one another.

A particularly sympathetic picture of Thompson at this time is given in Sarath Kumar Ghosh's 'novel' already mentioned, *The Prince of Destiny*. Although ostensibly fiction, this somewhat quaint book really offers the impression of an Anglophilic Indian on Anglo-Indian relations, Hindu mysticism and much else. Thinly disguised as Barath, the central character, the author records his impressions of several distinguished contemporaries, notably Thompson, of whom his sketch is of special interest as giving the reaction of a sensitive Oriental to this unusual man.

Barath, on a visit to his friend, Colonel Wingate, in the country, first encounters Thompson on a train going in the same direction. At that time, the poet is merely an odd stranger to him:

'He was of medium height, but very slight of frame, which made him seem taller than he really was. His cheeks were so sunken as to give undue prominence to a little grey beard that was pointed at the end but otherwise untrimmed. It was his garb that was against him, and in violent contrast to the traditional smartness of City men. His trousers were dark, far too dark for summer, frayed at the ends, spotted with tallow marks. His coat was grey—and did not match the trousers—stained with tea at the sleeves. The greatest incongruity was that he wore an ulster, though the heat was great. It had been originally brown in colour, but was of several different hues in patches.'

Later, Barath is astonished to find that this fellow-traveller to whom he surrendered his seat, is Francis Thompson, also Wingate's guest. From the beginning the two became fast friends: 'Instinctively the mind of the poet seemed to understand that some of the elements in his own nature, hitherto vaguely perceived and only partially understood, now stood before him in their fullest embodiment: that though he was wholly an Englishman in the body, he was partly an Easterner in imagination—and now for the first time met one who was wholly Eastern in body and perchance in thought.'

At a later meeting, Mr. Ghosh records, they discussed all manner of things, including Eastern mysticism. Barath introduced Thompson to the Sanskrit poets, including Kalidas, whose 'Sakuntala' he rendered into English prose, hoping that Thompson would recast it in verse. But Thompson never completed the task. Barath speaks of Thompson with immense affection, as a genuine sensitive, and stresses the physical weaknesses which made him cling to the drug in his later years. 'He knew more of the doctrine of pain than most European poets

and thinkers—nay, his insight was Eastern. . . . But to sustain
life the drug or the stimulant was as essential to his enfeebled
body as food or air. So he took it when needed—just to quench
the pain a moment, just to prolong the life and hour, till his
work was done, his mission fulfilled.'

According to Ghosh, Thompson at this time was forced 'to
devote himself to the journalism that was using up his genius and
sapping his life-blood'. In point of fact, Thompson turned to
prose because he had virtually ceased to write poetry. Thanks to
the good offices of Wilfrid Meynell, he found entry to the
columns of the *Academy* and the *Athenaeum*. In 1897, Lewis Hind,
then editor of the *Academy*, told Thompson that he would accept
weekly contributions from him; the poet continued to write
regularly for the journal right up to his death. Father Connolly's careful bibliography of Thompson's uncollected reviews
and articles lists 221 contributed to the *Academy* between 1896
and 1906, while for the *Athenaeum*, he wrote some 32 articles,
as well as pieces for the *Dublin Review*, the *Daily Chronicle*, *Merry
England*, the *Outline*, the *Tablet*, and the *Weekly Register*.

'A Thompson article in *The Academy* gave distinction to the
issue', Hind recalled. 'What splendid prose it was! Reading the
proofs, we would declaim passages aloud for the mere joy of
giving utterances to his periods.' Yet, elsewhere, Hind shows the
natural exasperation of a newspaper-man with a contributor
who could never be relied upon and whose copy rarely arrived
in time: 'I suffered for years from his—what shall I say?—un-
businesslike habits, inability to keep appointments, and indifference to the trouble he might cause his editors by unfulfilled
literary promises. Sometimes I would wonder what a mystical
Christianity is worth which, in everyday life, ignores the golden
rule. He could not discipline himself to consider the feelings of
editors and hostesses, and he lived in himself.' But, as always,
Thompson, if sparing of fulfilment, was generous in excuses, as
when he sold a review-copy before he had read it.

DEAR HIND—I regret exceedingly to find that the Menpes
was disposed of along with an accumulation of back review
books, nor can I get it back, for it sold almost at once. I am
very sorry it should have happened; because it should not and
would not have been sold, had it not gone among others

when I was in a hurry, and my mind occupied only with the work I had in hand. Of course, in such circumstances, I hold myself responsible for replacing it as soon as I can. Or if you cannot wait, I would suggest you get the book and dock it out of my extra money. The only alternative is for me to pick oakum (if they do that in debtors' gaols). And I have not the talents for oakum-picking. . . .

F. THOMPSON.

Like so many people who were irritated by Thompson, Hind felt a powerful obligation to father the poet. He came to realize that this man from whose pockets unopened telegrams would cascade and from between the crumbled pages of whose copy unposted letters would drift could hardly be trusted to make the best use of his money.

'I soon realized the folly of sending him a cheque in payment of contributions. Either he would never open the letter or, likely enough, he would light his obstreperous pipe with the cheque. . . . No, I sent him no cheques after the first month. A cheque was despatched to his landlady each week for board and lodging, and a few shillings was placed in the poet's hand, periodically, for pocket money, which he accepted with detachment, his flow of conversation uninterrupted.'

Wilfrid Meynell also acted as holder of the purse-strings. Like Hind, he knew that Thompson would spend money on laudanum if he had it; and so allowed him merely enough cash for his immediate needs. But the poet, skilled in the tricks of the streets and experienced in squeezing out a few extra shillings, was equal to the occasion. He sold his review-copies usually before the relevant article had appeared; when there were no books available he pawned his spare clothes, and his very few personal possessions, as the pawn-tickets found among his papers after his death attested. Laudanum cost little, but Thompson, being at the barest level of subsistence, and rationing the drug besides, could often scarcely afford it. Apart from what remained of the psychological compulsion which originally drove him to opium, there is much truth in Wilfrid Meynell's defence after the poet's death: 'The drug was, I think, some palliation of the disease from which he finally died—consumption.'

In any event, Thompson's dietary habits hardly helped his health. The Meynells fed him often, when he remembered to turn up in time, but he quite frequently forgot to eat his usual meals, and when he did do so, his fare was of the oddest. Toast sufficed for breakfast, and, on other occasions, beer and porridge were his staple, taken in the belief that they were the most nourishing, as well as the cheapest foods. For relaxation, there was reading, and cricket. Not that Thompson was ever an active player. E. V. Lucas, who, as a member of the staff of the *Academy*, met Thompson, wrote: 'Of all men Francis Thompson was to the casual observer least like a cricketer, in the ulster which he did not don until the swallows were with us nor doff until they had flown. It was not only his inverted affection for his overcoat, it was the whole effect, the *ensemble*, as Whitman would say. . . . And his eye supported it. His eye had no brightness: it swung laboriously upon its object; whereas the enthusiasts of St. John's Wood dart their glances like birds.' But he maintained his interest in the game, scanning the newspapers regularly for cricket-scores.

In later years he was seldom seen at Lord's, but he carried on a friendly war with Everard Meynell who upheld the cause of Yorkshire against Thompson's Lancashire. Thompson's nostalgic, sad recall of the great cricketers of the past, Hornby and Barlow, has already been mentioned. This poem, to quote E. V. Lucas again, 'imports a new note into cricket poetry. Cricket poetry hitherto has been descriptive, reflective, rapturous, gay, humorous. It has never before to my knowledge been made a vehicle for a lament for the past of profoundest melancholy.' Among Thompson's other cricket verses is a parody of FitzGerald's *Rubáiyát*, a very schoolboyish piece of humour, which begins:

> Wake! for the Ruddy Ball has taken flight
> That scatters the slow Wicket of the Night;
>   And the swift Batsman of the Dawn has driven
> Against the Star-spiked Rails a fiery Smite.

Of Thompson's academic knowledge of cricket there can be no doubt. In a lengthy criticism of *The Jubilee Book of*

Cricket written for the *Academy* in 1897, he displays considerable acumen in his analysis of various batting and bowling styles, and a sensitive perception of the balletic grace of a good player, as when he describes Vincent Royle, a Lancashire man, in action: 'In addition to his sureness and swiftness, his style was a miracle of grace. Slender and symmetrical, he moved with the lightness of a young roe, the fluxuous elegance of a leopard —it was a sight for an artist or a poet to see him field.'

The decade that straddled the centuries were, then, years of relative tranquillity for Thompson, in which prose articles poured from his pen in a constant stream. And it is to this aspect of his work that we must now turn our attention.

XII

The Infantries of Language

THE best-known of Thompson's prose-writings is the essay on
Shelley, written in the Storrington period, when he was making
his first recovery from opium, and composed side by side with
'Ode to the Setting Sun'. After Bishop Vaughan had suggested to
Thompson that he contribute something to the *Dublin Review*,
he worked hard at the Shelley paper, only to have it rejected
by the editor. In a letter to Canon Carroll, Thompson gave
the reasons he believed to be behind the editor's decision:

> 'First, you see, I prefaced it by a fiery attack on Catholic
> Philistinism . . . driven home with all the rhetoric I could
> muster. . . . Secondly, it is written at an almost incessant
> level of poetic prose, and seethes with imagery like my poetry
> itself. Now the sober, ponderous, ecclesiastical *Dublin* con-
> fronted with poetic prose must be considerably scared. The
> editor cannot make up his mind whether it is heavenly
> rhetoric or infernal nonsense.'

He goes on to say that Meynell thought the article splendid,
and that the prose poetry of some passages is like nothing else
in English prose. 'The editor', says Thompson patronizingly,
'feels himself out of his latitude. He is probably a person of
only average literary taste—that is, he can tell the literary
hawk from the literary handsaw when the wind is southerly.
He feels that discretion is the better part of valour. . . . So he
rejects it.'

Discovered among Thompson's papers after his death, it was
published by Wilfrid Ward, the editor of the *Dublin Review*, in

the issue of July, 1908; as a result, for the first time in its long history, the *Review* went into a second edition. The essay hit the taste of Edwardian critics; a typical reaction being that of the *Observer*, which called it 'a memorable masterpiece of English prose'. It was later issued as a separate booklet in 1909, with a preface by George Wyndham, who enthusiastically described it as 'the most important contribution to pure Letters written in English during the last twenty years'. Since that time, it has been often reprinted, and lavishly praised. Indeed there are some who affirm it to be Thompson's best work, superior to any of his poems.

As a piece of consciously 'artistic' prose, the Shelley essay has much to commend it to those with a taste for artificially manipulated English. But equally it shows up clearly all Thompson's inequalities as a writer, oddly mixing as it does lucid observation, clear critical thinking and relatively un-adorned statement with hectically over-elaborate passages of the deepest purple, enthusiastic errors of taste and perverse judgments. Even those passages of contrived ninetyish prose, which may be admired for their fine extravagance, are seldom carried through to a vigorous conclusion, but tail feebly away, as if the initial effort too quickly exhausted the writer's in-vention; for instance, the well-known passage which describes Shelley using the make-belief of a child in his poetry, and which, as we have seen, is so intimately related to Thompson's own vision:

'The universe is his box of toys. He dabbles his fingers in the day-fall. He is gold-dusty with tumbling amidst the stars. He makes bright mischief with the moon. The meteors nuzzle their noses in his hand. He teases into growling the ken-nelled thunder, and laughs at the shaking of its fiery chain. He dances in and out of the gates of heaven: its floor is littered with his broken fancies. He runs wild over the fields of ether. He chases the rolling world. He gets between the feet of the horses of the sun. He stands in the lap of patient Nature, and twines her loosened tresses after a hundred wilful fashions, to see how she will look nicest in his song.'

Much of the argument and appreciation in the essay is dis-guised in verbiage; and Thompson cannot make a point without immediately burying it beneath a mountain of vague imagery. For instance, speaking of Shelley's power to 'condense the most hydrogenic abstraction', he says: 'The coldest moon of an idea rises haloed through his vaporous imagination. The dimmest-sparked chip of a conception blazes and scintillates in the subtle oxygen of his mind. The most wrinkled Æson of an abstruseness leaps rosy out of his bubbling genius.' There are many glittering things said in the essay, too, that, upon examination, turn out to be virtually meaningless. 'His thoughts scorch through all the folds of expression. His cloth of gold bursts at the flexures, and shows the naked poetry.' How can poetry, naked or otherwise, exist independently of its expression? Even Mégroz, usually a doughty defender of Thompson on all fronts, finds that the essay lacks what he calls 'creative condensation'. 'The language', he goes on, 'is barely more than pseudo- or prose-poetry, because it is not fecund in a higher degree.'

What does Thompson's estimate of Shelley amount to? He identifies Shelley with himself, almost completely, as artist, as perpetual child, as imaginative manipulator of the cosmos. He romanticizes the sufferings of Shelley's childhood, and defends his adult personality as that of a child, who, like Peter Pan, never grew up. At the time the essay was written, Thompson felt that the wish to remain 'the enchanted child' was sufficient to explain his own evasions of adulthood; in the same way he excuses Shelley's shortcomings. Not wholly, however, for while 'we decline to judge so unhappy a being by the rules which we should apply to a Catholic', at the same time, 'No enmity of outward circumstances, therefore, but his own nature, was responsible for Shelley's doom.'

For Thompson, the chief excellence of Shelley's poetry lies in its wealth of imagery. In the passages about the 'box of toys', he attempts a justification of what he has persuaded himself was Shelley's normal practice, and, incidentally, of his own. Believing that imagery is the very stuff of poetry, and that the quality of a poem is to be measured by the number and variety of images in it, he greatly exaggerates the actual quantity in Shelley's poetry, and puts us off with what is, in fact, a description of his own early verse. 'For astonishing figurative opulence he yields only to Shakespeare, and even to

Shakespeare not in absolute fecundity but in range of images.'
But as J. A. Chapman has pointed out,[1] the poems of Shelley
praised by Thompson, 'The Cloud', 'The Skylark', and 'The
Sensitive Plant', contain much imagery that lacks the imaginative beauty of other Shelleyan imagery, and his more beautiful
poems are as bare of images as poetry can be.

Nowhere in the essay does Thompson suggest the special
quality of Shelley's poetry or of his mature mind, as expressed
in *Prometheus Unbound*, for instance, nor of the vision which
transcends the adolescent enthusiasms. He selects from Shelley's character and poetry those things which, real or imagined,
accord most with his own tastes and personality; he remakes
Shelley in his own image, as Coleridge remade Hamlet. At
the same time, he rebukes those who would idealize the poet;
and worship the 'sweetly pretty' Shelley. Yet to preserve his
own remodelled version, he is prepared not only to play down
Shelley's religious views, but also to strain analogies between
the poet and St. John the Evangelist (in 'Stray Thoughts on
Shelley') and to confuse the distinction between Shelley's
pantheism and Crashaw's Christianity. What has happened is
that Thompson, deeply attached to the image of himself he
has projected on Shelley, has become drunk with his own
imagery, and careless of logic, appropriateness or inner truth.
The essay on Shelley has little interest for the serious student
of Shelley's poetry, but appeals mainly to those enamoured of
fluid cadences, and liable to mistake flashiness for profundity.
Nevertheless, amidst the broken glass of Thompsonian rhetoric,
there glimmers more than one shrewd observation which
shows his lively intelligence. Although his claim that to be a
child is 'to believe in love, to believe in loveliness, to believe
in belief' is mere words, he does shrewdly see that Shelley's
remaining a child, in the good sense, consisted in retaining the
spontaneity of childhood without being childish; he recognizes
the central part myth played in Shelley's vision, and he ends
on a note of genuine charity: 'Let us hope rather that . . .
amidst the supernatural universe, some tender undreamed
surprise of life in doom awaited that wild nature, which, worn
by warfare with itself, its Maker and all the world, now

[1] 'Shelley and Francis Thompson', *Papers on Shelley, Wordsworth and others*,
Oxford University Press, 1929, pp. 9–10.

Sleeps and never palates more the dug,
The beggar's nurse, and Caesar's.'

There is also an astonishing passage on poetic diction which
Thompson seems not to have realized referred more immediately to his own poetry than to that of any of his contemporaries:

'The habit of excessive care in word-selection frequently
results in loss of spontaneity; and, still worse, the habit of
always taking the best word too easily becomes the habit of
always taking the most ornate word, the word most removed
from ordinary speech. In consequence of this, poetic diction
has become latterly a kaleidoscope, and one's chief curiosity
is as to the precise combinations into which the pieces will
be shifted. There is, in fact, a certain band of words, the
Praetorian cohorts of poetry, whose prescriptive aid is invoked by every aspirant to the poetical purple; against these
it is time some banner should be raised.'

Such unwitting condemnations of his own poetic vices are, as
we shall see, a constant feature of his prose criticism.

The celebrated essay, in short, is an arresting exercise in
verbal cleverness, rich in vocabulary, packed with images, an
over-loaded piece of self-conscious prose, bursting out at intervals into the bastard genre of 'prose-poetry'; it says very
little of any worth about its ostensible subject, but reveals a
great deal about the psychology of its author.

Some of the same charges can be made against the other
early essays. Those pieces collected by Wilfrid Meynell in the
third volume of the *Collected Works* (1913) are mainly essays
Thompson himself wished to reprint; they show him at anything
but his best, since they contain much florid over-writing and
mannered aestheticism. 'Finis Coronat Opus', for instance,
might have been penned by Oscar Wilde or J. K. Huysmans
in an off-moment. A laboured moral-fantasy clearly owing
much to opium-memories in its super-sensitivity to sound and
it swooning mood, it tells of Florentian, a poet 'in a city of the
future', whose place 'was high in the retinue of fame', but who
falls prey to the 'seductions of knowledge and intellectual pride',
and obeys the promptings of the evil power to kill his beloved,

Aster, as the price of his supremacy over a rival poet. The whole essay is stamped with the affectations of the Nineties, which it combines with opium-heightened hallucinations, as in the description of the hall of statues, where Florentian prays to the dark forces:

'At the extremity which faced the door there stood, beneath a crucifix, a small marble altar, on which burned a fire of that strange greenish tinge communicated by certain salts. Except at this extremity the walls were draped with deep violet curtains bordered by tawny gold, only half displayed by the partial illumination of the place. The light was furnished by lamps of coloured glass, sparsely hung along the length of the room, but numerously clustered about the altar: lamps of diverse tints, amber, peacock-blue, and changefully mingled harmonies of green like the scales on a beetle's back. Above them was coiled thinnest serpentinings of suspended crystal, hued like the tongues in a wintry hearth, flame-colour, violet and green; so that, as in the heated current from the lamps the smokes twirled and flickered, and their bright shadows twirled upon the wall, they seemed at length to undulate their twines, and the whole altar became surrounded with a fiery fantasy of sinuous stains.'

In the middle of the story, the narration changes from third to first person; Thompson becomes Florentian as he meditates over his crime: 'If confession indeed give ease, I, who am deprived of all other confession, may yet find some appeasement in confessing to this paper.' Just as Florentian is about to achieve the cherished prize of the laurel, he addresses the statue of Virgil: 'At length, Virgil, at length, I am equal with you; Virgil, magician and poet, your crown shall descend on me!' But the cathedral bell booms, and horror clutches at his heart. When the deputation of officials comes to take Florentian to his crowning, they find him dead beneath the statue: 'A dark pool almost hid that dark stain on the ground, the three lines on his forehead were etched in blood, and across the shattered brow lay a ponderous gilded wreath; while over the exhausted altar-fire the idol seemed to quiver its derisive tongue.'

A typical Decadent fable, written in a pastiche of Poe, Pater and Wilde (*The Picture of Dorian Gray*, in particular, is suggested), 'Finis Coronat Opus' today reads both artificially and melodramatically. Yet it does little violence to Thompson's underlying moral to find in it a projection of the same sense of guilt as runs through 'The Hound of Heaven', an interpretation assisted by Thompson's use of the first person through most of the piece. In Florentian we may see Thompson weaving a fantasy about himself, dramatizing in the poet's evil choice his own addiction to opium, in the murder of Aster and the surrender to demonic powers his own rejection of his family and home for the London slums, in Florentian's death the same death-wish which runs through his earlier verse.

Further signs of Thompson's kinship with the Decadents are found in another early essay, 'Moestitiae Encomium', which begins with a desolate picture of a fantasy landscape, clearly a reflection of laudanum sensations:

'Marsh, and night. There are sounds; no man shall say what sounds. There are shadows; no man shall say what shadows. There is light; were there not shadow, no man should call it light. The landscape is a sketch blotted in with smoke of Erebus, and greys from the cheek of death: those trees which threaten from the horizon—they are ranked apparitions, no boon of gracious God. The heaven is a blear copy of the land. Athwart the saturnine marsh, runs long, pitilessly straight, ghastly with an inward pallor (for no gleam dwells on it from the sky), the leprous, pined, infernal watercourse; a water for the Plutonian naiads—exhaling cold perturbation. It is a stream, a land, a heaven, pernicious to the heart of man.'

'Nature's Immortality' shows him in a better light. The style is still florid prose-poetry (in fact, Thompson translated the opening passage, with a minimum of change, into indifferent verse) and there is much typical rhetoric. But the essay carries an idea through consistently, and interestingly speculates upon the relationship between Nature and the Creator, rejecting poetic pantheism and sentimental Romantic personifyings of inanimate things. Nature has no heart, says Thompson; but all things reflect the immensity of God. And he speaks sound sense on the nature of artistic representation:

'The reality of the artist's ideal is not the reality of, e.g., a star; for one is man's creation, the other directly from God. Nor is the reality of the artist's ideal the same in kind as the reality of its objective image, of the painting. The one exists externally and the senses are cognizant of it; the other within his spirit, and the senses can take no account of it. Yet both are real, actual.' Nature, for him, is a phase of the Supreme Spirit. 'The Supreme Spirit, creating, reveals His conceptions to man in the material forms of Nature. There is no necessity here for any intermediate process, because nobody obstructs the free passage of conception into expression. An ideal wakes in the Omnipotent Painter; and straightway over the eternal dikes rush forth the flooding tides of night, the blue of Heaven ripples into stars; Nature, from Alp to Alpine flower, rises lovely with the betrayal of the Divine Thought.' And he ends the Romantic-Christian discussion of Nature:

'As in the participation of human spirits some are naturally more qualified for interpenetration than others—in ordinary language, as one man is more able than his fellows to enter into another's mind, so in proportion as each of us by virtue has become akin to God, will he penetrate the Supreme Spirit, and identify himself with the Divine Ideal. There is the immortal Sicily, there the Elysian Fields, there all visions, all fairness engirdled with the Eternal Fair. This, my faith, is laid up in my bosom.'

A more consistent and less rhetorical Thompson appears in the many reviews and critical articles he wrote from 1896 onwards, which show a wide, although not deep, knowledge of literature, discrimination, considerable sensitivity and even wit. As nearly all of these pieces were written while Thompson was taking laudanum, they indicate that he had attained something of the balance of de Quincey, who, taking as his maintenance dose a far greater quantity of opium than Thompson did, was able, over many years, to turn out a large volume of journalism.

The laudanum-fantasies of the earlier prose have almost completely disappeared, and, save for an occasional personal reference, the self-regard and self-pity have gone, too. At times, his Catholic concerns show through rather self-consciously. He

is less that kind of Catholic critic who can make literary judgments in which religious values and literary ones are nicely
balanced than he is the crusading critic, even the propagan-
dist. For instance, in an early essay, 'Bunyan in the Light of
Modern Criticism' (*Merry England*, November, 1888) he attacks Bunyan's popularity. 'How any man with imagination
can bear the book [*Pilgrim's Progress*] I do not know. Bunyan
had inexhaustible invention, but no imagination. He saw a
reason for things, but not the things themselves.' Clearly, he
is attacking Bunyan for not writing like himself, for using
selected, suggestive detail, instead of lavish, ornate 'poetic'
descriptions, for remaining close to every-day reality instead
of soaring beyond the stars, for using a plain style instead of a
rococo one.

A later essay, '*The Pilgrim's Progress*—After Two Centuries'
(*Academy*, August, 1898), shows little change in point of view.
Thompson still finds Bunyan deficient in imagination, regrets
the absence of 'a single touch of fancy or magic phrase' and
finds 'the tinker's allegory by comparison [with Spenser] a
tinker's allegory'. 'It is not', he ends, 'what it has hastily been
called—a work of strong imagination; unless we are to use
that word in a special and unauthentic sense.' The tone of the
second essay is kindlier than the first; it scores one or two
shrewd hits at Bunyan's more plodding passages and his
frequent literalness; and Thompson does say: 'The familiar
ingenuity of the imagery, the symbolism, the allegorical details,
make them admirably suited to impress the daily understanding', even though he is quick to follow this with the patronizing:
'Nor does the cultivated mind fail to admire them, as we
admire the shrewd practical instances of a clever peasant-
talker.' In other words, Thompson refuses to admit, or only
grudgingly admits, Bunyan's art. All through the essays the
reader has the uneasy feeling that Bunyan cannot be all-owed
art because of his Nonconformist religious views. Nor is there in
the essays a clear recognition that in his great allegory of man's
life Bunyan transcends the narrow sectarianism of his doctrine
of election.

In what are mainly occasional book reviews, we could hardly
expect to find any attempt to work out a consistent philosophy
of literature or an aesthetic. Nor is Thompson free from

inconsistencies of judgment. In the main, he expresses the conventional contemporary opinions on his subjects, preferring to paraphrase received views rather than to strike out new lines of his own. Nevertheless, he is always well-informed, frequently vivacious, and covers a very wide range, from Crashaw, Butler and Dryden to Burns, Coleridge, Patmore, Swinburne and Ruskin in English poetry, Henry James, Poe and James Russell Lowell in American writing, Irish, French and Italian poets. Amidst the courteously-phrased observations there are, too, many incidental revelations of Thompson's temperament, although nobody, reading these later essays, would suspect, on their evidence alone, that the same author wrote 'The Hound of Heaven' and 'Orient Ode'.

Perhaps the most striking feature of these critical essays is the many comments on diverse authors which may be taken as implying, unconsciously, criticism of his own earlier poetic practice. Grouped together, they provide impressive evidence of his changed attitude towards his poetry and of the whetting of his sense of self-criticism. Let us look at a few such statements. Writing on Crashaw, so influential in his own earlier days, he says: 'Had he but possessed the control of his own gift, indeed, no minor rank would have been his; for his great moments are unsurpassable in their kind. So rare an artist, he was also an unsteady artist, of the most capricious taste. . . . His sins are virtues which have overshot their mark'; and later: 'His most extraordinary conceits jostle the most triumphant imagery. And they are both of the one texture—the conceits are the images gone wrong, the images the conceits come right'; while this is the perfect comment on his own earlier verse: 'His fervour and sincerity are never doubtful when his taste is more than doubtful.'

Of Coleridge, whose influence he often acknowledged ('Coleridge was always my favourite poet'), he wrote: 'Yet these vast and varied powers flowed away in the shifting sands of talk; and what remains is but what the few and locked pools are to the receding ocean which has left them casually behind without sensible diminution of its waters', with which may be contrasted Patmore's infinitely more sympathetic understanding of Coleridge's character and accomplishment.

Among other relevant comments we find these: on Wilfrid

Scawen Blunt, 'When he writes free of bonds, he tends to diffuseness, to an over-lavish outpour of himself'; on Meredith's 'Ode on the French Revolution', 'Never has he been more intermittently careless of grammatical construction, obscuring what is already inherently difficult'; on Symons' view of the Decadents, 'We should certainly derive from him the impression that the nerves of the period had been cultivated at the expense of its brains'; on Thomas Davis, 'There is visible a tendency to cheap imagery, facile imagery devoid of selectness'; on Yeats' stories, 'For all that, we have no patience with the last and longest story, "Rosa Alchemica", which is totally distinct from the rest and resembles the recital of an opium-dream. Like everything else in the book, however, it is beautifully written—in long, slow, undulating sentences, easy and sinuous in their progress as the motion of a serpent'; on Swinburne's prose, 'The duplicative and triplicative pother of words never stops'; on Dowson's poetry, 'Derivativeness condemns him, as it would a French writer, to the minor ranks.' In short, it would be easy to compile from Thompson's essays a short anthology of comments which, although applied by him to other writers, would amount to a reasoned criticism of aspects of his own poetry.

Side by side with these are other passages which may be read as self-justifications, as, for instance, when he writes of Mangan's use of others' poems:

'Poetry is a rootedly immoral art, in which success excuses well-nigh everything. That in the soldier is flat blasphemy which in the captain, the master of his craft, is but commendable daring. Exactly as a great poet may plagiarize to his heart's content, because he plagiarizes well (since Spartan law holds good in literature, where stealing is honourable, provided it be done with neatness and dexterity) so the truly poetical translator may rewrite a foreign poem and call it a translation, nor will anyone seriously object except the excellent person who understands something of translation and nothing of poetry.'

The names of Mangan, Poe, Baudelaire and Coleridge, drug-takers and drunkards, appear frequently in his essays, sometimes in a context as revealingly personal as this, on Baudelaire and Poe:

'The Frenchman who had exchanged, as it were, his store of
human life-blood for strange artistic vibrations, fashioned from
those poisoned dreams masterpieces of form, permanent mani-
festations of what he purchased from art at the expense of
life. The American, abandoning the main currents of the
national life around him, nonetheless drew, from his very
loneliness, his suffering, his despair, the joy of the artist. Neither
of these could ever have regretted their strange barter. . . .
But it was quite otherwise with Mangan. . . . Mangan
was incapable of learning from realities—that was the secret
of his temperament. . . . Mangan, the poet-dreamer, who
sought vaguely from life the fleeting illusions of a lost poetry.'

Thompson is not uncritical of the writers he deals with, but
his approach is generally the 'appreciative' one. He writes of
his likes rather than his dislikes; he enjoys reading and tries to
communicate his pleasure. In fact, he wrote once: 'My editors
complain that I don't *go* for people—I am too lenient.' He is
happier with writers of the past, mediaeval lyrists, Goldsmith,
Crashaw, Coleridge, Mangan, than he is with more than a few of
his contemporaries. His taste is his guide, rather than any set
principles of literary judgment. On questions of prosody, he
tends to follow Patmore's theories, sometimes clumsily para-
phrasing him as in his article on 'Mr. Bridges and Metre'.
Elsewhere, his remarks on metrics are pedestrian.

I can find in Thompson's criticism little trace of a specifically
Catholic aesthetic, nor any real attempt to face up to the basic
problems of the relationship between literary and moral canons.
But much of it reflects the Catholic temper of his mind, not
so much in his reviews for secular papers as in those written
mainly for Catholic eyes. In an essay on D'Annunzio for the
Academy his Catholic values enable him to praise the Italian's
style, while condemning his 'morbid passions'. On the other
hand, his review of a book on mysticism by the Catholic,
Algar Thorold, is searchingly critical and unbiased.

The general impression left by the prose is of a lively mind,
well-read, sensible, and delighting in literature, but belonging
more to a 'bookman' than to a first-rate critic. Little in his
articles may not be found in the writings of a score of competent
book-reviewers of the time. Certainly, except for the unconscious

personal revelations and the recurrence of themes treated in his poetry, there is small evidence of an original vision. To read the essays is to take pleasure in a confident taste, a large sympathy and polished writing, but to find no special illumination. Occasionally, a forced comparison recalls the excesses of his verse, as, for example: 'The gods are in pairs, male and female; and if Dryden was the Mars of English satire, Pope was the Venus—a very eighteenth-century Venus, quite as conspicuous for malice as for elegance', or 'Were "Kubla Khan", for instance, mere nonsense-verse, it would still be enthralling poetry by the power of the sound alone.'

Yet there are also acute judgments tellingly phrased; for instance, on a play of D'Annunzio's: 'The very skylarks are *fin de siècle*. "One", says Alessandro, "fell, all of a sudden, at the feet of my horse, heavy as a stone, and lay there, dead, struck by its own frenzy, by having sung with too much joy." It is only a decadent skylark that would do that', or, on mysticism: 'The whole Quietist business turns on matters which John Bull has gruffly made up his mind no fellow can understand, and, therefore, they cannot be worth any fellow's understanding. The beef and pudding of spirituality are good enough for him, and should be good enough for everybody else'; and, on Dumas père: 'He retained from childhood all his natural virtues, his natural faults, unmodified and without a notion of modifying them.'

His point is sometimes made, too, with a pleasing gentle wit:

'It was long a conviction in the mind of the average English Protestant that Catholicity exerted a stunting influence on literary development, a belief which the educational disabilities incidental to English Catholicity for some time tended to confirm. The idea in the Protestant mind was something after this fashion—that from Martin Luther came the Reformation, from the Reformation came those twin gifts of Heaven, Good Queen Bess and William Shakespeare, from Good Queen Bess came our greatness, and from William Shakespeare came our literature. Q.E.D.'

And he writes of mysticism with something of Patmore's firm good sense: 'The mystic is not . . . a student of mysticism, any more than a scientist is one who studies books on science. Nor yet is he a *devotee*, a devout practiser of religion. Mysticism is an interior ladder, at the summit of which is God. The mystic endeavours, by a rigid practical virtue, combined with prayer, meditation, and mortification of the sense, to arrive at a closer union with the Creator.'

However, a consistent view of the nature of poetry is far to seek in Thompson's prose. At one time he would have it thus:

'The world—the universe—is a fallen world. . . . That *should* be precisely the function of poetry—to see and restore the Divine idea of things, freed from the disfiguring accidents of their Fall. . . . But of how many poets can this truly be said? That gift also is among the countless gifts we waste and pervert; and surely not the least heavy we must render is the account of its stewardship. . . . To be the poet of the return to Nature is somewhat; but I would be the poet of the return to God.'

Thus the poet's function is to penetrate beyond the accidents of the Fall, so as to restore the Divine Idea by making manifest a beauty which reflects Divinity. By presenting this to man, he can make him aware of the goal to which he should aspire. Since Nature has no heart, Thompson writes in 'Nature's Immortality', 'Absolute Nature lives not in our life, nor yet is lifeless, but lives in the life of God: and in so far, and so far merely, as man himself lives in that life, does he come into sympathy with Nature, and Nature with him.'

This is sound enough as the rationale of a Catholic poet. Love and Nature are seen as imperfect in themselves and as adequately understood only when viewed sacramentally. Unfortunately Thompson contradicts himself; he proposes several other ends for poetry which seem to run counter to the sacramental view. For instance, he sees poetry as teaching, and forming the personality: 'The main function of poetry', he declares in a notebook, 'is to be a fruitful stimulus. That is, to minister to those qualities in us which are capable of increase. Otherwise it is a sterile luxury.' Elsewhere, he speaks of the poet as the maker: 'For the poet is an Elias, that when he comes he makes all things new', and in the poem, 'Carmen Genesis':

> Poet! still, still thou dost rehearse
> In the great *fiat* of thy Verse,

Creation's primal plot;
And what thy Maker in the whole
Worked, little maker, in thy soul
Thou work'st and men knew not.

At other times, he would declare that poetry is suffering: 'Every great poem is a human sacrifice', he wrote, and 'A poet is one who endeavours to make the worst of both worlds. For he is thought seldom to make provision for himself in the next life, and 'tis odd if he gets any in this. . . . He alone of men, though he travel to the Pit, picks up no company by the way; but has a contrivance to evade Scripture, and find out a narrow road to damnation.' Yet this gospel of the suffering poet is explicitly contradicted elsewhere by: 'It is usual to suppose that poets, because their feelings are more delicate than other men's must needs suffer more terribly in the great calamities which agonize all men. But, omitting from the comparison the merely insensible, the idea may be questioned. The delicate nature stops at a certain degree of agony, as the delicate piano at a certain strength of touch.'

These varying ideas of poetry and the poet, the product of moods, rather than of reasoned thought, can scarcely be said to cohere; various passing impulses are raised to the status of oracular generalizations. The one statement most taken up by Catholic critics, 'I would be the poet of the return to God', seems to have been a more enduring idea than the others, yet it is scantily developed in his essays, or in his poetry for that matter. Most of the poetry is about himself, Alice Meynell or his own poetry; the religious verse itself is of that personal kind that only occasionally attains the grand impersonality of the finest religious poetry.

The concept of poetry as pain was very close to Thompson's heart, as witness the sense of desolation which is one of the most insistent moods of his verse. 'I never had your lightness of heart,' he wrote to Wilfrid Meynell, 'nor was I ever without sad overshadowings of the hurrying calamity.' In his later years, however, he viewed experience less masochistically, and learned to give a religious value to pain. He detested the perverse quality of Swinburne's algolagnic adoration of Pain, and contrasted it with the Christian view, in which suffering is offered up to God, for Christ's sake. So, in 'Sanctity and Song', an essay of 1894, the example of St. Francis of Assisi is invoked for support in saying: 'Pain, which came to man as a penalty, remains with him as a consecration; his ignominy, by a Divine ingenuity, he is enabled to make his exaltation.'

Thompson's rationalizations of his self-inflicted miseries play only a minor part in 'Health and Holiness: A Study of the Relations between Brother Ass, the Body, and his Rider, the Soul', which is perhaps his finest prose piece, as it is one of his most deeply sincere. It shows many of the vices of his early prose style, yet contains much sturdy common sense and many touches of dignified feeling.

In passages like this:

'To our generation uncompromising facts and severities of conduct are found to be piteously alien; not because, as rash censors say, we are too luxurious, but because we are too nervous, intricate, devitalized. We find our austerities ready-made. The east wind has replaced discipline, dyspepsia the hair-shirt. Either may inflict a more sensitive agony than a lusty anchorite suffered from lashing himself to blood. . . . Man is his own mortification. . . . Merely to front existence, for some, is a surrender of self, a choice of ineludibly rigorous abnegation',

Thompson, as Everard Meynell put it, 'generalized too liberally from his own disabilities'. True, and there are moments, too, in which Thompson canonizes his early behaviour: 'Both Saint and Poet undergo a preparation for their work; and in both a notable feature of this preparation is a period of preliminary retirement.'

Nevertheless, 'Health and Holiness' forces us again to recognize Thompson's duality. Thrusting through the brambles of self-justification comes a logical argument about the nature of asceticism, based upon Franciscan ideals and upon the teaching of Patmore, whose definition of the body, 'Creation and Creator's crowning good', is quoted in the essay. Thompson stresses the subordination of the body to the spirit, and to the demands of the creative impulse, and the increased spiritual energy which both saint and poet can win from ascetic practices. But he also points to the intricate relationship between soul and body, saying that the older rigid asceticism pressed too hard upon the latter: 'Brother Ass, poor Brother Ass, had been inhumanly ridden; and but for his stubborn constitution would have gone nigh to hamper the sanctity he could not prevent.' In words which presage modern developments in psychosomatic medicine and psycho-analysis, he says: 'We can no longer set body against spirit and let them come to grips after the light-hearted fashion of our ancestors. We realize that their intertwinings are of infinite delicacy, endless multiplicity; no stroke upon the one but is innumerably reverberated by the other. We cannot merely ignore the body; it will not be ignored, and has innumerable avenues of retaliation.'

This he pleads for health as well as holiness, for a respect for the body which will not submit it unthinkingly to the extravagant mortifications of the past, 'the showy austerities of our forefathers'. 'The co-operation of the body must be enlisted in the struggle against the body. It is the lusts of the healthy body which are formidable; but to war with them the body (paradoxically) must be kept in health; the soldier must be fed, though not pampered. Without health, no energy; without energies, no struggle.' This ideal is a wise asceticism so controlled as to preserve the best powers of the body, and he ends: 'Health, I have well-nigh said, is Holiness. What if Holiness be Health? Two sides of one truth. In their co-ordination and embrace resides the rounded answer. It is that embrace of body and spirit, Seen and Unseen, to which mortality, sagging but pertinacious, unalterably tends.' There are some biographical touches in the essay, including an odd episode, reminiscent of one of Conan Doyle's flights of self-deception, in which Thompson claims to have seen a fairy, although he at once dismisses it as a hallucination. Yet, if we overlook the simplified picture of mediaeval asceticism, the essay speaks with stirring sincerity of a balanced Catholic outlook that recognizes the claims of the spirit but does not, on that account, despise the body, and, equally important, expounds the naturalness of sanctity.

Thompson's other prose works may be passed over very briefly. Two biographies, of St. John Baptist de la Salle and of St. Ignatius Loyola, fall into the category of hack-work, being commissions obtained for him by Wilfrid Meynell and conscientiously carried out, under what spurs we do not know,

with little real enthusiasm for the subjects. Both consist largely
of compilations from encyclopaedias and earlier biographies in
the British Museum. In the case of the book on Loyola, Meynell, with his usual caution, doled the money out to Thompson
at the rate of £1 for every three pages of manuscript handed in
to the Serendipity Shop. This, the longest of his prose works,
was published posthumously in 1909, after revision by an Ignatian scholar, Father J. H. Pollen. The style is quite undistinguished, save for a mixed metaphor here and there, reminiscent of his poetic practice: 'The Excalibur of Ignatius was
now forged; the Spiritual Exercises which he had evolved from
his own experience at Manresa—a graduated process of religious preparation based on subtle spiritual psychology—a
turn-stile through which only the fit and few could pass.'
Neither in this work nor in that on the founder of the Christian
Brothers were the sympathies of the ailing Thompson engaged.
He did what he was paid to do, but the works are dispirited.
No trace of the energy of the flamboyant poet emerges from the
grey, tired, plodding pages.

XIII

Alone in Crowded Life

TIRED Thompson undoubtedly was in these later years, spiritually fatigued with the exhaustion of a man who knows that his
creative powers are exhausted, and physically worn out with the
debilitations of tuberculosis. His weariness of soul is plain enough
in the few poems he published after 1897. These were mostly
lengthy odes in the by now faint carbon of Patmore's *Unknown
Eros* form, produced, nearly all of them, as pieces of versified
journalism for importunate editors.

H. M. Massingham's request for a poem on Queen Victoria's
Diamond Jubilee for the *Manchester Guardian* ('We must have the
copy by the afternoon of the 21st') was supplied within the
given three weeks by an ode full of hollow rhetoric and assumed
feeling, but containing a flash or two of the old Thompson,
especially in the lines commemorating the Victorian poets,
Tennyson, Browning, the Rossettis, Arnold, and, inevitably,
Patmore; who is described in these lines:

> Last came a shadow tall, with drooping lid,
> Which yet not hid
> The steel-like flashing of his armèd glance;
> Alone he did advance,
> And all the throngs gave room
> For one that looked with such a captain's mien.

But the real poetry in this lengthy ode comes in the opening
lines, which give a vivid, objective picture of the London streets
as Thompson remembered them in his days of desolation:

> Night; and the Street a corpse beneath the moon,
> Upon the threshold of the jubilant day

That was to follow soon;
Thickened with inundating dark
'Gainst which the drowning lamps kept struggle; pole
And plank cast rigid shadows; 'twas a stark
Thing waiting for its soul,
The bones of the preluded pomp.

For the *Academy* was written a similar poem to mark the close of the age, 'The Nineteenth Century', another rhetorical ode stuffed with the pompus platitudes of commissioned verse:

Thou, spacious Century!
Hast seen the Western knee
Set on the Asian neck,
The dusky Africa
Kneel to imperial Europe's beck,

and so on; but at its heart is a long passage on the scientific discoveries of the time, showing that something of his early desultory studies still clung to him, providing him with images more precise and apt than his customary vague references:

The unwonted green scale cleaving to the moist earth's face
Behold disclosed a conjugal embrace.

The passage immediately before this blatantly paraphrases Patmore's 'Crest and Gulf', and the succeeding lines owe a good deal to 'Comus'. But whereas Patmore, limiting science to its own sphere, had no doubt that the conflict between science and religion was more apparent than real, Thompson, after paying tribute to individual scientists, calls science 'a thing of sightless prophecies . . . working dull way by obdurate, slow degrees'.

The high-falutin language of these journalistic odes in which Thompson endeavours to lend some emotional grandeur to his subject is a measure of the hollowness of their sentiments. Their mechanical quality comes, of course, partly from the circumstances of their composition. 'Peace', which celebrates the signing of the treaty which ended the South African War in 1902, with lines like these:

Peace:—as a dawn that flares
Within the brazier of the barrèd East,
Kindling the ruinous walls of storm surceased
To rent and roughened glares,

was actually written some time before the occasion it purports to commemorate, at the request of the editor of the *Daily Chronicle* who wanted something standing that he could print at once when news of the treaty came through. It is no wonder that Thompson's jubilation sounds empty and that the chief burden of the ode is a doleful warning against a forgetful, false peace.

Thompson has ceased to find much point or purpose in poetry. He merely put on what he considered to be the appropriate expression for the occasion, and turned out the required number of lines, booming emptily from the page, and written in a vacuum of experience. What, for instance, had he in common with Cecil Rhodes, on whose death he wrote an ode for the *Academy* on April 12, 1902?

C. Lewis Hind tells how it was written:

'His chief regret was that his Muse had deserted him; so when on the morning after the death of Cecil Rhodes, I managed to lure him to the office and persuaded him that his Muse had not deserted him, and that he could write an "Ode on the Death of Cecil Rhodes" better than anybody else, he flushed, and his strange eyes sparkled. He brought in the "Ode" on press day, hours late; he fumbled in various pockets of his time-worn clothes for the bits of paper on which it was written, thanked me profusely when I gave him half-a-crown to purchase some dinner, and promised to return at 9 p.m. to read a proof. He arrived at ten, *exalté* with port and laudanum; he read the proof standing and swaying. When he had finished it he said, his enunciation a little blurred, "It's all right, Hind. No corrections." '

No corrections, indeed. The Rhodes poem is the versified equivalent of an obituary editorial, with, scattered pathetically among the verbiage, echoes from Thompson's heart, now virtually dry of poetry, little whispers from the empty shell of his earlier self. He praises Rhodes' vision rather than his acts, and when speaking of this 'dreamer', speaks of himself:

> But for the dreams,
> For those impossible gleams
> He half made possible; for that he was
> Visioner of vision in a most sordid day.

The last line is certainly a more appropriate description of Thompson than of Rhodes. And, at the end, his own sense of deprivation and his wish for death, expresses itself in the quiet sadness of

> There let him cease from breath,—
> Alone in crowded life, not lonelier in death.

One later poem, 'To the English Martyrs,' stands out from the stodgy inflation of the newspaper odes. This was inspired by the former site of Tyburn Tree, on Edgware Road, part of Thompson's normal beat. The poem shows Thompson seized by a subject which genuinely moved him—the personalities and the courage of the English Catholics who died for their faith—More, Fisher, and the others. From the impressive opening:

> Rain, rain on Tyburn tree,
> Red rain a-falling;
> Dew, dew on Tyburn tree,
> Red dew on Tyburn tree
> And the swart bird a-calling.
> The shadow lies on England now
> Of the deadly-fruited bough;
> Cold and black with malison
> Lies between the land and sun;
> Putting out the sun, the bough
> Shades England now!

to the end, there are many felicitous lines; for instance, his description of More contains a touch of that gaiety of heart so typical of the great English Chancellor:

> Ah, happy Fool of Christ, unawed
> By familiar sanctities,
> You served your Lord at holy ease!
> Dear Jester in the Courts of God—
> In whose spirit, enchanting yet,
> Wisdom and love, together met,
> Laughed on each other for content!

The poem is, however, long-winded, and, even in this tribute to the 'purple dynasty', the poet's own concerns must obtrude. Towards the end, he expresses his consciousness of the superiority of real life to poetic fantasies, the power of action as against the inertia of empty dreams:

But more lofty eloquence
Than is writ by poet's pens
Lives in your great deaths. O these
Have more fire than poesies!
And more ardent than all ode
The pomp and raptures of your blood.

So, as the old century yielded place to the new, Thompson
lived out his last sad, exhausted years, industriously penning his
reviews, living in numerous lodgings in the northern town,
including various houses where his landlady was the wife of
Meynell's printer, reading and dozing in the British Museum,
sitting long hours in the 'thirty public-houses in the immediate
neighbourhood of this house' of which he once claimed intimate
knowledge to a guest of the Meynells, and sometimes blowing on
the ashes of his poetic gift. The Meynell children were fast
growing away from him; the household which had for years
been his only real home was beginning to break up, as the elder
children sought their independence. Alice Meynell, too, while
still generous and kindly, had less time for him. Thompson had
long known that her affection for him came from the merest
corner of her crowded heart, and that his own romanticized
adoration was as unrealistic as that for his Manchester statue.
'I am unhappy', he wrote to her, 'when I am out of your sight,
but you, of course, have no such feeling in reference to me. Now
my sense of this inspires me with a continual timidity about
inflicting my society on you in any way, unless you in some way
signify a desire for it.'

His indolence of spirit increased. He lay later and later in bed,
ignoring his own injunctions written in exercise-books or stuck
on his wall. He missed more and more appointments. Alice
Meynell wrote to one of the family during this period: 'Francis
Thompson has just arrived, at about eight-thirty to the seven
o'clock dinner, or rather to the one-thirty luncheon, for that was
the meal he chose, as he was going to confession tonight. I
think it is the same confession that kept him many moons ago.'
He could not bring himself to rise for Mass every Sunday morning. He was so late with his copy that the *Athenaeum* staff pretended that the paper was going to press some days earlier, in
the hope that they might have his contribution in time for the
actual printing day. Thompson saw through the device, however,

and recorded in a notebook: 'Remember the new *Athenaeum* dodge testifies against you.'

Unquestionably, this increased lassitude was in great part the result of failing health. The cheap exercise-books, filled with jottings, aspirations, diary entries and drafts of poems, and the mass of journalism he wrote testify to the fact that his accidie was no permanent state. At times, however, it was a close go. More than once, he was seen standing late at night in the light of the flares on the bookstalls in Bishop's Road hastily scribbling in pencil the final pages of some over-due article. He would write until the very last instant before the light was extinguished, dash into the shop to sell his review-copy, then rush to the post-box to despatch his article—if he had a stamp.

During these last years, Wilfrid Meynell, despite his own complex problems of writing and family cares, treated the poet with unfailing tact and friendliness. When, one Christmas, Thompson wrote to his benefactor: 'Every happy wish to you, dear Wilfrid, and may God be as kind to you as you have ever been to me', the wish came from the very centre of his heart. The shrinkage of the Meynell household meant a move for the remaining ones to an apartment in Granville Place, whither Thompson would tramp from his lodgings in Elgin Avenue and elsewhere, in the rain or sleet. There must have been occasions on which all Meynell's resources were put to the test, as commissions and agreements carefully obtained for the poet were forgotten in his erratic alternations of activity and idleness, of optimism and pessimism. The papers left behind him at his death yielded a rich harvest of unopened or unanswered letters requesting articles for encyclopaedias promised but undelivered, books of poetry or anthologies planned, essays projected. And yet Thompson would inflate the slightest reverse into a world-shaking calamity. When a magazine rejected a poem 'of an Imperialist nature' he had submitted to it, he lamented to Meynell, 'Try as I will, all doors are shut against me.'

After his friend, C. Lewis Hind, left the *Academy*, Thompson wrote more frequently for the *Athenaeum*, whose editors offered him every indulgence and accepted work from him until almost the time of his death. Perhaps the most grotesque of his ventures at this time was into the field of drama. We can only wonder what freakish impulse persuaded him, who had so little understanding of human beings, and not the faintest knowledge of the needs of the theatre, that he could write plays. His lack of self-criticism can hardly be better illustrated than by the two plays, 'Napoleon Judges: A Tragedy in Two Scenes' and 'Man Proposes, But Woman Disposes; Un Conte sans Raconteur. In Two Scenes.'

The first is a miniscule piece of crude melodrama about one of Napoleon's officers who callously shoots a deserter, the officer's mistress, and Napoleon's intervention in the affair. This speech provides a fair specimen of the dialogue:

Napoleon: Aye, the harlot's mercy he shall have. Habitation of lust and death! he had better have stroked the sabre's edge than you, kissed the musket's mouth than yours! The sword sometimes spares, the musket sometimes misses; the harlot, never! Fair Destruction! he has clasped you a thought too close to his breast.

Thompson submitted the playlet to William Archer, whose reaction, not surprisingly, was unfavourable; it was also rejected by *T. P.'s Weekly* in 1903. 'Man Proposes, But Woman Disposes' is a dreadfully laboured contemporary comedy, almost completely static, with speeches of Shavian length, but no trace of Shavian wit, all about nothing in particular and amounting to a painful pastiche of Oscar Wilde and nineteenth-century 'tea-cup' comedy.

His health became more and more of a burden to him. A typical complaint to Wilfrid Meynell says: 'I have been full of worry, depression, and unconquerable forebodings.' From about 1903, he became steadily worse; what had before been to some extent a self-indulgence in thoughts of death and a melancholy scrutiny of his face in the mirror of the cosmos became inescapable realities. The very streets of London, which had been his true home, where he had loved to walk and dream in all weathers, which had provided him with bed, sitting-room and library, now became oppressive to his sick nerves. His talkativeness increased; his repetitions piled up still more maddeningly; his constant need for opium nagged at him like a rotten tooth. 'When he spent an evening explaining that last August was hot, but this hotter', wrote Everard Meynell, 'his cry really was "Where is my laudanum?" ' At the end of 1905, his illness had advanced so far and the prospects of his surviving another London winter seemed so slender that Wilfrid Meynell felt it imperative to send him to lodge at Crawley, in Sussex, close by a monastery of his beloved Franciscans.

The Prior at Crawley was Thompson's old friend, Father Anselm. The two had kept in touch since Pantasaph days. But the poet was reluctant to go, feeling that, as the end was near, any severance from his dear friends might be the last. 'I feel depressed at going away from you all' he wrote to Everard Meynell; 'it seems like a breaking with my past, the beginnings of I know not what change, or what doubtful future.'

When he got to Crawley, in 1906, the friars did all they could to make him welcome; he was invited to the various ceremonies at the monastery; biting his great pipe, he discussed cricket and philosophy with the Prior. His early letters show him suffering from the cold: 'I just manage to get on when it's not cold, and have a horrible time when it is. . . . O for Spring! and not the fraudulent substitute which of late years has been rather worse than winter.' But as the season changed he cheered up somewhat: 'I am, thank God, far from being as bad as I was in London last winter, and should have been again, or rather worse, had I been exposed to the condition of my life in London and its horrible fogs and smoke, which are killing to me.'

He stayed at Crawley until well into 1906. In April, Father Anselm quitted the monastery to take up duties at a foundation at Oxford, leaving Thompson desolate at the loss of this understanding friend whom he was never to see again; when Thompson died, the Franciscan was in Rome. The poet was becoming increasingly sensitive to heat and cold, to noise and the company of others, and he kept himself in bed as long and as often as possible. His will on worldly matters seems to have diminished to vanishing point, yet he could still rally to protest at the suggestion that he was seriously ill, and must go to hospital. 'It is all baseless nonsense', he expostulated to Wilfrid Meynell.

When the weather improved, he came back to London, to lodge at Kilburn and to sink into an even greater lethargy, broken only by spasms of journalistic work. The staff of the *Athenaeum*, aware of his condition, handled him as gently as the Meynells did. But nothing could now halt Thompson's steep descent down the slope towards death.

In August, 1907, Wilfrid Meynell was shocked by his looks—
the gaunt bones of his face standing out, his little body emaciated,
his hands and limbs trembling. With his one thought to get the
poet out of London again, he approached his friend, Wilfrid
Scawen Blunt, who readily agreed to the request that Thompson
be allowed to stay at a cottage on Blunt's estate at Newbuildings
in Sussex. When Blunt first met Thompson in 1898, he had
already had his curiosity aroused by Meynell's story of the
poet's early life and experiences as a vagrant, and he responded
warmly to Thompson's personality. 'On the whole, I liked him,'
he records in his diary for October 12, 1898, 'for he is quite simple
and straightforward.' 'Only,' he adds, 'it was difficult to think
of him as capable of any kind of strength in rhyme or prose.'

Yet Thompson was not easily persuaded to Sussex. He made
all kinds of excuses; he delayed; he changed his mind. Finally,
Everard Meynell had to agree to accompany him and stay for
a few days before Thompson would take the, to him, perilous
journey. Wilfrid and Everard arranged to call one day for the
poet at eleven. But when they arrived, his bed was empty and
his landlady could throw no light on his disappearance, being
as astonished as the Meynells that he should set out so early.
When Thompson at length turned up, he explained that he had
been to a distant part of London to purchase a special kind of
pork-pie on whose powers of sustenance he relied to keep up his
strength for the journey.

On August 24, the two men arrived at Newbuildings Place.
Here, since 1895, Blunt had made himself a hermitage. The
grey stone house, dignified and comely, stood on a hilltop looking across the oak-rimmed fields, farms and hedged meadows
towards the long blue line of the Sussex downs. Blunt delighted
in the woods 'lovely in green and gold, nightingales singing
night and day from every hedge'; in his Arab robes he strolled
along the box-edged paths among attar roses imported from the
East and the more familiar flowers of England; he luxuriated in
the peacocks flaunting themselves on his lawns and the Arab
mares prancing in the fields. Perhaps, on the surface, nobody
could have been less congenial to the devout, sickly poet than
this burly, healthy, ambiguously Catholic convert, who doubted
the reality of a future life, who openly professed Mohammedan-
ism, who was to receive the Last Sacraments on his death-bed,

yet stipulated in his will that he be buried in unconsecrated ground, without church rites, and wrapped in his Eastern travelling carpet. Blunt, aristocratic rebel, anti-imperialist, passionate Sussex-lover, picturesque defender of the rights of Ireland, devoted to Oriental ways and culture, diplomat and traveller, English squire, poet of love and action, and crank, had kept in close contact with Wilfrid Meynell for some years, and transcribed into his diaries many of his friend's opinions on such things as Modernism, and long accounts of Francis Thompson's career.

At the time of Thompson's visit, Blunt was sixty-seven, tall, robust, with a big, flaming beard, and had still fifteen vigorous years ahead of him. He is almost the only independent witness who has left a full account of the poet's last days, apart from the frankly partial Meynells. His evidence is coloured somewhat by the patronizing attitude of a healthy extravert who loved nothing better than to gallop his Arab horses through the English lanes, while he stood upright in the stirrups, his Eastern robes streaming behind him, for an ailing introvert, but otherwise it is dispassionate, and valuable for the fullness and frankness of its picture of the poet at the end of his tether.

When Everard arrived from London with his charge, they were lodged at Gosbrook, a guest-cottage on the estate.

'The poor poet seemed to be in the last stage of consumption', Blunt recorded. . . . 'He is emaciated beyond credibility, his poor little figure a mere skeleton, under clothes lent him for the occasion by the Meynells. He has the smallest head and face of any grown man I ever saw, colourless, except for his sharp nose, where all light is concentrated, and his bright eyes. It is the face of a Spanish sixteenth-century Saint, almost that of a dying child. When he had rested a bit at Gosbrook, I drove him down to tea at Newbuildings, and he revived there a little and began to talk with Everard and me. I took him a toddle round the garden, but he does not know one flower from another any more than twelve years ago when he could not distinguish an oak from an elm. The poppy was the only flower he recognized. "Ah, there's a poppy", he said, as if greeting a friend.'

The two dissimilar men talked much together, Thompson

agreeing, perhaps out of lethargy, with Blunt's hatred of European civilization, and the 'destruction wrought by it on all that was beautiful in the world'. But he opened his heart to Blunt's questions about himself, told him of his relations with his father and his wasted years of pretended study. 'I was in every way an unsatisfactory son', he said. 'On the whole', Blunt wrote, 'I find Thompson much saner and more sensible than I expected. Of his poetry he talked reasonably and said that he took a soberer view of his talents now than he had done as a boy.'

At Gosbrook, David Roberts and his wife, both servants of Blunt, provided fires and breakfast for Everard and Francis. Thompson rose very late, as usual, but also went to sleep late. Everard used to see him in the small hours, propped up in bed with pillows, reading his prayer-book by the light of a candle. Blunt summoned Neville Lytton, his son-in-law, to Newbuildings Place to make a profile drawing in chalks of the poet. Thompson was so weak that he could pose for only a few minutes at a time, but in his admirable sketch, Lytton caught the poet's lean, haggard look and straggling beard, and his sad introspective glance and tense mouth which tell of immense suffering. He looks like a very ill, very devout Franciscan. A priest, Father Gerrard, who visited him at Blunt's, found him 'a dying man, and an old man, although only forty-eight years of age'. But he added, 'Still, even in his extremity, the characteristics of his life were manifest, a shrinking from fellowship, a keen perception and love of the Church, a ready and masterful power of language.'

As the days crept by, Thompson wrote a little, but was too debilitated to do much. Everard Meynell had to return to London, so Blunt had Thompson removed to one of his cottages called Rascall's Corner, Southwater, where David and his wife lived. Blunt's own nurse and a doctor visited him there, although Thompson's evasions made a diagnosis of his real condition very difficult. Late in September, Blunt wrote to Wilfrid Meynell: 'I shall be very glad to keep Thompson on here as long as the weather continues fine.' He was, at that time, according to his host, 'somewhat better in health, but intellectually defunct'. He did, however, manage to complete his last article for the *Athenaeum*, written with great labour, a piece on Sir Thomas Browne, which appeared in the October 19th issue.

Every day, Blunt had the poet brought over by carriage to luncheon, 'very feeble and quite silent, except it be on some trivial subject. He seems incapable of bringing his mind to bear on any complex thought, and sits through the afternoon with a volume of Dickens' *Martin Chuzzlewit* sometimes held upside down in his hand, which he does not read, nodding, and three parts asleep, like a very aged man. He seems happy, however, and I do not disturb him, nor does he ask that anyone should talk to him.' They used to lunch in the garden, where the wasps, particularly prevalent that summer, bothered Thompson.

'He used to appeal to me to help him when they got into his wine, "Will you please kill this wasp for me, I cannot do it, I have never killed anything in my life." At last one bit him, and he had his wrist bound up in lint with a strong solution of ammonia, and going to sleep soon after, it raised a blister which remained an interest to him till he died, wearing the rag, as saints are represented carrying the instruments of their martyrdom.'

Blunt soon became aware that, for all the generous care the poet was receiving, he was steadily sinking.

'We had become alarmed about him latterly, as since the weather began to break up, he has remained entirely indoors, shut in David's cottage with a big fire and windows carefully closed, a bottle of laudanum, David tells me, and ill with diarrhoea. It has reduced him to a skeleton. Meynell has sent a priest to see him, and I felt that any day he might go suddenly. He needs some one with him who can exercise control over him, but I doubt his living over Christmas. As an intellectual force he is already dead, and his poor body is dying too.'

Blunt was so afraid that the poet would die separated from his friends that he wrote urgently to Wilfrid Meynell, and, on October 16th, Everard came down to bring the wraith of Thompson back to London.

In his extremity, the whole world seemed to him to be his enemy. When an umbrella fell against him in the railway carriage, he said, seriously, 'I am the target of all disasters.' On arrival at London, he was put in lodgings where Wilfrid

Meynell came at once and was horrified at what he saw. 'Wilfrid,' said the poet, 'I am more ill than you think. I am dying of laudanum poisoning. I put myself in your hands.' The word that had been unspoken for a decade dropped between them like a curse. But Thompson was wrong; consumption, not laudanum, was killing him. At once, Meynell urged his friend to enter the Hospital of St. John and St. Elizabeth. Thompson, his resistance gone, made no protest, and on November 1st, he was placed in the care of the nuns. He weighed only five stone.

During his twelve days in the hospital, he was, for the most part, comfortable, save when the approach of his normal time for opium caused his body to cry out for it. He read W. W. Jacobs' *Many Cargoes* and his prayer-book, he dozed, and he tightly clasped the hand of Wilfrid Meynell who kept long vigils at the bedside.

When the end was near, a priest came and administered the Last Sacraments to him, which he received with great devoutness. The nuns who nursed him reported that he was 'all brow', and that his wide open eyes seemed always to be looking upwards. They heard him talking to himself, repeating the same thing over and over again, and at length they discovered that it was 'My withered dreams. My withered dreams.' He died at dawn on November 13, 1907, his medal of the Blessed Virgin still around his neck. All that he left was a tin box of rubbish, crammed with broken pipes and pens, unopened letters, a wickless spirit lamp, his toy theatre, as well as his notebooks, and, of course, his poems. He was buried in St. Mary's Cemetery, Kensal Green.

XIV

In No Strange Land

AFTER Thompson's death, there was that spontaneous revival of interest in him that usually, if temporarily, follows a poet's passing. Obituaries in the leading journals, such as Blunt's in the *Academy*, praised his religious sentiment, the originality of his vision, and the variety and colour of his imagery. Few of these, however, were without their reservations. As Christian Gauss, for instance, wrote in the *Nation*, three weeks after the poet's death: 'His execution is often inexcusably wretched; he cannot strike his note and hold it; when hard pressed he stuffs the gap with monstrous words and his ear fails him. The technical accomplishment which is always there to save Verlaine's worst is not evident even in Thompson's best, and it is perhaps for this reason that he has fallen so hopelessly far behind even his own deserts.'

Wilfrid Meynell, as Thompson's literary executor, had taken charge of the poet's papers. Loyal to his friend's memory and supremely confident of his greatness, he set about capitalizing, with all the force at his command, upon the interest revived by Thompson's death. Finding the essay on Shelley, rejected eighteen years before, he sent it again to the *Dublin Review*, with what result we have already seen. The great success of this piece gave a tremendous fillip to Thompson's reputation, and Meynell was not slow to take advantage of the excitement.

In 1908, he issued *Selected Poems by Francis Thompson*, a skilful culling from the poet's best work. Although the poetry had been neglected for years and almost forgotten, and the edition of *New Poems* had been a miserable failure, Meynell's selection sold over

20,000 copies in a couple of years. Thompson was entering his years of greatest popularity. The pedestrian biography of Loyola following in 1909 did nothing for his reputation, but it was a different matter with the three volumes of the *Works*, with which, in 1913, Meynell crowned his labours on Thompson's behalf. The first two volumes contained the poems issued in the three books published in Thompson's lifetime together with several uncollected poems and others found in manuscript, and the third consisted of a selection from the essays and reviews. This full-scale presentation of Thompson the writer was rounded out by Everard Meynell's admirable study of the man published in the same year. This first full revelation of Thompson's life and personality, which did much to dispel the rumours that had grown up of a hopelessly disordered and dissipated life, rivalled the *Works* in popularity.

On this solid basis of devotedly and intelligently presented work, Francis Thompson's writings became widely known and gained a renown which was to last for less than a decade. After that, his fame steadily declined, and he will never again recover the stature he had in the years just after the 1914–18 War. 'The Hound of Heaven', constantly reprinted, and frequently quoted, has become an integral part of the English poetic heritage, so, too, has 'In No Strange Land', from which a phrase, out of context, 'the many-splendoured thing' has been exploited to celebrate adultery in a book and a film, something stupefyingly different from what Thompson intended. Apart from these poems, Thompson's achievement is little known and revered today, except in Catholic circles.

He has, in fact, become a touchstone of literary quality for some Catholics. Chesterton was fond of him, and once wrote, in an oft-quoted phrase: 'Perhaps the shortest definition of the Victorian Age is that he stood outside it.' Father Joseph Husslein, S.J., found in his work 'something Teresian, something Ignatian, something, we may say, strictly Pauline, that is matched, too, by the Pauline vigour and subtlety and Franciscan simplicity with which he pursues his thoughts', and his old friend, Archbishop Kenealy said, 'The intellect of the world has been corrupted. Francis Thompson is the antidote.'

Because they prize his doctrine, such critics have given Thompson a supreme place in English poetry ('only beneath

Shakespeare', as Canon Sheehan wrote), and attribute non-Catholic lack of enthusiasm to an antipathy for his Catholic subjects and background. (It does not seem to occur to them that Hopkins should be subject to even more of the same disqualifications.) It is true that some writers, Austin Harrison and A. J. Symons among them, reacting against exaggerated Catholic estimates of Thompson's worth, have made it their business to treat him as a narrowly sectarian poet. Yet it is not only from the secular critic that serious attacks on Thompson's work have come recently. John Heath-Stubbs, a Christian poet and critic, whose sympathy with, for instance, Patmore, is strong, says in *The Darkling Plain:* 'He was a remarkable and unlikely phenomenon, but serious criticism cannot for a moment contend that he was a good poet.' And, writing in the Jesuit monthly, the *Month,* J. M. Cohen, a decade ago, said: 'He savours all the paraphernalia of the Church ritual with the shut-eyed rapture of a child sucking a particularly luscious sweet', and, 'As a mystic Thompson seems curiously uncritical of the relative intensities of his experience, relishing them all alike, I feel, with the same sensuous naïvety with which, on another plane, he revelled in the sound of words.'

The truth of the matter seems to be that while, at the present time, the bulk of Thompson's poetry is almost unknown to the ordinary reader or even to the student of literature, save for 'The Hound of Heaven', 'In No Strange Land', and perhaps 'Little Jesus' and 'To a Snowflake', among the inevitable anthology pieces, his reputation among possibly the greater number of Catholics is higher than Patmore's—higher indeed than it should be poetically, and yet lower than it deserves with those who do not share his faith.

For Thompson has suffered, with other poets of his generation, from the inevitable reaction of the post-World War I years and from the changed ideas of the nature of poetry shaped by Hulme, the Imagists, Pound and Eliot. A taste for a more cerebral style, care and economy in language and new concepts of rhythmical appropriateness has shown up the poverty of thought in Thompson's poems beneath the flamboyant words and the brash images. The discovery of Hopkins, too, with his fresh, energetic language, his emotional and intellectual power, his strong, yet sensitive personality, and his exact, searching vision made Thompson's achievement seem slight where it was not outdated.

As the nineteenth century receded too, it became manifest that Thompson had very little in common with the Metaphysical poets some of his contemporaries thought he resembled. There is a kinship with Crashaw, perhaps, the most baroque of the Metaphysicals, in his ecstatic flights, as well as in his frequent lapses of taste. But his roots, it is now plain, are in the nineteenth century; he shares his vision with that of the stricken band which includes Poe, Mangan, de Quincey, Baudelaire, Rimbaud, even James Thompson, as well as Francis Thompson's own co-religionists, Lionel Johnson and Ernest Dowson.

All of these, impelled by physical stresses, weakness of will, psychological inadequacy, or a combination of all three, to drink or drugs, are poets of the tainted vision, writers in whose work it is often difficult to distinguish the effects of their particular narcotic from the expression of a genuine imaginative experience. Most of them, too, were poets whose racked bodies compelled them to renunciations only half-elected, and who yearned for a peace which, however closely identified it may appear to be with religious concepts, must always arouse the suspicion that it was most passionately desired by them as a relief from the imperious claims of a craving or from the burden of a pain-wracked and enfeebled body.

And here we come up against the chief problems which arise from a study of Thompson's life in conjunction with his poetry. To what extent is he, as he has been claimed, a mystical poet, or, indeed, a religious poet? By this I mean to what degree does he make immediate in his poetry an awareness of God and of the poet's, and man's, relation to Him? How much of his poetry is visionary and how much merely hallucinatory? To what degree is his explicitly religious poetry diluted by self-pity, memories and escapism? As Paul Elmer More wrote, just after Thompson's death: 'Who shall untangle the threads of such a life, and say that this peace is born of faith's vision and this ecstasy is wrung from the body's defeat?'

I have tried, in the preceding pages, to show how much in Thompson's work is the direct product of his sense of personal inadequacy, his revulsion from normal adult life, his various shifts to evade mature responsibility, and the pains of the deprivation of opium. It does no real service to the poet to refuse to acknowledge that much of what he wrote is both a confession and an attempt at obfuscation, as well as a substitute for laudanum-fantasies, that his religious vision is frequently warped by a morbidity which comes from a sense of physical and spiritual desolation, that his love-poetry is gelid and unreal, and that, in his earlier phases, his praise of asceticism and his notion of the poet as one whose experience is won only through suffering are a rationalization of the wretched state to which an enfeebled will had reduced him. It is hard, too, to escape the conviction that Catholic praise for mediocre poems like 'Assumpta Maria', 'The Passion of Mary' and 'Lilium Regis', is mere family praise. One may be tempted to leave it at that, to say: 'Well, if Catholics find Francis Thompson a satisfactory poet for them, let them do so. There is no reason why, if they find his doctrine sound and his expression of it stimulating, they should not write books on "Francis Thompson as a Guide to Devotion" "The Message of Francis Thompson", providing they do not confuse doctrinal appropriateness with literary excellence.'

But the matter is not quite so simple. Not every Catholic is prepared to accept indifferent poetic workmanship as great poetry for the sake of its doctrine, especially when there can be found in Hopkins, for instance, a poetry which satisfies in both respects. At the same time, we cannot ignore the fact that five or six poems of Thompson have become part of the popular heritage of English poetry, and that, for every one person who knows a line of Donne, Crashaw, Mangan, or James Thompson, there are thousands for whom many lines of Francis Thompson are as familiar as lines of Shakespeare.

There is, therefore, a danger of stressing Thompson's weaknesses at the expense of his genuine talent, of falling into the Pelagian trap of attributing everything in his life and work to psychological factors, and thus of overlooking those things which give some of his work permanent value. The basic reality in his life was his deep and abiding religious faith, which was the source of a genuine power. We must face the fact that, for most of his life, Thompson was addicted to a drug, and simultaneously experienced agonies of guilt for this sin against the spirit. In so far as the drug-habit was an indulgence, a calculated retreat from the real world, it was a fault, and grievously did Thompson suffer for it, both as a man and as a poet. Yet who can judge him harshly, when we can only surmise what torments of mind and soul the man endured in his years of isolation, loneliness and pain?

For there is ample evidence that, his drug-habit, his social ineptness and his ignoring of the feelings of others aside, he was an innocent and a good man. For all his exasperating impact upon the lives of others, the words of reproof that have come down to us are few indeed. 'There was something lovable about him,' wrote the clear-eyed Katharine Tynan, 'about his simplicity, his humanity, his humbleness, which perhaps made the burden of his faithful friends lighter, as it made their grief heavier when he died.' And Patmore paid him the highest compliment he could when he said: 'He is of all men I have known most naturally a Catholic. My Catholicism was acquired, his inherent.' A cousin of the poet averred that the whole cause of his life-long trouble was that he had not succeeded in becoming a priest. We are reminded of the effect on Belloc's life and thought, even on the melancholy that seems so integral a part of his outlook, by his failure to secure a Fellowship at All Souls.

A recognition that Thompson's Catholicism went very deep ought not to prevent us recognizing that he had to struggle towards an understanding of its innerness and that in his poetry can be found the chart of his movement deeper and deeper into the heart of his faith. His was no steady development but a series of rises and falls. His soul was a constant battle-field between a genuine, sincere religious feeling and his accidie, between his anxious wish to fulfil the obligations of his faith by Sunday Mass and the inertness which kept him in bed so that he forgot the day or arrived to find the cleaners at work in the empty church. Yet Jesuit critics can find in his work, notably 'The Hound of Heaven', a habit of thinking which they characterize as Ignatian.

We may take it that Thompson, nourished in the provincial piety of his home, left Ushaw with normal devoutness, but with little real intellectual apprehension of his faith, or even a particularly warm feeling for it, as, in fact, the priests recognized. After Meynell rescued him from destitution, he had a breathing-space during which, in 'The Hound of Heaven', he looked

back over the false trails he had followed, and turned to God
with a sincerity which is manifest, even though to modern taste,
its expression may seem to show undue softness of feeling and
lack of incisiveness. But this was no Augustinian conversion, a
change of heart followed by a purified, resolute life. What was
to happen in Thompson's case is expressed in the words of St.
Paul: 'For I am delighted with the law of God, according to the
inward man. But I see another law in my members, fighting
against the law of my mind and captivating me in the law of sin
that is in my members' (*Romans* vii. 22–3). His struggle with
himself is mirrored in the extravagance of the early odes, with
their tearing nostalgia for laudanum, their attempts to escape
life in riotous capers of images, their confronting of the secret
places of the heart, their pathetic attempts to make Alice
Meynell and her children vessels for his pent-up affections.

Little of this poetry is overtly religious; although his devotion
to the Blessed Virgin sometimes adds a touch of tenderness to
otherwise desolate poems. Many of the early pieces are, in fact,
not even quasi-religious; yet his first two volumes reveal an
undercurrent of strain having its origin in a complex set of
moods, one of which is religious. And amidst so much worthless
verse, the other, durable Thompson is seen in, for example, 'A
Fallen Yew' and 'The Hound of Heaven', giving universal
meaning to his personal misfortunes. This is the Thompson who
tried to break into the ways of normal life through the Meynell
children and their mother; while the other Thompson be-
devilled the busy writing family. But his failure to cultivate adult
affections is reflected in the hyperboles, chill conceits and stale
bombast of 'Love in Dian's Lap' and *Sister Songs* and in the
poems on his loss of Katie King, such as:

> O Christ the Just, and can it be
> I am made for love, no love for me?
> Of two loves, one at least be mine;
> Love of earth, though I repine,
> I have not, nor, O just Christ, thine!
> Can life miss, doubly sacrificed,
> Kiss of maid and kiss of Christ?
> Ah, can I, doubly wretched, miss
> Maid's kiss, and Thy perfect kiss?

Years of self-involvement, of evasion, dreaming, and egocentric living had virtually dried up whatever capacity he may have had for human love. But he longed for it, and he continued to lament its absence from his life.

> Implacable sweet daemon, Poetry,
> What have I lost for thee!

he cries at the beginning of 'Laus Amara Doloris', and, in a poem 'A Double Need', addressed to Wilfrid Meynell, he mourns that, with the passing of his poetic gift, he has nothing at all to give his friend.

> Ah, gone the days when for undying kindness
> I still could render you undying song!
> You yet can give, but I can give no more;
> Fate, in her extreme blindness,
> Has wrought me so great wrong.
> I am left poor indeed;
> Gone is my sole and amends-making store,
> And I am needy with a double need.

This being so, we can hardly interpret Thompson's celibacy as a voluntary sacrifice in the interests of asceticism. He had just that kind of pyschology which would try to erect a principle of willed lovelessness out of a temperamental inadequacy.

Still even in the depths, the love of God was alive in him, and from his successive encounters with the Franciscan friars he came to see in the Franciscan ideal the fulfilment of what he had unwittingly sought for in poetry. One notebook entry shows his developing awareness of the inadequacies in his own experience:

'It is this lofty and unsought genuineness which makes the true poet like to the Franciscan, and the true Franciscan to the poet. For the Franciscan embodies in himself the poet's ideal, which is sensitive and candid self-realization—the spontaneous candour of a child combined with adult consciousness: while he has the native amity towards his fellow-mortals which, in the poet, is too often absorbed by egoism. Two things in this world *are* poetry, and luckily do not know it—the child and the Franciscan.'

The Pantasaph sojourn, in particular, reinforced the second

Thompson, especially when the influence of the friars combined with that of Patmore. The adolescent delight in liturgical trappings and incense disappears, and is replaced by the more profound religious and poetic insights of 'Contemplation' and 'The Mistress of Vision'.

At Pantasaph, Thompson realized that what he had taken for granted as a religious vision had been flawed by evasion, and egoism. It is a measure of the real depth of his capacity for religious experience that he did reach this point of self-appraisal, for there are many who never perceive how much their piety is diluted by such unworthy elements. He came, too, to realize how little real knowledge he had of life, and how little understanding of people, and that, once the vessel of his fantasies was shattered, he had too limited a human experience to provide him with material for true poetry. Thus his verse became clogged with laments for the fading of his vision, and for his slender hold on the mundane realities. 'The perceptions of the spirit', he admitted, 'are not indefinitely credible and sufficing without the occasional confirmation and assurance of the body.'

From the ashes of his despair arose a purer, more wholesome and more profound vision, of the innermost peace of God, of the real innocence of the uncorrupted spirit, of Divine love, of the glory of pain endured for God's sake alone, a vision which seemed shattered again by Patmore's death. It appeared at first that this event and Thompson's new maturity of insight as a man destroyed the poetry in him. The journalistic odes, save for an occasional flash, are hollow things, with thoughts and attitudes put on, like Sunday clothes, for the occasion only. With the reversion to laudanum, his book reviews take the place of his poetry, showing, if nothing else, a quick adaptable mind. Had the two Thompsons, then, disappeared, to be replaced by a competent Catholic journalist? Had the struggle between the real and the hallucinatory been abandoned by Thompson the man?

The answer comes in a ringing negative from two of his last poems, 'All Flesh' and 'In No Strange Land', the latter more than likely the very last poem he wrote. Here he passes beyond the merely devotional or pietistic to the mystical, and crowns his sad life with the attainment of the vision he had sought in many strange places. The best of the earlier religious poems, tend to identify religion with deprivation, to imply that to win the love of God one must pass by the joy of God's world. There is in them barely a whisper of the ecstasy of the mystic's union with God, which Patmore expressed in the Psyche odes. Of course, there are religious motifs and ideas in the early poems— the emptiness of Nature without God, the triumph of the soul over Death (although Death is itself often seen as a maternal bosom on which the tired soul finds oblivious rest), the dependence of man upon the sustaining power of God, the secret heart of man where God alone is at home, the place of the Blessed Virgin in the Divine dispensation. But much of the poetry itself is life-denying, which religion is not, and often enough the poem is wrenched back from indulgence in laudanum-memories to a religious context by a hasty last-minute reference.

Before the end, a chastened humility makes itself felt. In 'Any Saint', for all its echoes of Patmore, its halting metre and confessional quality, Thompson tries strenuously to make a self-denying approach to the divine humanity and to fling himself, with no reservation at all, on the mercy of God.

> Gird, and thou shalt unbind;
> Seek not, and thou shalt find;
> To eat
> Deny thy meat;
> And thou shalt be fulfilled
> With all sweet things unwilled.

In 'The Cloud's Swan-Song' he stills his clamorous despair at the fading of his poetic talent, with the resolve to accept life as it is, even though it means life stripped of fantasies.

Such poems lead up to 'All Flesh' and 'In No Strange Land' which, almost alone of Thompson's poems, might be called mystical. Here is the last fruit of his war with himself, a reconciliation of the physical and spiritual realities, a sudden blazing realization of the Incarnation, that central doctrine of Christianity which is barely mentioned or realized in his earlier poems. In these poems, Thompson wins by the inner religious strength of his heart, from his life of pain and desolation, a tremendous apprehension of the interdependence of the spiritual and the

material, which enables him both to recognize that he had previously tried to evade sustaining reality and to joy in his gain
without mourning his loss. It is not unlike the cries of Rimbaud
in 'Une Saison en Enfer': 'Cela s'est passé. Je sais aujourd'hui
saluer la beauté', and, 'Moi! moi qui suis dit mage ou ange,
dispensé de toute morale, je suis rendu au sol, avec un devoir
à chercher, et la réalité rugueuse à étreindre!'

In these last two poems, we find completed ideas intimated in
'To a Snowflake', with its not wholly congruous use of Thomas
Hood's 'Bridge of Sighs' metre, in which Thompson sees God's
power and presence in the perfection of the snowflake, and in
'Field-Flower' where he forsakes his cosmic roaming to peer
into the heart of a flower. Patmore's voice is still heard in 'All
Flesh':

> Mastering littleness
> Which the wise heavens confess,
> The frailty which doth draw
> Magnipotence to its law—

but now, instead of using the planets as playthings, Thompson
finds all wisdom in a humble blade of grass; this thing, product
of sun, moon and wind, this union of substance and essence, of
God and Nature, is like Patmore's violet:

> Epitomized with thee
> Was the mystery
> Which shakes the spheres conjoint—
> God focussed to a point.

Transferring the concept of 'To a Snowflake' to flesh and
human personality, the poet sees himself as the link between
God and the world of things, a bridge between two realities:

> Unfathomably framed
> Sister, I am not shamed
> Before the cherubin
> To vaunt my flesh thy kin.
> My one hand thine, and one
> Imprisoned in God's own.
> I am as God; alas,
> And such a god of grass!

214

In No Strange Land

> A little root clay-caught,
> A wind, a flame, a thought,
> Inestimably naught!

The vision here is as pure as Blake's; in and through the concrete Thompson sees the greatness of God; he sees, too, man's greatness and littleness.

The insight of 'All Flesh' is completed in the poem which Wilfrid Meynell found amongst Thompson's papers at his death, and gave the title of 'The Kingdom of God' above the poet's own 'In No Strange Land'. This, unfinished or not, unrevised or not, is Thompson's most perfect poem:

> O World invisible, we view thee,
> O world intangible, we touch thee,
> O world unknowable, we know thee,
> Inapprehensible, we clutch thee!
>
> Does the fish soar to find the ocean,
> The eagle plunge to find the air—
> That we ask of the stars in motion
> If they have rumour of thee there?
>
> Not where the wheeling systems darken,
> And our benumbed conceiving soars!—
> The drift of pinions, would we hearken,
> Beats at our own clay-shuttered doors.
>
> The angels keep their ancient places;—
> Turn but a stone, and start a wing!
> 'Tis ye, 'tis your estrangèd faces
> That miss the many-splendoured thing.
>
> But (when so sad thou canst not sadder)
> Cry;—and upon thy so sore loss
> Shall shine the traffic of Jacob's ladder
> Pitched betwixt Heaven and Charing Cross.
>
> Yea, in the night, my Soul, my daughter,
> Cry,—clinging Heaven by the hems;
> And lo, Christ walking on the water
> Not of Gennesareth, but Thames!

Now brought unforgettably together are the experience of

the streets and the experience of the heart, the certainty of the
continual Incarnation, the whole Divine economy, the sense of
God at one's hand and of the intersection of the timeless world
with the world of time. Here, in the repudiation of fantasy,
human responsibility is accepted and joyed in, the doctrine of
the Mystical Body asserted, and reality defined in its fullness.
Thompson had emerged from the dark forest of his life with a
vision we may call truly mystical; and he expressed it here in
language purged of affection and elaborations, with the plain
poetic beauty of his true self. Here was emergent that trait
which Father David Bourne found in him when he spoke to the
poet at Pantasaph: 'As men commonly understand the word,
there was no "fascination" about Thompson. There was something better. There was the *sancta simplicitas* of the true poet and
the real child.'

It was the potentiality in him for such a vision as 'In No
Strange Land' incarnates that drew people to him, and made
those who knew him best make light of his faults. Thompson
may, for most of his life, have done grievous harm to himself;
but he never injured anyone else. It may be that, in a half-
century or less, many readers will find the praise of Dylan
Thomas's earlier poems as incomprehensible as others now find
that of Thompson's earlier work; yet how different the ends of
these two men, how rounded and complete at last in Thompson
the religious vision, how imperfect and stammering the expression of it in Thomas. For, in the last analysis, the poet in Francis
Thompson is less important than the religious man. Finally,
from beneath the self-praise, the assertions of poetic immortality, there sounds the inner humility which can mock thus in a
notebook at a newspaper critic who called him a 'mystic': 'I
conclude that a mystic must be a person who mystifies people—
anything, probably, between a card-trick man and a Russian
Minister. It seems possible, therefore, that despite a virtuous life
I may be a "mystic"; but then it is clear that I am a very little
one. *Parturiunt montes, nascetur ridiculus m(ystic)us.* Would it be
better—*mus(ticus)*?' F. T.

This life was no disaster which was crowned with a good death,
and with the achievement of the tranquil integration that saw
Christ walking on the water of the Thames. The handicaps he
had to overcome—physical and moral weaknesses, tempera-

mental shyness, the impulse to dream, not do, the frustrations of his priestly ambition, his lack of self-criticism—all of these, and laudanum too, might well have destroyed a man in whose heart, however remotely at times, there did not burn a genuine and sincere love of God. Thanks to the Meynells and Patmore, he was reclaimed from the depths and led up mountain-heights. Yet his own will took him first to Wilfrid Meynell, and in the very extremity of his last illness, he saw the world of things and of the spirit plain and flung aside his withered dreams to float away for ever on the surface of the Thames.

The greater part of his poetry has already faded, and is unlikely ever to arouse interest again. Its borrowings dull the edge of husbandry; the multicoloured trains of images, the conglomerate vocabulary, and the cosmic vagueness belong to a trumpery tradition and have died with it. But there remains the other Thompson, him whose nuclear force, as Leone Vivante says[1] lies in the discovery of the immanent spirit, the poet of 'The Hound of Heaven', 'The Mistress of Vision', 'All Flesh', 'Contemplation', 'A Fallen Yew', and 'In No Strange Land' wherein precious experience is distilled in a bare, simple style and which we must acknowledge as enduring poetry. It is by such poems that Francis Thompson still lives; it is through these poems that we are brought to the heart of a vision so true and so profound that a life of suffering may seem small enough price to pay for it. For Thompson was right when he mused in a casual note: 'Where I find nothing done by me, much may have been done in me.'

[1] *English Poetry*, Faber & Faber, 1950, p. 317.

Select Bibliography

(Unless otherwise stated, the place of publication is London)

I. THOMPSON'S POETRY

(a) First Editions

Poems (Elkin Matthews and John Lane), 1893
Sister Songs: An offering to Two Sisters (John Lane), 1895.
New Poems (Constable and Co.), 1897.
    (In addition, several collections and individual poems were printed for private circulation, such as *Songs Wing to Wing*, an early version of *Sister Songs*, printed in 1895.)

(b) Collections and Selections

Selected Poems by Francis Thompson. Edited by Wilfrid Meynell (Burns, Oates and Methuen and Co.), 1908.
The Works of Francis Thompson in three volumes, Vols. I and II, poetry. Edited by Wilfrid Meynell (Burns, Oates), 1913.
The Collected Poetry of Francis Thompson (Hodder and Stoughton), n.d.
Le Lévrier du Ciel, etc. Translations of five poems by Francis Thompson, with notes, by Auguste Morel (Paris: La Maison des Amis des Livres), 1921.
Selected Poems and Prose of Francis Thompson. 'Wells of English' series (A. and C. Black), 1929.
The Poems of Francis Thompson. Edited with notes by Terence L. Connolly, S.J. (New York: Century), 1932.
The Poems of Francis Thompson. Edited by Wilfrid Meynell. Oxford Standard Authors (Oxford University Press), 1937.
Poems of Francis Thompson: Collected Edition (Hollis and Carter), 1946.

(c) Additional Poems, Formerly Uncollected

Juvenilia of Francis Thompson. Reprinted in the *Ushaw Magazine*, St. Cuthbert's College, Ushaw, March, 1908.
Eyes of Youth: A book of verse including four new poems by Francis Thompson. With a preface by G. K. Chesterton (Herbert and Daniel), 1909.
Youthful Verses by Francis Thompson (Preston: Privately printed by Harold Halewood), 1928.
The Man Has Wings. New Poems and Plays by Francis Thompson. Edited with Introduction and Notes by Terence L. Connolly, S.J. (New York: Hanover House), 1957.

Select Bibliography

II. THOMPSON'S PROSE

The Life and Labours of St. John Baptist de la Salle (J. Sinkins), 1891.

Health and Holiness. With a preface by George Tyrell (Burns, Oates), 1905.

St. Ignatius Loyola. Edited by John H. Pollen, S.J. (Burns, Oates), 1909. Reprinted with an introduction by Hugh Kelly, S.J. (Dublin: Clonmore and Reynolds), 1951.

Shelley: An Essay. With an Introduction by George Wyndham (Burns, Oates), 1909.

A Renegade Poet and Other Essays. With an Introduction by E. J. O'Brien (Boston: Bell Publishing Co.), 1910.

The Works of Francis Thompson. In three volumes. Vol. III, prose. Edited by Wilfrid Meynell (Burns, Oates), 1913.

Sir Leslie Stephen as a Biographer. With a bibliography and chronology of Thompson by Clement Shorter (privately printed by Clement Shorter), 1915.

Literary Criticisms by Francis Thompson. Newly discovered and collected by Terence L. Connolly. S.J. (New York: E. P. Dutton and Co.), 1948.

Minor Poets. Criticisms by Francis Thompson, newly discovered and edited by Terence L. Connolly. S.J. (Los Angeles: Anderson and Ritchie), 1949.

III. BOOKS ON FRANCIS THOMPSON, BIOGRAPHICAL AND CRITICAL

CONNOLLY, TERENCE L.: *An Account of Books and Mss. of Francis Thompson* (Newton, Mass.: Boston College), n.d. 1938?

—— *Francis Thompson: In His Paths* (Milwaukee: Bruce), 1944.

DE LA GORCE, AGNES: *Francis Thompson et les Poètes Catholiques d'Angleterre* (Paris: Libraire Plon), 1932.

—— *Francis Thompson.* Translated from the French by H. F. Kynaston-Snell (Burns, Oates and Washbourne), 1933.

DE LEON, JACK: *Francis Thompson.* A play in Nine Scenes. (Fortune Press), 1945.

DOHERTY, FELIX: *Song Out of Sorrow.* A biographical Play on Francis Thompson (Boston: Bruce Humphries), 1942.

DOOGAN, FRANCIS: *The Catholicity of Francis Thompson* (Melbourne: Australian Catholic Truth Society), n.d.

HUTTON, JOHN A. : *Guidance from Francis Thompson in Matters of Faith* (Hodder and Stoughton), 1926.

LEBUFFE, FRANCIS P., S.J.: *The Hound of Heaven: An Interpretation* (New York: The Macmillan Co.), 1921.

MÉGROZ, R. L.: *Francis Thompson. The Poet of Earth in Heaven* (Faber and Gwyer), 1927.

MEYNELL, EVERARD: *The Life of Francis Thompson* (Burns and Oates), 1913. Fifth edition, revised and condensed, 1926.

MEYNELL, VIOLA: *Francis Thompson and Wilfrid Meynell* (Hollis and Carter), 1952.

Select Bibliography

O'CONNOR, REV. JOHN, S.T.P.: *Commentary on 'The Mistress of Vision'* (Sussex: Ditchling Press), 1918.

O'CONOR, J. F. X., S.J.: *A Study of Francis Thompson's 'Hound of Heaven'* (New York: John Lane), 1912.

OWLETT, F. C.: *Essay on Francis Thompson* (John and Edward Bumpus), 1936.

ROOKER, K.: *Francis Thompson* (in French) (Herbert and Daniel), 1913.

THOMPSON, JOHN: *Francis Thompson, The Preston-Born Poet* (Simpkin, Marshall, Hamilton Kent and Co.), 1912.

—— *Francis Thompson, Poet and Mystic* (Simpkin and Marshall), 1923.

WRIGHT, REV. T. H.: *Francis Thompson and His Poetry* (George G. Harrap and Co.), 1927.

IV. BOOKS CONTAINING ESSAYS ON, OR EXTENDED REFERENCE TO, FRANCIS THOMPSON

ALEXANDER, REV. CALVERT, S.J.: *The Catholic Literary Revival* (Milwaukee: Bruce Publishing Co.), 1935

BATHO, EDITH, and DOBRÉE, BONAMY: *The Victorians and After, 1830–1914* (Cresset Press), 1938.

BLUNT, WILFRID SCAWEN: *My Diaries* (Martin Secker), in two volumes, 1919–20.

BRÉGY, KATHERINE: *The Poet's Chantry* (Simpkin, Marshall, Hamilton Kent and Co.), 1912.

BURDETT, OSBERT: *The Beardsley Period* (John Lane), 1925.

BURNE-JONES, LADY GEORGINA: *Memorials of Edward Burne-Jones* (Macmillan and Co.), 1912.

CAZAMIAN, LOUIS: *Symbolisme et Poèsie: L'Exemple Anglais* (Neuchatel: Editions de la Baconnière), 1947.

CHAPMAN, J. A.: *Papers on Shelley, Wordsworth and Others* (Oxford University Press), 1929.

CHESTERTON, G. K.: *The Victorian Age in Literature* (Williams and Northgate), 1913.

—— *Selected Essays* (Methuen and Co.), 1949.

—— *The Common Man* (Sheed and Ward), 1951.

DE LA MARE, WALTER: *Private View* (Faber and Faber), 1953.

ELTON, OLIVER: *The English Muse* (G. Bell and Sons), 1933.

EVANS, B. IFOR: *English Poetry in the Later Nineteenth Century* (Methuen and Co.), 1933.

FIGGIS, DARRELL: *Bye-Ways of Study* (Dublin: Talbot Press), 1918.

FREEMAN, JOHN: *The Moderns* (Robert Scott), 1916.

GAUNT, WILLIAM: *The Aesthetic Movement* (Jonathan Cape), 1945.

GHOSH, SARAT KUMAR: *The Prince of Destiny; The New Krishna* (Rebman Ltd.), 1909.

GRAVES, ROBERT: *The Common Asphodel* (Hamish Hamilton), 1949.

HAMILTON, G. ROSTREVOR: *Poetry and Contemplation* (Cambridge University Press), 1937.

HEATH-STUBBS, JOHN: *The Darkling Plain* (Eyre and Spottiswoode), 1950.

Select Bibliography

HIND, C. LEWIS: *Authors and I* (New York: John Lane Co.), 1921.
—— *Naphtali* (John Lane, The Bodley Head), 1926.
HUTTON, EDWARD: *Catholicism and English Literature* (Frederick Muller), 1942.
JACKSON, HOLBROOK: *The Eighteen Nineties* (Pelican Books), 1939.
JULIAN, CONSTANCE: *Shadows Over English Literature* (Milwaukee: Bruce Publishing Co.), 1944.
KELLY, BLANCHE MARY: *The Well of English* (New York: Harper and Bros.), 1936.
KENNEDY, J. M: *English Literature* (Stephen Swift and Co.), 1912.
KENT, WILLIAM (ed.): *An Encyclopedia of London* (J. M. Dent and Sons), 1951.
LE GALLIENNE, RICHARD: *The Romantic Nineties* (G. P. Putnam's), 1926.
LITTLE, REV. ARTHUR, S.J.: *The Nature of Art* or *The Shield of Pallas* (Longmans, Green and Co.), 1946.
LONG, VALENTINE, O.F.M.: *They Have Seen His Star* (New Jersey: St. Anthony Guild Press), 1938.
MASON, EUGENE: *A Book of Preferences in Literature* (John G. Wilson), 1915.
MEYNELL, ALICE: *Prose and Poetry*. Edited by F. P., V. M., O. S. and F. M. (Jonathan Cape), 1947.
MEYNELL, EVERARD: Article on 'Francis Thompson' in *Dictionary of National Biography*, 2nd Supplement 1910–11, Vol. 1 (Oxford University Press).
—— *A Catalogue of the Library of Coventry Patmore* (Serendipity Shop), 1921.
MEYNELL, VIOLA: *Alice Meynell: A Memoir* (Jonathan Cape), 1929.
MEYNELL, WILFRID: Preface to *Selected Poems of Francis Thompson* (Methuen and Co.; Burns and Oates), 1908.
MUSSER, BENJAMIN FRANCIS: *Franciscan Poets* (New York: The Macmillan Co.), 1933.
O'NEILL REV. G.: *The Story of Catholicism in English Literature* (Melbourne: Australian Catholic Truth Society), 1941.
PATMORE, DEREK: *The Life and Times of Coventry Patmore* (Constable), 1949.
SCOTT-JAMES, R. A.: *Personality in Literature* (Martin Secker), 1913.
SHEEN, BISHOP FULTON: *Life is Worth Living: Fifth Series* (Peter Davies), 1958.
SHUSTER, GEORGE N.: *The Catholic Spirit in Modern English Literature* (New York: The Macmillan Co.), 1922.
—— *The Catholic Church and Current Literature* (Burns, Oates and Washbourne), 1930.
SYMONS, ARTHUR: *Dramatis Personae* (Faber and Gwyer), 1925.
TUELL, ANNE KIMBALL: *Mrs. Meynell and her Literary Generation* (New York: E. P. Dutton and Co.), 1925.
TYNAN, KATHARINE: *The Middle Years* (Constable and Co.), 1916.
VIVANTE, LEONE: *English Poetry* (Faber and Faber), 1950.
WALKER, HUGH: *The Literature of the Victorian Era* (Cambridge University Press), 1910.
WHITE, HELEN C.: *The Metaphysical Poets* (New York: The Macmillan Co.), 1936.
WILLIAMSON, REV. CLAUDE, O.S.C. (ed.): *Great Catholics* (Catholic Book Club), 1939. Essay by C. Williamson.

Select Bibliography

ANON: 'Recent Poetry', *Edinburgh Review*, CCCLXXVI, April, 1896, pp. 493–502.

—— 'Francis Thompson', *Times Literary Supplement*, November 21, 1907, p. 355.

—— 'The Vision of the Unseen', *The Nation*, December 12, 1907, p. 535.

—— 'William Barnes and Francis Thompson', *Contemporary Review*, Vol. 95, No. 19, April, 1909, pp. 19–21.

—— Review of *Selected Poems 1908*, *Athenaeum*, January 9, 1909, pp. 37–8.

ARMSTRONG, MARTIN D.: 'The Poetry of Francis Thompson', *The Forum*, Vol. L, November, 1913, pp. 721–33.

BOURNE, RAYMOND: 'Thompson's "Shelley": A re-appreciation', *The Month*, Vol. CLXIX, No. 874, April, 1937, pp. 327–32.

CHAMBERS, EDMUND K.: Review of *Sister Songs*, *The Academy*, No. 1219, September 14, 1895, pp. 198–9.

COCK, ALBERT A.: 'Francis Thompson', *Dublin Review*, Vol. CXLIX, October, 1911, pp. 247–77.

COHEN, J. M.: 'Francis Thompson', *The Month*, Vol. 2, No. 6, n.s., December, 1949, pp. 390–401.

CORBISHLEY, PHILIP D.: 'Famous British Catholics: VI Francis Thompson', *Heritage*, Vol. 2, No. 3, June, 1956, pp. 116 and 137.

DAVIES, W. H.: 'Francis Thompson' (a poem), *The Nation*, Vol. XII, No. 23, March 8, 1913, p. 928.

DELATTRE, FLORIS: 'Le poète Francis Thompson', *Revue Germanique*, July, 1909, pp. 422–54.

FIGGIS, DARRELL: 'Francis Thompson', *Contemporary Review*, Vol. CIV, No. 72, October, 1913, pp. 487–95.

FINBERG, H. P. R.: 'Francis Thompson', *English Review*, Vol. XII, No. 6, December, 1925, pp. 822–31.

GAUSS, CHRISTIAN: A Letter on Francis Thompson, *The Nation*, December 5, 1907, pp. 513–14.

HAMILTON, G. ROSTREVOR: 'Wit and Beauty: a Study of Metaphysical Poetry', *The London Mercury*, Vol. XIV, No. 84, October, 1926, pp. 606–20.

HARRISON, AUSTIN: 'The Poetry of Francis Thompson', *English Review*, Vol. XV, No. 1, August, 1913, pp. 103–16.

HENNESSY, DOYLE: 'Did Francis Thompson Attempt Suicide?' *The Catholic World*, Vol. CLXX, No. 1019, February, 1950, pp. 346–50.

HIND, C. LEWIS: 'A Letter on Francis Thompson', *The Nation*, Vol. XII, No. 24, March 15, 1913, p. 990.

—— 'Francis Thompson: Another Book' (review of Mégroz's study), *The Bookman* (London), Vol. LXXII, No. 429, June, 1927, pp. 164–5.

JOHN, PHILIP: 'A Poet of the Church', *The Catholic World*, Vol. CLI, No. 903, June, 1940, pp. 320–5.

JOHNSTON, LESLIE: 'Modern Mysticism: Some Prophets and Poets', *Quarterly Review*, Vol. 220, No. 438, January, 1914, pp. 220–46.

Select Bibliography

J. W. B.: Review of Lebuffe's study of 'The Hound of Heaven', *Modern Language Notes*, Vol. XXXVII, No. 2, February, 1922, pp. 124–8.

KENEALY, ARCHBISHOP ANSELM: 'Francis Thompson; Some Personal Recollections', *Carmina*, May, 1931, pp. 170–4.

—— 'Francis Thompson; The Man and his Poetry', *Capuchin Annual*, 1933, pp. 39–59.

(LANG, ANDREW): 'The Young Men', *Contemporary Review*, No. 338, February, 1894, pp. 177–88.

LESLIE, SHANE: 'Francis Thompson', *Spectator*, No. 5446, November 11, 1932, pp. 657–8.

LUCAS, E. V.: 'Francis Thompson's Cricket Verses', *The Cornhill Magazine*, Vol. XXV, July, 1908, pp. 58–66.

MADELEVA, SISTER MARY: 'Religious Poets of the Nineteenth Century', *The Catholic World*, Vol. CXX, No. 716, November, 1924, pp. 212–24.

MARTINDALE, REV. C. C.: Review of Meynell's *Life of Thompson*, *Dublin Review*, Vol. 154, No. 308, January, 1914, pp. 172–4.

MEYERSTEIN, E. H. W.: ' "Epipsychidion" and "The Hound of Heaven" ', *Times Literary Supplement*, March 17, 1945.

MEYNELL, ALICE: 'Some Memories of Francis Thompson', *Dublin Review*, Vol. CXLII, No. 284, January, 1908, pp. 160–72.

MEYNELL, EVERARD: 'The Notebooks of Francis Thompson', *Dublin Review*, January, 1917, pp. 109–22.

MEYNELL, WILFRID: 'Mr. Francis Thompson' (Obituary), *The Athenaeum*. No. 4178, November 23, 1907, pp. 654–6.

MOORE, THOMAS VERNER: 'The Hound of Heaven', *Psychoanalytical Review*, Vol. V, No. 4, October, 1918, pp. 345–60.

MORE, PAUL ELMER: 'Francis Thompson', *The Nation*, November 19, 1908, pp. 486–9.

O'LEARY, P. I.: 'Francis Thompson: Do Catholics Know Him?' *Father Mathew Record*, September 8, 1935, pp. 385–9.

(PAGE, FREDERICK): 'Memorabilia', *Notes and Queries*, April 21, 1945, p. 55.

PATMORE, COVENTRY: 'Francis Thompson: A New Poet', *Fortnightly Review*, January, 1894. Reprinted in *Courage in Politics*, edited by Frederick Page, pp. 157–66.

POPE, MYRTLE PIHLMAN: 'A Critical Bibliography of Works by and about Francis Thompson'. Four articles in six sections. *Bulletin of the New York Public Library*, Vol. 62, No. 11, November, 1958; Vol. 63, No. 1, January, 1959; Vol. 63, No. 3, March, 1959; Vol. 63, No. 4, April, 1959.

PRUNTY, MAURA: 'Great Poet of the Celestial Vision', *Catholic Herald*, No. 3736, November 8, 1957, p. 6.

SHARPE, ELLA FREEMAN: 'Francis Thompson: A Psychoanalytical Study', *British Journal of Medical Psychology*, Vol. 5, 1925, pp. 329–44.

SMITH, FRED: 'Francis Thompson: "Some Sort of Derelict" ', *The Catholic World*, Vol. CLVI, No. 934, January, 1943, pp. 430–3.

SQUIRE, J. C.: ('Solomon Eagle') 'Francis Thompson's Notebooks', *New Statesman*, Vol. VIII, No. 199, January 27, 1917, p. 401.

Select Bibliography

STANFORD, DEREK: 'Francis Thompson's Prose', *The Month*, Vol. 18, No. 5, November, 1957, pp. 299–306.

SYMONS, ARTHUR: Review of *Poems* by Francis Thompson, *The Athenaeum*, No. 3458, February 3, 1894, pp. 143–4.

TOLLES, FREDERICK B.: 'The Praetorian Cohorts: A Study of the Language of Francis Thompson's Poetry', *English Studies* (Amsterdam), Vol. 22, No. 2, April, 1940, pp. 49–64.

TOMAN, GRAHAM R.: Review of *Poems* by Francis Thompson, *The Academy*, No. 1145, April 14, 1894, pp. 302–3.

TRAILL, H. D.: 'Mr. Thompson's Poems', *Nineteenth Century*, Vol. XXXV, No. CCIV, February, 1894, pp. 229–33.

TWITCHETT, E. G.: 'Francis Thompson', *The London Mercury*, Vol. XXVII, No. 157, November, 1932, pp. 58–64.

TYNAN, KATHARINE: 'Francis Thompson', *Fortnightly Review*, No. DXVIII, n.s., February 1, 1910, pp. 349–60.

—— 'Francis Thompson', *The Bookman* (London), Vol. LIV, No. 321, June, 1918, pp. 87–9.

WEYAND, N. T.: 'Francis Thompson: His Theory of Poetry', Abstract of thesis for Ph.D., St. Louis University, 1934, *Microfilm Abstracts*, Ann Arbor, 1938, pp. 51–2.

WHITTEN, WILFRID: 'Francis Thompson', *T. P's Weekly*, November 29, 1907, p. 696.

WILSON, WINIFRED GRAHAM: 'His Fruit Not Bread', *Quarterly Review*, Vol. 276, No. 548, April, 1941, pp. 273–86.

YOUNG, JOAN COCKERILL: 'The Strange Story of Francis Thompson', *Catholic Herald*, No. 3736, November 8, 1957, p. 6.

VI. NARCOTICS

ANON: 'Treatment and Care of Drug Addicts: Report of the Study Group of the World Health Organization, 1957', *Bulletin on Narcotics*, United Nations European Office, Geneva, Vol. IX, No. 3, July-September, 1957, pp. 36–8.

COCTEAU, JEAN: *Opium* (translated by Margaret Crosland and Sinclair Road), (Peter Owen), 1957.

GOODMAN, LOUIS S., and GILMAN, ALFRED: *The Pharmacological Basis of Therapeutics* (New York: Macmillan Co.), 2nd edition, 1955.

SCHNEIDER, ELISABETH: 'The "Dream" of "Kubla Khan" ', *P.M.L.A.*, Vol. LX, No. 3, September, 1945, pp. 784–801.

—— *Coleridge, Opium and 'Kubla Khan'* (University of Chicago Press), 1953.

STARKIE, ENID: *Baudelaire* (Faber and Faber), 1957.

WHOLEY, C. C.: 'The Mental and Nervous Side of Addiction to Narcotic Drugs', *Journal of the American Medical Association*, Vol. 83, No. 5, August 2, 1924, pp. 321–5.

Index

Index

Index

Index

Index

Index